Praise for

LA DOLCE VITA UNIVERSITY

◆ ◆ ◆

"The title—*La Dolce Vita University*—captures the great virtues of this reader-friendly book perfectly: it's delicious and educational at the same time, with each virtue reinforcing the other. *Dulce* blended with *utile,* as the great ancient Roman poet Horace recommended.

"This book sustains that combination masterfully. It's a complete delight to read, but (as a professor of Renaissance literature for many decades) I'm happy to report that the authors know their stuff. The research is careful and the analysis is intelligent and witty. I learned amazing new things about dozens of topics—Artemisia, Burano, Casanova, Dante, and onward through the alphabet to *zanni. La Dolce Vita University* also seasons lots of popular myths with just the right number of grains of salt. It's written in prose as clear, bright, crisp, and lively as a spring morning in the Dolomites. Add to that graceful but also playful prose, the talent of skilled storytellers, and it's no wonder that the entries stay so fascinating.

"*La Dolce Vita University* makes me crave a return to Italy, and helps me daydream that I'm already there. Like an ideal platter of antipasti, it's made of deliciously varied bites you can pick your way through. If you want—or want to give a friend—an appetizer that will rouse up a hunger for the glory and festivity of that wonderful place and its no less wonderful culture, this book is perfect."

—Robert N. Watson, PhD.
Distinguished Professor of English,
Associate Vice-Provost for Educational Innovation, UCLA

"Imagine it as a dessert course of dark chocolates, filled with exotic fruits and nuts, packed with knowledge and love of history and art, wisdom and wit, Italian, American, global.

"The chocolates are alphabetically listed, described and presented beautifully, and offered as something to dip into as you wish. You open it, choose the one you think you will like best, then another, and another. Suddenly it's gone.

"Because Carla wears her scholarship lightly, you don't feel over full, but what a feast!"

— Denise Scott Brown RIBA, Int. FRIBA
Winner of the Jane Drew Prize for Women In Architecture

"Carla is the consummate Italian. *Mille grazie* for sharing your extensive knowledge, insights and fascinating little-known backstories with such affection and humor!"

—Joan Tucci
Co-Author, *The Tucci Cookbook*

"Excellent! Bravissima! Delightfully informative, a book to enrich any reader's life with a greater appreciation of Italian culture—even in everyday experiences here at home, from visiting an art museum to dining in a local Italian restaurant, or from cooking for friends and family to the usage of common expressions and words. Not to mention, it might just inspire you to hop on a plane!"

—Commendatore Professor Carlo Sclafani
SUNY Distinguished Professor and Former Chairperson of the
Modern Languages Department at Westchester Community College

"*La Dolce Vita University* is an authentic full immersion in Italian culture, history, art, traditions, and more. Fun, funny, and informative. Brava!"

—Cristiano Bonino
Founder, Food, Stories, Travel

"An enlightening, entertaining guide to the history behind so much of what we love about Italian cuisine and culture. As a chef and cooking enthusiast I enjoyed the variety of information and perspective on the Italian and Sicilian culture. From antiquity to today, reading this special history written with color and style is a pure joy for the food aficionado and any lover of Italy. You won't want to miss reading through any part of this book."

—Chef Bert Cutino, CEC, AAC, HOF, WCMC
Co-Founder/COO, The Sardine Factory Restaurant, Cannery Row, Monterey, CA

"An obvious love of all things Italian is evident in every essay of this quirky, delicious, and absolutely delightful book. From A to Z topics are peppered with insights, memories, fun factoids, and the intrigues of history. Whether you are a seasoned globetrotter or an armchair-traveler, *La Dolce Vita University* will inspire you to dig deeper into the magic and allure of *Italia*."

—Tara Coniaris
Secretary, Board of Trustees at Katonah Museum of Art

"The enthusiasm that Carla brings to her work is unmistakable and contagious. *La Dolce Vita University* merits many "students" and readers who share a passion for Italy."

—Commendatore Stefano Acunto
Hon. Vice Consul, Republic of Italy

"I believe that most rewarding travel experiences are those that engage the senses and enrich you emotionally and intellectually. Reading *La Dolce Vita University* is a great armchair vacation that captures the essence of Italy. This is the one book to read before visiting Italy—or to put you in the mood for your next one."

—Lauren Hefferon
Founder & Director
Ciclismo Classico and Travel Vision Journeys

LA DOLCE VITA UNIVERSITY

◆ ◆ ◆

An Unconventional Guide to Italian Culture from A to Z

CARLA GAMBESCIA

WITH MICHAEL STEIN

ILLUSTRATIONS BY LANNIE HART

TRAVELERS' TALES
AN IMPRINT OF SOLAS HOUSE, INC.
PALO ALTO

Travelers' Tales and Solas House are trademarks of Solas House, Inc., Palo Alto, California. travelerstales.com | solashouse.com

Art Direction and Cover Concept: Carla Gambescia
Illustrations: Lannie Hart
Cover Design and Interior Layout: Ronda Taylor

Library of Congress Cataloging-in-Publication Data

Names: Gambescia, Carla, author.
Title: La dolce vita university : an unconventional guide to Italian culture
    from A to Z / Carla Gambescia with Michael Stein ; illustrations by Lannie
    Hart.
Description: Palo Alto : Travelers' Tales, an imprint of Solas House, Inc.,
    2017.
Identifiers: LCCN 2017050614 (print) | LCCN 2017050981 (ebook) | ISBN
    9781609521325 (ebook) | ISBN 9781609521318 (pbk.)
Subjects: LCSH: Italy--Civilization.
Classification: LCC DG450 (ebook) | LCC DG450 .G295 2017 (print) | DDC
    945.003--dc23
LC record available at https://lccn.loc.gov/2017050614

First Edition
Printed in the United States
10 9 8 7 6 5 4 3 2 1

♦ ♦ ♦

To my mother and father,
Anna and Pasquale Gambescia,
whose greatest gift, after their love,
was the love of Italy they instilled in me.

L'amor che move il sole
e l'altre stelle.

Contents

Introduction

I've been writing this book my entire life ... though I only realized it a few years ago.

My earliest sense of myself was not just that I was a little girl but that I was Italian. This made me feel special. I don't know why I felt this, but I did. As it happens I wasn't born in Italy, and Italian was spoken only rarely in our household by my father and grandmother and occasionally by visiting relatives.

Three of my four grandparents immigrated at the turn of the nineteenth and twentieth centuries and my parents came of age during the Depression. A favorite family story was that when my father was courting my mother, he once gave blood for a small payment so he could buy her a Coke. He graduated from medical school, they married, war was declared, and my father joined the Navy. Like so many Italian-Americans, my father was eager to defend the country of his birth. (During the war his troop ship participated in the invasion of Sicily.) After the war family life resumed, and eleven years later I made my grand entrance. My parents were fiercely proud of being Americans, but within the family there was also tremendous pride in our Italian heritage. Both my parents imparted this to me in ways that were more than just a "feeling." I learned to appreciate being Italian through the lenses of their personal interests and passions.

Every Sunday after church, my father gave me my Italian lessons. Lessons always began with words and pronunciation but inevitably lead to what I loved best, stories—the stories of my father's favorite Italian geniuses throughout Italy's history, beginning with the Romans. Daddy admired Julius Caesar and was named for him: Pasquale Julius Caesar. Julius Caesar had been captured by pirates when he was a teenager, crossed a famous river, and triumphally returned to Rome as one of the most brilliant military leaders who ever lived. I had several favorite stories: the story of Galileo dropping a big ball and a little ball off the Leaning Tower in Pisa; of Mr. Vivaldi teaching young orphan girls to sing and play violin in Venice; of Michelangelo painting the great ceiling upside down all by himself; and a sad story of Dante who couldn't marry Beatrice, the girl of his dreams, but who instead wrote the greatest love story in the world, dedicated to her. Like all children I loved to hear my favorite stories over and over, and they imprinted on me just like "Hansel and Gretel" and "Little Red Riding Hood."

My mother much preferred art to history and loved Italian Renaissance art in particular. She had several big beautiful books of paintings which we would often look at together. By the age of seven, I could reliably identify a Raphael from Michelangelo or a Botticelli from a Titian, and began forming my own artistic opinions. My parents were very proud of my precocious skill which I was called upon to display for relatives, all of whom were naturally impressed! But I can also remember feeling frustrated with Mom's love of Madonna and Child scenes, especially during the Christmas season. I would beg her to choose a family Christmas card with Santa Claus, Frosty or, better yet, Rudolph—yet she would not relent and stuck with her beloved Madonnas or a Holy Family, even on the postage stamps! One year she selected a card with Raphael's Madonna Della Seggiola which caused me to impertinently ask why the baby Jesus was so chubby. There was no critiquing Raphael, her very favorite artist. When I was eight we all traveled to Italy and visited the Vatican Museum; my mother was so moved by Raphael's Transfiguration she wept.

My father died prematurely three years later. By that time I had outgrown his storytelling, but I can still remember those stories almost word for word. My mother lived a long life, and art and painting and applied arts—not just by great Italians—always filled her with wonder, and she passed that passion on to me.

I passed through my teen years and young adulthood with the typical detachment young people can have from their childhood. Italy receded into the background as I built a career in advertising and marketing while also traveling widely across six continents for work and play.

Then in 1995 I signed up for a cycling trip in Sicily with a boutique travel company specializing in "authentic" Italy with native guides. A magical thing happened: I rediscovered my roots and I fell deeply in love with the land of my ancestors. Following that fateful trip, I took dozens more (eleven by bike) exploring the cities and the countryside in every region, seeing Italy in summer and winter and spring and fall, and delighting in the richness of its cultural gifts. In 2007, while a consultant to the Ciao Bella Gelato company, I co-created and co-led a unique tour dubbed the *Giro del Gelato* which went on to be awarded "Best Trip in Western Europe" by *Outside Magazine*.

But that original "Bella Sicilia" tour was life-changing, and that is no exaggeration. As a result, I resolved to open an Italian-inspired restaurant, not because I was a foodie—though I love food!—but because I wanted to create a place through which my guests could feel they too were "there" even when they were still "here." About twelve years later I made that dream a reality and operated a very special restaurant for nearly a decade. It was called *Via Vanti!* (a contraction of *via* and *avanti* for "the way forward") and was very popular, not just because its food was *delizioso*—we were a top Zagat®-rated restaurant for years—but because of the experience we created for our guests. We transformed the interior of a landmark train station into a veritable jewel box decorated with colorful Murano light fixtures, a Carrera marble bar, and assorted Venetian design motifs. Patrons were greeted with a dazzling gelato case offering 18 award-winning flavors daily. I took on the role of both Culinary and Cultural Director and became the impresario of all sorts of special dining events with catchy titles like *Carnevale Evening in Venice*, *Swept Away in Sardinia*, *Sicilian Summer* and *Fichi Fantastici*, during which, between courses, I'd share the "back story" of the food and wine, surprising historical facts about the region, and the like.

I discovered I loved to share with others the things that gave me pleasure, most especially talking about Italy and all things Italian. The restaurant's food and wine were "portals" though which I could share my stories, stories that I built into the menu and weekly specials. A favorite annual event included our own unique take on New Year's Eve *Neapolitan Plate Tossing* based on a quirky "out-with-the-old" custom originating in Naples (yes, we actually threw plates, though the paper variety, out through a window frame positioned on the bar). I enjoyed creating all sorts of "edu-taining" touches and souvenirs for my patrons, including laminated "La Dolce Vita University" fun fact discovery cards and "Parliamo Italiano" vocabulary cards placed at each table, which guests often collected. In addition, I authored a monthly column titled "La Dolce Vita U" for a local newspaper. Frequently I shared my "thesis" with guests that all of us, regardless of ethnicity, possess an Inner Italian—that part of us which is most joyful, spontaneous, and expressive. This was invariably met with a knowing smile and unanimous nod of understanding and agreement. *La Dolce Vita University* began to take on tangible form through the restaurant.

I never imagined I would write a book as I've always had difficulty sustaining much of a written narrative, but *La Dolce Vita University* is different. Its "stories" are shorter than short stories—mini-essays, really, designed to impart surprising or intriguing nuggets that will enrich and enliven your appreciation of all that is Italian, whether you are an armchair or seasoned traveler, a lover of art, food, history, or of any other facet of Italian culture. What I have chosen to write about in *La Dolce Vita "U"* is what has most captured my imagination, so I have not attempted to be comprehensive or scholarly—just to share my passions.

Special thanks go to Mauro and Claudio, the guides on that fateful cycling tour, for being inspiring catalysts to my own Italian renaissance. Most of all, I shall be always grateful to my sweet and humble parents who cherished me and gave me the confidence to feel that anything is possible. I know they would be so very proud *La Dolce Vita University* is dedicated to them, and I hope that they would be able to see a small part of themselves in its pages.

I hope you love it too!

Author's Note

*T*he mini-essays that follow each treat a topic that I found surprising, intriguing, quirky, fun, or some combination of those qualities. Collectively they begin to express what I find so endlessly captivating about "the Boot."

Their organization appears as alphabetical. But nothing is ever quite that straightforward when it comes to Italy. Even if you choose to read these mini-essays sequentially you may very well feel as though you're wandering the mysterious alleys of a medieval town, the hidden *vicoli* of a larger city, or even along the serpentine canals of *La Serenissima*. Unexpected connections emerge and fresh discoveries await around each corner. Or perhaps you'll choose to dip in and out of this volume at random. Either way, just relax—you're in *Italia!*—and enjoy the *passeggiata*. It will lead you to new insights and marvelous revelations, as it has, on my own journey, for me.

Readers who are planning to visit a specific Italian city or region may wish to consult the special Traveler's Topic Index at the end.

Italy is a glorious and fascinating mosaic. Consider the following passages just a few of its glittering tesserae.

♦ A IS FOR ARLECCHINO

Endearingly transgressive, Arlecchino is a universal symbol of fun and creativity and can be instantly recognized by his iconic colorful diamond-patterned patchwork costume. You may know him by the similar sounding "Harlequin," which is Frenchified, but his roots are pure *Italiane*.

He is the true star of Italy's *Commedia dell'Arte*—where improvisational theatre took root. The ever-clever servant, Arlecchino can be counted on to innocently thwart the plans of his master while pursuing his own interests, often love-oriented. Naturally inventive and entertaining, he routinely displays acrobatic agility with a quick flip or a somersault for physical "punctuation." His engaging trickster antics kept audiences coming back for more.

♦ ARRANGIARSI, THE ART OF "MAKING DO"

A recipe begins with a spontaneous and opportunistic organization of whatever is available. So goes just about all of life in Italy. *Arrangiarsi* means the art of working your way through, often through obstacles, and making do—even if it's making something out of what seems to be nothing.

Is it a skill? That would be much too cerebral, too much like management. In Italian it's *un'arte*. In the kitchen or the winery, it's all about skillfully improvising and, always in the moment, adapting to ever-changing circumstances. In life, it involves putting aside too much premeditation in favor of acceptance and creative problem solving, occasionally reinforced with political maneuvering (possibly payoffs!) and sometimes just ignoring the "rules" that somebody else or some authority is trying to impose.

It's not overthinking and having too much of a plan, but it's not laziness either—there isn't a single word in English to encompass its full meaning because, as in so many things Italian, there's body language involved just as there is a melody to the word. When asked in astonishment "how did you get this done?" or "how are you going to get yourself out of this jam?" one says with a shrug and raised eyebrows "*si arrangia*," the last syllable trailing off as the listener is given a wink.

In Italy you get praised for having a good "*naso*" (nose), or being "*in gamba*" (as in another body part, a leg), but what it really means idiomatically is "being on top of your game." All ways of putting imagery, as Italian so often does, to the combination of instinct and intuition. Fearlessness tempered by cleverness, that's *arrangiarsi*. Italians know it well, and have needed it often. Every day, Italians face complex and mutable situations with no clear rules but plenty of amorphous threats, all overlaid with a faceless and self-contradictory bureaucracy overseen by a constantly changing government (an average of more than one a year since World War II). Throughout history, Italians have dealt with oppressors of every stripe: marauding barbarians from the north, fundamentalist religious leaders like Savonarola, bombastic dictators like Mussolini, self-appointed emperors like Napoleon.

When another one comes along, you shrug, raise an eyebrow, sigh "*s'arrangia*," and ask "*cosa mangiamo*?" What's for dinner?

♦ ARTE

Art is to Italy what oxygen is to the human bloodstream.

Art is everywhere. Art, beauty, and aesthetics have been integral to life on the Italian peninsula for millennia. Italy is home to the highest concentration of art in the world, with the most masterpieces per square mile, and possessing an estimated 60 percent of the world's art treasures (not to mention all the Italian paintings and sculpture that grace museums throughout the world).

The great art may go back to the pre-Renaissance and Renaissance, but appreciation of manmade beauty and aesthetics goes back to the Romans, who appreciated Greek art the only way they knew how: they took it (although the more respectable word is "appropriation"). But while they may have conquered Greece politically and "appropriated" the culture (including the sculpture and architecture) of classical Greece, Greece "conquered" Rome in a cultural sense as its artistic output became part of the Greco-Roman style, which became one of the main foundational cornerstones of Italy's artistic standing in subsequent centuries.

But it took awhile before there were "artists." One thousand years ago the term *artigiani* (artisans) referred to members of craft guilds, with no particular word for those who did artwork, and no particular distinction for, say, anonymous stone carvers who worked on a cathedral. Painters belonged to the same craft guild as doctors and apothecaries; sculptors were associated with stone masons and woodworkers who were low-paid and anonymous.

The revelation that catapulted individual artists into Italian awareness came in the late 1200's with the emergence of the painter Cimabue and his apprentice (who surpassed his teacher) Giotto. With Giotto painting became realistic portrayal of human drama. As Kenneth Clark pointed out in *Civilization*, for Giotto to break through the two-dimensional Byzantine style of painting, and "evolve this solid, space-conscious style was one of those feats of inspired originality that have occurred only two or three times in the history of art."

Mathematics became art's handmaiden with the science of spatial perspective and fostered the new realism of artists like Masaccio. Donatello learned from Greco-Roman influences how to, for example, represent bodily weight and movement under drapery, and Masaccio learned from classical portraiture and from Giotto realistic roundedness and portrayal of human emotion.

This placing of the human figure front and center ignited Renaissance art. The Renaissance in full bloom witnessed the glorification of art for art's sake—not simply as a means to express religious devotion, but also to portray humanity, and (not surprisingly) put one's patrons into the newly realistic human scene, to demonstrate their erudition, power, and prestige. "Artists"—painters, sculptors, poets, and architects—became the local heroes and the celebrities of the day, no longer anonymous craft people but the equivalent of today's rock stars.

3

And no city rocked harder, so to speak, than Florence. The Florentines had the Athenian appreciation of beauty and, through the guilds, the skills and power to manifest that passion. They also had the wealth to support it, thanks to their mastery of international finance, or as their guilds called it, the *Arte de Cambio*, moving money from one city to the next in their phenomenally successful banking system. One "Arte" here definitely supported another.

But all Italy shared in this creative explosion. All over the various city-states were patrons (apart from the usual kings and religious leaders) with a broader appetite for artistic subject matter and approaches. Up and down the peninsula were great mercantile centers with a growing and developing bourgeoisie supportive of the new humanism and the new art. And all through Italian culture was a pride in handmade workmanship, fostered by the pre-Renaissance craft guild system, that buttressed the culture of artistic creation. That enhanced the pursuit of the most talented and creative artists, and then the rewards (material and reputational) for the most accomplished, all of which led quite naturally to ever greater artistic competition and achievement.

And so *arte* became celebrated and learned and passed down through individual practitioners freely and harmoniously developing all sides of their nature and craft, and, as Clark writes, "the most profound thought of the time was not expressed in words, but in visual imagery": the heroic vision of man being raised above simple earthly consciousness by the power of God in the Sistine Chapel, or the harmonization of classical reason and Christian wisdom in Raphael's *School of Athens*, or the ever-fascinating beauty of the *Mona Lisa*.

Today, the great art of the past is a part of Italy's civic pride (in contrast to the United States being more about the "now"). Art, architecture, poetry, literature, and music, whether Dante or Leonardo or opera, live on today and still have currency, and not just among *cognoscenti*, opinion-makers, and Italy's flock of art students and tourists, but for the man (and woman) on the street. You can even sit down to dinner almost anywhere, sip a Bellini first, savor some Carpaccio, and have shared in a bit of Venice's art legacy.

♦ ARTEMISIA'S REVENGE

Does art imitate life or the other way around? One could well answer "both" in the case of Artemisia Gentileschi, the foremost woman artist of the Italian Renaissance.

Like nearly all female artists of the period, Artemisia was the daughter of an artist father; there were simply no other avenues open at that time for young Italian women who wished to develop such skills. To even desire an artistic career was suspect, if not down-right suspicious, in the patriarchal society of 17th century Rome.

Orazio Gentileschi's daughter proved a precocious student; at age 17 she painted a stunning *Susanna and the Elders* based on an Old Testament story. In the story a fair Hebrew wife was spied on at her bath by two lecherous elders who then pressed her for sexual favors in exchange for their silence about an adulterous liaison between her and a fictional lover. The virtuous Susanna refused to comply with their blackmail demand. In the subsequent trial, our heroine was exonerated when obvious differences arose in her accusers' testimonies, and they were subsequently put to death for their treachery.

Artemisia's masterful painting proved eerily prescient in certain ways. Within two years of its completion Artemisia herself was to become the victim of sexual assault—outright rape—at the hands of an artistic associate of her father's, the Florentine muralist Agostino Tassi. A sensational seven-month trial ensued. Artemisia was falsely accused of having had numerous lovers prior to her encounter with Tassi, a charge that gained temporary traction because she had stepped outside the narrow limits imposed on women of her time. Ultimately Tassi was convicted on the testimony of a former friend to whom Tassi had boasted of his conquest.

But despite having previously been imprisoned for incest with a sister-in-law and charged with arranging the murder of his wife, Tassi served less than a year for his crime, a far less severe penalty than that exacted upon Susanna's false accusers. Meanwhile Artemisia's reputation lay in tatters.

During and after the trial ordeal, Artemisia executed *Judith Beheading Holofernes*, based on another Old Testament story about a virtuous Jewish woman who, in this instance, took up her sword to defend her people from the Assyrian general Holofernes. Artemisia used her likeness for Judith, and Tassi's, minus his body below the neck, for Holofernes. Thus she achieved in art the justice she could not be granted in life.

Artemisia would go on to become a highly regarded artist, receiving the patronage of Grand Duke Cosimo II in Florence and, in 1616, becoming the first woman admitted to the *Accademia dell'Arte del Disegno*. And while it would take hundreds of years, in the latter part of the twentieth century, her work would revive from obscurity and receive due critical recognition and a series of retrospectives. She would become something of a feminist celebrity, featured both in Wendy Wasserstein's Pulitzer Prize–winning Broadway drama *The Heidi Chronicles* (1988) and in Judy Chicago's seminal *The Dinner Party* (1979) installation at the Brooklyn Museum. In the latter case, Artemisia's place setting on the triangular table is in clear view of the Biblical Judith's.

And so Artemisia's revenge has become part of Western art history, in which Artemisia has finally been properly recognized for her talents and innovations. Agostino Tassi is but a smudged footnote.

♦ APERITIVI TO DIGESTIVI

Italians care deeply about the dining experience, making sure it moves beautifully through its arc of different courses. And they care just as deeply about digestion of the meal as the enjoyment of it. There's an art and science that come together though the proper sequencing of an Italian meal. If the dining has its courses, digestion has its course, almost like a workout: it moves in a trajectory from warmup to cool down, dining and digestion rising and falling together for optimal pleasure.

The meal opens with an *aperitivo*, derived from Latin *aperire* which means to open, as in opening the stomach for the meal. The ancient Romans did it with honey wine and spices, while modern Italians do it with those *aperitivi*: drinks thought to kickstart your digestion, get the juices flowing. They are usually relatively low in alcohol content and dry or even bitter rather than sweet. Popular *aperitivi*—Campari and Aperol (both "branded" in the glass with their signature red and orange colors, respectively) or *spumantes* like Prosecco—are drunk with something salty as an accompaniment to further stimulate the palate; Italians believe appetite is properly stimulated when you begin to eat.

So here's an example of an Italian meal done right: begin with Campari and soda with some olives, follow that with *salumi* (Italian cold cuts) or *crostini* (bruschetta), and that can lead to pasta, risotto, or a soup or stew, which culminates in a meat or fish portion or a combination thereof. Then the digestive "cool down" begins with *insalate* (always after the main course to facilitate the digestive process, which makes sense when you think about it . . . not the American way with salad first) followed by some fruit and/or cheese and perhaps gelato or *sorbetto* or a light regional dessert.

Finally comes a *digestivo*, an after-dinner drink to ease digestion. And you'll need it after a meal like that! It's easy to remember: the more indulgent your meal, the more likely you'll benefit from a quick drink at the end of it.

The best *digestivi* are distillations of aromatic herbs, barks, roots, seeds, and plants believed to have stomach-settling properties (after being steeped in alcohol, usually 45 percent). The first attempts to aid digestion using aromatic herbs and seeds steeped in liquids were made by the Greeks and Romans, and they do work, then and now: by stimulating digestive enzymes they can soothe bloating, relieve occasional heartburn after meals, and calm potential upset stomach and nausea.

Here are some popular *digestivi* and their key ingredients:

Cynar—artichoke leaves and 13 select herbs (considered both an aperitivo and digestivo)

Fernet Branca—a secret recipe of 40+ herbs and spices

Averna—a combination of blood orange, lemon peels, and aromatic herbs

Mirto—typical of Sardinia and consisting of myrtle, juniper, bark of strawberry bush, and sage

Grappa—fermented grape residue after pressing

Sambuca—star anise and white elderflowers . . . when three coffee beans are floated on the surface it's called *Sambuca con la mosca*—"Sambuca with the fly"

Those coffee beans on the Sambuca have come to signify health, happiness, and prosperity, a fitting way to end the kind of Italian meal that embodies those delights in every serving.

✦ ANACAPRI, THE OTHER CAPRI

Ah the isle of Capri, as in Sinatra's enjoyable tune off his *Come Fly With Me* album, where Frank turns a charming if creaky romantic ballad from the '30s into a jet-set ring-a-ding-ding, tragically cut short by the "meatball" on the romantic target's finger. It's a playboy and playgirl's paradise, still known for its marina, Piazzetta of fashionable sidewalk cafes, snugly inviting "Capri pants" of the '50s and early '60s—made a fashion sensation by Grace Kelly— and ultimate upper-crust lifestyle and nightlife. But take a public bus just three kilometers to another part of the figure-eight-shaped island, Anacapri's higher elevations, and you're in another world. "Ana" is a Greek prefix that means "up" or "above" but it could just as well be "anti-Capri."

Located on the slopes of Monte Solaro, Anacapri has about 7,000 residents, as well as visitors who don't love crowds and want to experience the more authentic, timeless side of the island. Here are walking and backpacking trails that lead you to rocky pine-and-brush covered terrain and the citizens who still scratch out vegetable gardens and lemon groves amid the sunlight and fragrances of the Italian Mediterranean. In the town center are little Neapolitan tailor and shoemaker storefronts and narrow side-streets where you may have to press against a wall to let by a businessman or nun on a Vespa. You'll find fewer luxury boutiques and more artisan workshops on the Via Giuseppe Orlandi, along with superb secular and religious architecture and art.

These are the charms of Capri's golden age, and, while it's a nineteenth-century creation, the epitome of that beauty is the Villa St. Michele. Swedish physician Axel Munthe, as he described in his bestselling *The Story of St. Michele*, built the villa on the ruins of an ancient chapel dedicated to Saint Michael, with the idea that it be as filled with Mediterranean light as a Greek temple. And indeed its main architectural features are a loggia, pergolas, and columns that lead one to a magnificent circular viewing spot overlooking the Bay of Naples. Ancient objects on display include fragments of sarcophagi, busts, genuine Roman paving, and a Greek tomb and granite sphinx sharing the view.

Munthe lived in his villa for fifty-six years, often playing host to the ailing Swedish queen, Victoria. He lived long enough to see Capri become an international playground but, along with creating a sanctuary for migrating birds on Barbarossa Mountain, he kept his villa just as he loved it, which makes it now, along with Grotta Azzurra, the most visited place on the whole of the island.

Along with the villa, one of the great architectural treasures of Anacapri is the Chiesa Monumentale di San Michele, a crowning example of Neapolitan Baroque architecture that's one of the most stunning churches in the Campania region. The church, with its simple and white exterior, sits in a quiet, pretty little square keeping its charms modestly hidden and only for those who would revere them the right way. That includes walking on a narrow wooden walkway and up a spiral staircase so as not to mar the incredible hand-painted majolica tile floor of the church, a giant representation of the expulsion of Adam and Eve from a luxuriant Garden of Eden, painted by Leonardo Chiaiese. The marble high altar of the church is another work of art, including a painting of Saint Michael the Archangel by the Neapolitan artist, Nicola Malinconico.

There is also the beautiful Chiesa di Santa Sofia and the Piazza Boffe with its remarkable barrel-vaulted homes. But the hiking and picnicking, with views everywhere of Mediterranean macchia and white-walled houses spilling over with bright purple-pink bougainvillea, is one of the main joys of Anacapri. And the Phoenician Steps (the Scala Fenicia), restored in 1998, and connecting the port of Marina Grande with Anacapri, remains one of the most rewarding challenges to any backpacker or walker. The steps were chiseled out of the rock face by not Phoenicians but 7th and 6th century BCE Greeks. You can now take the climb that used to be taken by women lifting burdens like water jugs on their heads (when it was only way to carry water up from the Marina Grande's Truglio spring) while marveling at their ancient strength.

And should you continue hiking (or just take the funicular)—ah, the views from Monte Solaro, including the sight of the glowing chapel of Sant'Antonio of Padua, the Patron Saint of Anacapri. If you get tired, no one will blame you for frequently stopping. Such Mediterranean beauty, artistic splendor, and peace will give you what you truly desire from Italian towns, without any "meatball" standing in your way.

♦ AMARETTI, AMARETTO, AMARONE

They're three very similar words, but they refer to very different and vital parts of the Italian culinary and viticultural heritage, and the differences are the key to relishing a delightful range of Italian desserts and wines.

All share the same root, "amaro," which means bitter, although none are actually bitter and the first two are sweet. Amaretti and amaretto are both flavored with bitter almonds and use a diminutive ending, suggesting just a little or just a hint. Not so much bitter as sharp, with a bit of an edge.

Amaretti cookies were the original macaroon, predating French-style macaroons by over 150 years. They are thought to have been first created in the mid-17th century by Francesco Moriondo, pastry chef of the Court of Savoy in Northern Italy (their close cookie relative, biscotti, (*biscotto* singular), has been around since ancient Roman times (see "Vin Santo e Biscotti"). These delectable little morsels are crisp and crunchy on the outside and soft on the inside; they're ideal as an after-meal treat and can lend an unexpected sweet note and textural accent when crumbled over pasta dishes such as *Pasta con Zucca e Amaretti*—pasta with pumpkin and amaretti.

Amaretto, the after-dinner liqueur, is made from bitter almonds and the pits of apricots. There has been an unsurprising conflation of amaretto and *amore* ("love") and natural associations with romance. Perhaps it's just a sentimental legend, but a Renaissance-style "love story" has been promoted by the di Saronno family as to the "origin" of this velvety-rich amber-colored spirit:

> In 1525, a church in the town of Saronno (not far from Milan) commissioned a star pupil of Leonardo di Vinci—Bernadino Luini—to paint its frescoes. The church, like so many in Italy, was dedicated to the Virgin Mary, requiring Luini to find a model as an inspiration for his Madonna. He chose a lovely young widow innkeeper of limited means as his model ... and then lover. As a humble gift, she steeped apricot kernels in brandy and presented her sweet intoxicating creation to Luini.

Amaretto, like Limoncello, is made as an infusion, which means that, like the legendary lovely widow, you can create your own by yourself at home. It also means, as the story shows, that actual almonds need not be used. So if you have a nut allergy you can still feel the love!

As for **Amarone,** that means "big" or "great bitter"—even though it's paradoxically not bitter at all, and, as often in Italy, there's an anecdote for that. *Amarone della Valpolicella,* from the Veneto region, is one of Italy's most distinctive and appreciated robust red wines. Its contradictory name came out of its accidental discovery: the story goes that a winemaker found a forgotten barrel of sweet dessert wine that had not been properly sealed, allowing the yeast to continue to ferment. He tasted the wine, expecting it to be bitter, and cried out enthusiastically "*questo non è amaro, questo è un amarone!*" (this is not bitter, this is a great bitter!).

Today to replicate the winemaker's happy accident and make Amarone takes a lot of time, labor, and grapes for every bottle. To produce one bottle of wine, a winemaker in any other part of the world will vinify approximately 2 1/4 pounds of grapes. For each bottle of Amarone approximately 23 pounds are required. And those grapes must dehydrate into raisins before vinification truly begins. Amarone is high in alcohol, with intense aromatics and complex flavors that can range from dark fruits like berry, cherry, and plum to licorice, coffee, and chocolate.

You'd think a wine like that would be better known, and it almost was. In the classic crime thriller *Silence of the Lambs*, Hannibal Lecter spoke to Clarice Starling about savoring "fava beans and a nice Amarone"—underscoring that it goes quite well with liver, though Lecter's choice of the liver source would not be anyone else's. But in the movie Anthony Hopkins turned that, in a brilliant moment of improvisation, into "Chianti," having devilish fun with the "eeee." And so Amarone was ready for its closeup, and just missed it.

Still this is a glass of rich, figgy tannic red wine (which goes well with fava beans and, yes, liver), and one can definitely follow it with an amaretti cookie, and amaretto liqueur, an excellent combination for finishing a meal, and so a sequence well worth remembering.

♦ AMORINI, THE FLYING BAMBINI

Plump, naked, and *piccoli*—in short, very cute indeed—*amorini*, or *putti*, are those androgynous winged babies that tumble and flutter through Renaissance, Baroque, and Rococo art. Both terms are Latin diminutives; *amorini* for love and *putti* for "putus," meaning "boy child." They are typically depicted as angels or cherubs in religious scenes, but in an earlier form are frolicking young cupids in mythological narratives. In both cases, the presence of *amorini* symbolize love and joy, whether divine or earthly, and they are always ever so fetching. There is nary an ugly *putus*.

However young these flying bambini look, they're quite old . . . going back to classical antiquity, when they were winged messengers of the Greek gods and were known are *"erotes,"* forms of Eros and members of Aphrodite's train who conveyed various forms of love to humans. They were recast as angels in early Christian imagery, messengers now between the human and the divine, or in some cases, especially when carved on sarcophagi, symbols of the cycles of the seasons and the joys not only of the earth being left behind but the afterlife. However, they fell out of favor during the dour Middle Ages.

Then came their rediscovery, along with a cornucopia of other classical images, in the Renaissance. In Donatello's *Cantoria* (in Florence's Museum of the Duomo) the sculptor breathes new life into them; his new breed were as bacchanalian as their ancestors yet infused with a new Christian context as they appear in the guise of musical and dancing angels. During the Quattrocento, they once again took on the role of heavenly emissaries, reappearing on sarcophagi, especially of unfortunate children.

Still, most Renaissance *putti* are like the adorably curious ones who appear at the foot of Raphael's *Sistine Madonna* in the Uffizi, essentially decorative and ornamenting both religious and secular works without usually participating in the great events. Whether religious, mythological, or beautifully spectatorial, the *amorini* bring a host of classical and religious nuances to the tableaux they join, as well as their enchanting grace.

◆BARBELLS AND BIKINIS

◆BELLINI

◆BERNINI'S ANGELS

◆BEATRICE, LOVE AT FIRST SIGHT

◆BOTTICELLI'S VENUS

◆BONFIRE OF THE VANITIES

◆BURANO'S CANDY-COLORED CASAS

◆BOLOGNESE ... SAUCE OR DOG?

$\mathscr{B}$

♦ BARBELLS AND BIKINIS

If you thought the bikini was invented by the French after the war (and cleverly named for the Bikini Islands where "explosive" atomic tests were being conducted), think again. There are floor mosaics of athletic women in Sicily, with very well-toned abs, competing in running and weightlifting in what would pass for bikinis on any beach in Europe, and that predate the post-WWII bathing sensation by about seventeen hundred years.

The "Bikini Girls" are perhaps the most astonishing, unexpected, and famous mosaic in the Villa Romana del Casale in the town of Piazza Armerina (see "Hall of the Hunt"). When these 4th-century Roman mosaics were unearthed, to quite a bit of publicity, one hundred years ago, these portraits of stunningly modern-looking young women were originally thought to be part of a beauty contest. Closer analysis (of what clearly seem to be barbells and a discus) reveals that they most likely depict a kind of montage of female athletes in a competition; in the center is the winner with her trophies of a floral crown and palm scepter.

This interpretation is supported by evidence from the 4th century that it was expected for a wealthy aristocratic Roman woman to participate in sports—these were not Stephen Sondheim's "ladies who lunch." The sponsorship of contests of female athletes was clearly an elite pursuit attesting to the elevated status of the owner of the Villa Casale, no doubt one reason for the celebratory mosaic. Also, this sort of garb was for female participation in sport, since Romans swam nude.

Which means that the young women in the mosaic don't just anticipate the bikinis of the 1950s, but the sports bras and female triathlete gear of the 21st century! Well, Italians have always been "fashion forward."

✦ BELLINI

Ever consider why the Bellini cocktail is called the Bellini?

It's definitely a beautiful cocktail —"*bella*" and so *bella* one might even say *bellissima*—but there's more to it than meets the eye.

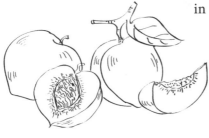

The Bellini (a luscious mixture of Prosecco and peach purée and sometimes muddled raspberry) was invented in the 1940s by Venetian-born Giuseppe Cipriani, founder of Harry's Bar in Venice. The cocktail's vibrant color reminded Cipriani of the luminous palette of the paintings of 15th-century Venetian artist Giovanni Bellini, who shaped Venetian artistic tradition with his innovative use of color and oil paint—sumptuous, richly jewel-like tones, sensuously detailed shading, and atmospheric landscapes. It's just another example of how, thanks to civic pride in general—and the astute good taste, knowledge, and cultural patriotism of one citizen in particular—great Italian art makes itself felt in contemporary Italian life.

Looking for examples of Cipriani's inspiration in Bellini's oeuvre is not difficult; whether in the lustrous robes of a Madonna, the toga of a saint, or an achingly beautiful sunrise, you can also find the classic cocktail.

The Bellini is, in fact, an official IBA (International Bartenders Association) Cocktail. The IBA suggests celebrating other great Italian composers and artists by substituting the peach puree with mandarin juice to create a Puccini, strawberry purée for a Rossini, and pomegranate juice for a more intense Tintoretto.

• BERNINI'S ANGELS

Make yourself familiar with the angels, and behold them frequently in spirit; for, without being seen they are present with you.
—St Francis de Sales

Connecting the Eternal City to Saint Peter's Basilica in Vatican City is Ponte Sant'Angelo, one of the most serenely beautiful bridges in the world. Ten marble angels on the parapets are graced with the most lifelike and delicate of movements, their draped clothing seemingly flowing in the breeze. The harmonious symmetry, openness to light, and the above all, the sheer grouping of the *angeli* create a monumental impact.

Ponte Sant'Angelo, however, is not named for its extraordinary baroque angels, but instead for Castel Sant'Angelo, which in turn was named for the Archangel Michael, who stands on top the cylindrical castle with his sword stretched to the sky. During the plague of 590 ACE, Pope Gregory I saw a vision of the Archangel standing there signifying the end of the deadly epidemic, and the statue was erected in gratitude and celebration.

Castel Sant'Angelo itself has a colorful history. Originally the mausoleum of Emperor Hadrian, it was later used as a fortress and "safe house" for Popes. They would hole up there during sieges and wars, as there was a secret escape route connecting the Vatican to the castle. (Castel Sant'Angelo is also featured in Puccini's opera *Tosca;* Floria famously throws herself off the Castel rooftop to evade capture.)

In 1667 Pope Clement IX commissioned Bernini to "stage set" the bridge, originally built for Roman funerals, to be a principal part of the walking route taken by pilgrims visiting St. Peter's Cathedral. Bernini designed a "living" Via Crucis (Way of the Cross) so pilgrims could emotionally participate, as in a theater (and what was the Baroque if not theatrical), in the story of Jesus's suffering and crucifixion. Each angel holds an instrument of the Passion serving as a point of reflection for pilgrims. Bernini sculpted only two of the angels (although he designed them all): the one holding the crown of thorns, and the one with the inscription

INRI (the initials for the Latin title *Iesvs Nazarenvs Rex Ivdaeorvm*—Jesus of Nazareth, the King of the Jews—which was written over the head of Jesus on the cross). They are meant to complement each other: the first, with a more masculine feel, appears serene in his confidence of the Resurrection, and second more compassionately lyrical and feminine in sensibility.

Before dying in 1669, Pope Clement IX not only contemplated the statues but, ironically, decided they were too magnificent to be exposed to the elements on the bridge and had them replaced with copies. Bernini's originals can be seen in the church of Sant'Andrea delle Fratte, a short walk from Piazza di Spagna. As so often in the Italian Renaissance, an earthly compromise was struck between the spiritual realms of religion and art.

✦ BEATRICE, LOVE AT FIRST SIGHT

The Taj Mahal, perhaps the world's most exquisite monument, stands as a lasting expression of one man's love for a woman. Dante Alighieri's *Divine Comedy*, a monumental work of world literature, stands as a lasting expression of one boy's love for a girl.

In May of 1274 the nine-year-old Dante accompanied his father to a party held at the home of the Portinaris, another upper-class Florentine family. There the lad beheld Beatrice, daughter of the party's host and a girl several months his junior. The impressionable Dante was instantly besotted. Despite only a few chance encounters between the two of them after that fateful day, the flame of Dante's love for Beatrice was never extinguished, even after they both went on to arranged marriages and Beatrice died at the age of only twenty-five. Beatrice's untimely death, in fact, spawned the extended love poem *La Vita Nuova* (The New Life) recounting their "relationship." This work cemented Dante's reputation as a poet without equal.

But Dante's crowning achievement, the *Divine Comedy*, established him as a poet for the ages. Beatrice's transformation into a heavenly presence is complete in Dante's masterwork. At her behest, the poet Virgil is summoned from the afterlife to escort a wayward Dante through Hell and Purgatory en route to her post in Heaven. When Dante the pilgrim finally reaches Beatrice in Heaven, what kind of reception does Dante the poet prepare for him? Beatrice chastises him for having squandered his talents! But things improve markedly from there (this being Heaven, after all).

♦ BOTTICELLI'S VENUS

Surely one of the high-water marks in the humanist revival of the Renaissance is the painting of the first pagan female nude since classical antiquity. That landmark was the *Birth of Venus (Nascita di Venere)*, a depiction of the Roman goddess of love and also one of the first large-scale canvases in Italian art.

Sandro Botticelli (1445–1510), one of the most acclaimed artists of Italy in his lifetime, painted the work, commissioned by Lorenzo de Medici, in the spirit of a Neoplatonic theme emerging from Lorenzo's humanist "salon": a belief that spiritual uplift was achieved though love, harmony, and ideal beauty. Lorenzo had this theme set to verse by a humanist poet in his circle, Angelo Poliziano, and Botticelli followed the poem in designing the painting.

It's a wonderful tableau of the wind gods Zephyr and Aura wafting with their breath a shell from beneath the sea, on which is perched the gloriously beautiful Venus. You can almost feel that motion and sense the miraculous distance from which the goddess is emerging in the composition of the painting. Her modest stance is borrowed from a classical statue, *Venus Pudicae*, that had just been unearthed. Meanwhile one of the Graces is there to cover her beauty with a cape and in effect sanctify her to be not just an image of beauty but a mother of creation, a kind of spiritual intermediary between the earthly and the divine.

Botticelli brought to the work the best of his highly identifiable style: refined delicacy, elegance, and a gift for the portrayal of sublime feminine beauty. So inevitably viewers ask: who was the mesmerizing woman with the golden strawberry blond hair—an idealization of such beauty or a real flesh and blood woman?

It is generally believed there is a real woman who inspired both Birth of Venus and Primavera (looking closely at the two paintings' models they appear very similar) and that she was Simonetta Vespucci, considered the most beautiful woman of Florence (and therefore, to Florentines, the world). She was born in a Ligurian town just south of Genoa, Portovenere, which coincidentally means "port of Venus." She arrived in Florence at the age of

15 or 16 as the bride of Marco Vespucci (cousin to the navigator Amerigo) whose family had the Florentine gold standard: advantageous connections to the Medici.

Given her grace and beauty, she was immediately accepted and appreciated. In spite of her marriage, Lorenzo's brother Giuliano publicly declared his great affection for her and entered a jousting contest bearing a banner with her image painted on his helmet along with words meaning "unparalleled one." Giuliano commissioned Botticelli to paint her portrait (which he did twice).

Sadly, La Bella Simonetta died of consumption at the age of 25. There is debate among art historians as to whether there was a love affair between her and Botticelli, but most feel that, as Beatrice was for Dante, Simonetta was an unrequited love transformed into his muse. Botticelli, who never married, lived another thirty-four years and then asked to be buried at Simonetta's feet. His wish was granted and you can find them both in the Church of Ognissanti (All Saints) in Florence.

At the time of Botticelli's death, his reputation had already begun to wane. It's not that he hadn't continued to paint after *Birth of Venus*; in fact, he was summoned (along with other contemporaries) by Pope Sextus IV to take part in the decoration of the Sistine Chapel. He would paint many Church-approved religious subjects, as well as portraits. But his iconic works would remain paintings pagan in their themes and expressing the revival of interest in the classics and the humanist concepts of beauty that so characterized the Quattrocento Renaissance. And so, he would be overshadowed and then eclipsed with the establishment of High Renaissance style and the paintings of Leonardo, Michelangelo, and Raphael.

But Botticelli's genius was rediscovered in the latter part of the 19th century and embraced by the Aesthetic and Pre-Raphaelite movements, most notably by Gabriel Rossetti and Edward Burn-Jones in Great Britain. Today it's unimaginable that Botticelli, even for a time, had nearly been forgotten. The large Botticelli room in the Uffizi is always packed with viewers silently enraptured by the great beauty of Florence and the great creator of beauty, linked with her in life and death, who immortalized her and the world she represented.

◆ THE BONFIRE OF THE VANITIES

It's a phrase that for many colorfully and comically satirizes the excesses of the 1980s, thanks to Tom Wolfe's novel of the same name. But for the people of 15th-century Florence, there was nothing funny about these bonfires that consumed so much of not only their culture, but their belief in the glowing humanism that had sustained the Renaissance.

The "bonfires of the vanities" were the creation of a Florentine government presided over by the Dominican friar and would-be prophet Girolamo Savonarola. If Lorenzo the Magnificent was the ultimate Renaissance man, leading a society where the finest of human abilities were expressed in literature and the arts, Savonarola, who came to power after Lorenzo's death and the expulsion of the much weakened Medici family, was the anti-Renaissance man, plunging Florence back into the torments of medieval puritanical Catholicism.

Once his party, the *piagnone* (the "weepers"), came to power, the bonfires of the vanities began. The flames were meant to consume all that was vain and impious and wicked in Florentine life. First and foremost were the books, which made Savonarola's bonfires the precursors of all the book-burnings by fascist dictators in the twentieth century.

Then, most tragically, irreplaceable paintings that violated Savonarola's strict guidelines for permissible Christian art. The immortal Sandro Botticelli became a *piagnone* and threw some of his great works into the flames.

Finally, and most absurdly, the *piagnone* went house-to-house collecting makeup, playing cards, jewelry, carnival masks, mirrors (which reflected people's vain earthly images), perfumes, elegant clothes, and underclothes. Even the obese were set upon outside of bakeries for the sin of gluttony and ordered to throw their baked goods into the flames.

In 1498 came the reaction to the reactionary Savonarola; such has often been the dark grand guignol theater—the elaborate horror show—of Italian politics. Savonarola's old enemy Pope Alexander VI (Rodrigo Borgia) excommunicated him; the suggestion he undergo a trial by fire to prove God was on his side never quite came off, and he lost his credibility. Charged with heresy, false prophesy, and sedition by his enemies in the republic, he was dragged from his cloister and tortured on a rack for three days, breaking almost every bone in his body except his one hand needed to sign a confession. His reign was over.

Savonarola foreshadowed, in his fire and brimestone anti-papacy crusade, the grim religious warfare of the Reformation and papal Counter-Reformation. In a sentence that mirrored the *contrapasso* punishments of Dante's *Inferno*, where sinners suffered penalties that reflected their crimes, the monk's last giant bonfire was lit for him. He was hanged and his body was burned before a partially weeping but mostly cheering crowd in the Piazza della Signoria, the same site where he had burned the works of others.

✦ BURANO'S CANDY-COLORED CASAS

Forty minutes from Murano, world famous for its glass, is the island village of Burano, famous for its lace. Many visitors to Venice, perhaps forgetting one out of confusion with the other, or perhaps due to a tight schedule, choose to go to Murano and not take a second 40-minute valporetto journey to its less-well-known almost-namesake. But those who do are treated to one of the most beautiful vistas in Italy.

Burano is where the dazzling colors of locales like the Caribbean meet the haunting qualities of the Venetian lagoons. Along the canals are charming two-story houses—cherry, pink, chartreuse, azure and canary yellow, with contrasting-hued shutters, brightly patterned curtains for doors and window boxes, and ceramic pots overflowing with flowers (and arguably the best art-directed clotheslines in all of Italy).

No one really knows how all this exuberant beauty began, but there are many legends about the origin of Burano's vivacious color scheme. One plausible suggestion was that in earlier days, painting each house a different color was useful in defining the separate properties and property lines. Another more enjoyable and at least remotely plausible suggestion is that on days of winter fog or very rough seas, the fishermen could not go fishing and spent their day playing cards and drinking wine. In the evening they were so wasted they couldn't even recognize their own houses. So it was decided to paint every house a different color so every wife could be sure that the right man would return to her after a day of carousing (well, at least somewhat sure).

The drunken fishermen have faded into history, leaving behind lacemakers and a lace museum, and that long tradition of rainbow-colored house facades, which now guide not fishermen, but photographers. In a city where the mirror images of beautiful houses on the canal waterways have an eternal allure, there is no better place than Burano for vistas that combine the fabulous, fantastical spirit of Venice's reflections (literal and poetic) with the most delightfully lively bursts of color in *La Serenissima*— The Serene Republic.

♦ BOLOGNESE ... SAUCE OR DOG?

The answer is ... both! But let's first explore the city of Bologna, home of both the legendary pasta sauce and noble breed of dog.

All too often overlooked on the basic Italian tourist itinerary: a buzzing prosperous city renowned as the gastronomic center of Italy and capital of the Emilia-Romagna. It has an opulent feel reflecting both its present and illustrious past. Bologna is *bellissima*. The center is quintessentially medieval with red tiled roofs and balconies radiating out from the great central square of Piazza Maggiore and a harmonious ensemble of porticoed walkways, red-brick *palazzi,* and charming squares. There are numerous monuments and curiosities including plenty of small quirky museums and, most conspicuously, the *Due Torri*, Bologna's own *two* "leaning towers."

Italians refer to Bologna as *la dotta, la rossa, e la grassa,* "the erudite, the red, and the fat." "The erudite," because it is home to the oldest true university in the world—known as *La Dotta* (The Learned)—which first achieved its worldwide fame as a law school and then medical school. Thomas Becket, Petrarch, Copernicus, and Erasmus studied at Bologna. Marcello Malphighi, the great pioneering physician, Luigi Galvani, one of the first biologists, and novelist Umberto Eco taught there. Today 100,000 Italian and foreign students attend the university, making up about 20 percent of the city's population, and bringing a true "happening" energy and vibe to the city, whether in theater, music, summer festivals, or just the café and bar scene, which is among northern Italy's liveliest.

Bologna "the red" because of the vivid color of the roofs and buildings—and because Bologna has a reputation and long history of left-wing politics and is home to the former Italian communist party and its newspaper, *L'Unita*.

And finally, Bologna "the fat" because of its legendary gastronomy, prominently featuring meats, ham, salami, and, of course, the famous Bolognese sauce. *Ragu alla Bolognese* is typically served with tagliatelle or lasagna. Today it's thought of as a red sauce but many recipes only add a small amount of tomato and the "original" did not; it was really all about the meats. The first recipe came from Pellegrino Artusi and is included in his cookbook published in 1891. Artusi's recipe, *Maccheroni alla bolognese*, thought to have originated in the 1850s when he spent time in Bologna, called for lean veal filet, pancetta, onions, and carrots all finely minced, cooked with butter until brown, then cooked with broth. Artusi also suggested enhancements, like the addition of dried mushrooms or truffle slices, or finely chopped chicken liver cooked with the meat. He further suggested as a final touch the addition of cream to make an even smoother, richer-tasting dish.

The *Accademia Italiana della Cucina* (Italian Academy of Cuisine) registered the "authentic" recipe for Bolognese Ragù with the Bologna Chamber of Commerce on October 17, 1982 in the Palazzo della Mercanzia. The recipe features beef, pancetta, carrots, celery, onions, tomato sauce, whole milk and red wine.

Now the dog. A member of the *bichon* group, the Bolognese breed is thought to have descended from that type in southern Italy around the 11th or 12th century—making the dog senior to the sauce, and, as it turns out, just as well-liked domestically and abroad. The Bolognese became very popular among the royal courts of Italy and other parts of Europe from the 16th century to the early 19th century. The little dog is featured in several famous paintings by the Venetian master Titian (as well as some of those by Spain's Goya) and was the "it dog" and a pampered companion of the Italian nobility. Cosimo de Medici took eight Bolognese to Brussels as gifts for Belgian noblemen. Both the Gonzagas and Medicis bred them. The Duke d'Este gave a pair to King Phillip II of Spain as a gift; he was thanked by the king who wrote, "These two little dogs are the most royal gifts one can make to an emperor."

Many famous personalities in history had a Bolognese: Madame Pompadour (1721–1764), Czarina Catherine the Great of Russia (1729–1796), and Maria Therese, Empress of Austria and mother of Marie Antoinette (1717–1780). Maria Therese loved her Bolognese so much that after its death she had it preserved, and it can be seen in the Natural History Museum in Vienna.

With the decline of the aristocracy in Europe, the Bolognese fell from favor and by the end of World War II the breed became almost extinct. But with the hard work of some dedicated breeders in Italy and Belgium it has been resurrected. So, when in Italy, visit Bologna, try the delicious sauce, and if you can't quite pick up a sample of what is now a highly uncommon breed, you can always select the adorable and energetic consolation prize: the breed most closely related to the Bolognese is the popular Bichon Frise.

- CARNEVALE

- CARPACCIO

- CATERINA'S CARCIOFI

- CASANOVA, SO MISUNDERSTOOD

- CENTENARIANS OF SARDINIA

- CARPET SLIPPERS

- COSIMO,
A CAESAR OF THE RENAISSANCE

- CANTICLE OF THE CREATURES

- CAVE CANEM

- THE CASTRATI

♦ CARNEVALE

"The season of Carnival changes the whole world," wrote Carlo Goldoni, the 18th-century Venetian comic playwright. "Whether you are doing well or doing badly, Carnival cheers you up."

At the mention of Mardi Gras or Carnival, images of revelers in New Orleans or of wild abandon in Rio likely come to mind. However, the history of Mardi Gras began long before the Europeans set foot in the New World. The word carnival (*carnevale* in Italian) comes from the Latin *carne + vale*, meaning "farewell to meat," and is associated with the pre-Lenten festivals prior to Fat Tuesday or, in Italian, *Martedí Grasso*: the period of merriment and temporary abandon that precedes the penance of Lent, lending a Christian interpretation to the ancient rites of spring.

During the Middle Ages and Renaissance, Italian cities, and most notably Venice, developed a tradition and reputation of *Carnevale* feasting (it was declared an official holiday in 1296). *Carnevale* grew into a season of celebration and as it flourished added more and more elaborate costumes, lavish masquerade balls and other events, and performances by roving minstrels and actors. By the eighteenth century, the Venetian Republic was in serious decline; however, the Venetians were still having plenty of fun masquerading for more than half of the year with the original religious significance of *Carnevale* utterly diminished and mostly forgotten.

But then abruptly Carnevale was kaput. On February 28, 1797, Venetians celebrated what turned out to be their last *Martedi Grasso* for a very long time, for the Venetians would soon surrender without a fight to Napoleon, who banned Carnevale, and sadly future *Martedí Grassos* came and went without the revelries of the past.

On February 27, 1979, almost exactly 182 years to the day, pipers piped and revelers once more reveled in Piazza San Marco on *Martedi Grasso*. Municipal authorities and Scuola Grande di San Marco, along with a flock of young art students, joined forces to revive the grand festivities and pageantry with the same spirit that inspired American historical societies to organize mock battles or to stage charity balls with Victorian costumes and themes (not to mention revive Mardi Gras in Mobile in 1867 once the Union occupation ended). The one missing ingredient was the masks. However, serendipitously a few local artisans, not anticipating the return of *Carnevale*, were already making masks to keep the old traditions alive.

And so, Venetians being Venetians, amid the modern day merchants of Venice a traditional craft was reborn. In fact, it exploded, and can now be seen everywhere you turn, from fantastical high-end workshops to small shops specializing in masks to "tobacci" shops, newsstands, and kiosks. Venetians may no longer have the elaborate system of social, religious, and sexual evasions and liaisons that characterized the old customs of mask wearing; it's more a fun way these days to honor a tradition and of course participate in *Carnevale*.

Should you want to join in the merriment and purchase a mask, you'll find most sold are plastic and not all are Venetian; the Chinese, for example, have figured out the market. You may find more artful papier-mâché masks, though most are not truly "handmade" (Italian law permits an article be labeled "handmade" if some percentage came from somebody's hands … somewhere … so there's a lot of leeway as to what qualifies) and these cost about ten to twenty Euros. A handful of artists, however, in the true *Carnevale* and Venice spirit, are producing amazingly phantasmagorical masks, and you can, of course, commission your own concept. These can cost hundreds or thousands of euros and be fabricated elaborately out of leather, clay, papier-mâché, or plaster of Paris and gauze, with feathers, beads, and brocade to decorate ever more lavish versions limited only by the imagination.

Thanks to these artisans dedicated to the craft of make-believe, fantasy still has its place, especially at carnival time, in the magical, mysterious city of watery reflections, color, and light.

◆ CARPACCIO

Recognized by the Oxford English Dictionary as a noun rather than a name, carpaccio bars can be found the world over. A special dish of raw meat thinly sliced or pounded thin, carpaccio was invented at Harry's Bar in Venice, where it was first served to an eccentric countess whose doctor recommended she eat only raw meat. The dish was named "Carpaccio" in reference and as homage to the Venetian painter Vittore Carpaccio, who loved the color red and was known for the use of distinctively vivid pigments in his paintings. The dish was on the Harry's Bar menu before it was given its name; in 1963 it was officially dedicated to Vittore Carpaccio at the same time as a major exhibition of the painter's work was taking place in Venice. As with the Bellini before it, Harry's Bar gave an unexpected but naturally welcome boost to Italian art history.

A native of Venice, Carpaccio developed an engaging storytelling style suited to the painting of incident-filled scenes. As a proud citizen of Venice, he managed to depict La Serenissima everywhere; even Britain and Brittany were transformed into the legendary canal city in one of his most famous fresco cycles. He was terrifically popular in his time, painting his huge canvases for the Venetian *scuole* (charitable and religious organizations), and delighting his fellow Venetians with scenes of pomp and pageantry, the sounds of drums and trumpets, and endearing details of familiar sights: dogs, birds, pet monkeys, lounging cavaliers, flying flags, and bustling activity everywhere. One suspects this master of richly colored panoramas celebrating his beloved city would have appreciated being "consumed" for centuries not only in galleries but also as a signature dish in its most famous restaurant. (And likely be astonished that his namesake's popularity

has proliferated far beyond "red meats" to include tuna, salmon, beetroot, octopus, and even kangaroo carpaccio).

✦ CATERINA'S CARCIOFI

There was a time when the consumption of certain foods by women was simply not allowed in France. Not *comme il faut*, very much *de trop*. And why? Because they were con-sidered too sexually stimulating (I know … that doesn't sound quite right … but hang on …).

This was in the mid-sixteenth centu-ry, when morals were somewhat stricter, certainly with regard to women, and even in France. It took a strong Italian woman to break through that boundary, just as she would break through so many boundaries in France during her lifetime.

Caterina de Medici, great-granddaughter of Lorenzo the Magnificent, was married to Henry of Orleans—the son of King Frances I of France—by her cousin, Pope Clement VI, when they were both only fourteen years old. It was a marriage made in supposed strategic alliance heaven, but its consequences would prove more culinary than political.

Caterina introduced a wide variety of Italian foods to French cook-ing including the *carciofi* or artichoke, which she brought to France as part of her wedding dowry. It's hard to think of that as the exotic move it once was, since few vegetables are as central to Roman cuisine today as this round, prickly member of the thistle family. *Carciofi alla romana* artichokes are stuffed with a mixture of oil, lemon, garlic, parsley, and mint. They are then braised until tender. The result is as scrumptious as it is simple to prepare.

In ancient Roman times, the artichoke was a menu item for feasts and special occasions. The plump globes at their centers were considered to be an aphrodisiac (because of their phallic shape) and it was even believed that their consumption could be effective in securing the birth of boys.

After the fall of the Empire, the cultivation of artichokes declined and they became a rarity. However, they regained popularity during the Renaissance. Caterina made the *carciofi* a staple of the French diet but scandalized French society with her own love of them. For she brazenly defied the popular convention which dictated that women were not to eat foods considered to be aphrodisiacs, and certainly not in public.

Catherine ate them openly, and in large quantities. One historian who observed her unabashed passion is quoted as saying that she "liked to burst," such was her affinity. She also encouraged her entourage of female attendants to enjoy the culinary pleasure of *carciofi*. By the end of Catherine's reign, the artichoke had become one of the most popular vegetables in France. She and her staff were no doubt very skilled at preparing them and very persuasive. And perhaps Frenchmen reconsidered that whole no-sexual-stimulants-for-women rule.

◆ CASANOVA, SO MISUNDERSTOOD

He was perhaps the greatest living example of the Don Juan figure, the unrepentant compulsive seducer of women, a character first brought to life in a Spanish play, celebrated by a British poet, made the central character in an immortal opera by a German, and described by a French philosopher as an example of a man living in a godless world with dignity, passion, and humor. So perhaps the world can be forgiven for its first misunderstanding about this international cultural history icon: that he wasn't Italian. He was indeed—from Venice, to be exact.

Of course, Casanova fed that misunderstanding by being very much a pan-European figure and by writing his autobiography in French. He had lived much of his life in Paris, French was the language of intellectuals and the main language in Europe (as in the phrase "lingua franca") in the 18th century, and he hoped for the widest possible readership. He would ultimately receive a greater readership than he ever imagined, or would get to imagine, since it was posthumous. But the misinterpretations and misunderstandings that dogged his life almost prevented the world from ever knowing about him and about what is now regarded as one of the great memoirs of all time.

It's certainly true that this brilliant self-made Venetian social climber was a notorious womanizer. That aspect of his life began early when he was dismissed from the priesthood because of his "involvement" with nuns who were the daughters of nobles. Despite being plagued by a gambling habit that often ruined him, he would lead the high life for many years thanks to various patrons, even taking the famous Grand Tour of Europe, but ultimately his blasphemies, affairs, and fights with prominent men would catch up with him. He was arrested for sedition, jailed in the Doge's Palace in Venice, and escaped with a fellow prisoner.

His life's extraordinary encounters and events would ultimately fill a 3700-page book. He crisscrossed Europe and got to know popes, royalty such as Catherine the Great, and luminaries like Voltaire, Mozart, and even Ben Franklin. He was spy, gambler, astrologer, and freemason. His life had such mythological dimensions that many still believe him to be a fictional character.

He was also a writer, an extraordinarily prolific one, having penned forty-two books including a translation of the *Iliad* into his Venetian dialect, numerous mathematical treatises, a history of Poland, and a five-volume fantasy novel. He was a true Enlightenment era polymath, a kind of eighteenth-century descendant of the "Renaissance man." Insofar as this whole aspect of his life has been neglected in favor of making his name a synonym for "seducer" and "libertine," he may be history's most misunderstood intellectual.

In his herculean effort to set the record straight, he wrote his legendary memoir, *Histoire de ma Vie* (The Story of My Life) in his penniless old age while working as a librarian in Bohemia. On his deathbed (he died in 1798) he bequeathed it to his nephew, having no idea if it would ever be published. His nephew's descendants sold it to a German publisher, whose family kept the original manuscript under lock and key for nearly 140 years. The Church got to exact its long-delayed punishment on Casanova when a highly censored version was first published in 1821 and immediately placed on the Vatican's list of Prohibited Books. The most misunderstanding of Casanova's misinterpreters appeared to have the last word.

But perhaps the Vatican's ultimate Master thought differently: the original manuscript escaped destruction in World War II, even though the building it had been kept in sustained a direct hit. At the end of the war the Allies were able to unearth the book and transfer it back to its original German owners.

Only in 1960 was the first uncensored edition published. The tales of his notorious love affairs constitute no more than a third of the book, and, being a religious man despite all his problems with the Vatican, he actually self-censored some parts he considered particularly offensive. The rest consists of wonderful stories of duels, adventurous journeys, arrests, and escapes, but also a priceless record of the social life and customs of the period, and passages of great wisdom and intellect that attest to Casanova's curiosity, his skills as an observer and journalist, and his grasp of human nature. Both the characters and events he describes have been verified.

In 2010 the Bibliotheque Nationale de France in Paris purchased the original manuscript for $9.6 million and the French government subsequently anointed it a "national treasure." Perhaps it took the French to understand that Casanova was a lot more than the ultimate example of the Italian stereotype of the inveterate skirt-chaser: he also exemplified Italian wit, culture, spirit, literary facility, and appreciation of all the goods of this world.

◆ CENTENARIANS OF SARDINIA

In Sardinia, when the traditional toast *"A kent' annos!"* ("May you live to be 100 years!") is shouted, it's not just an expression of affection; it might mean "May you live as long as my grandfather/grandmother/brother/sister." For Sardinia, with a population of 1.6 million, has the world's highest recorded percentage of centenarians. And unlike in some of the world's "Blue Zones"—where life spans of the local population often exceed one hundred years—that holds true for men as well as women.

Theories abound. Ask the Sardinians and they say it's a diet of fresh homegrown beans, potatoes, *minestrone* (soup vegetables), olive oil and spices, and very little meat, along with a hard-working but low-stress farmer's or shepherd's lifestyle. Or, as one villager put it, their own breathable *la dolce vita*, "something in the air" in the *monte e mare* (mountain and sea) Mediterranean climate. And especially the warmth of a society where elders are still very much a beloved, respected, and vital part of an extended family community; there's no assisted living exclusion for these cherished grandparents.

Scientists and health specialists, as part of an AKeA program—yes, that's an acronym for "*A kent' annos*"—are trying to dig a little deeper into this Sardinian mystery. They're considering, for example, how the rugged, rocky coast of the island has deterred both invaders and intermarriage, and thus may have preserved genetic traits for long life.

But the most intriguing (and happiest) theory has to do with the local red wine of the region, grown from the Cannonau (or Grenache) grape. Like all such wines it contains antioxidant sources in its grape skins, which may help guard against heart disease and cancer. Cannonau especially has greater amounts of resveratrol, a protective compound against insects, fungi, and UV radiation that has been experimentally shown to extend life in animal subjects. This may be due to a Sardinian traditional longer wait before their grapes are pressed, which gives them a higher resveratrol content, and British scientist Roger Corder has theorized that the vineyards' higher altitude causes the grapes to percolate more resveratrol protection against UV rays, making the local vintage even more beneficial.

But you don't have to be a scientist to perform this experiment. You just need to know that this robust wine goes especially well with thick red sauces, meats, pasta, and the local Sardinian goats' milk cheese, *Pecorino Sardo*. It also has a beautiful dark ruby red color, an aroma of violets, plum and berry notes, a hint of spices, and a warm rustic earthiness. It may not guarantee you a hundred years, but you'll enjoy more of the days you get.

✦ CARPET SLIPPERS

It might surprise you that this rustic, slipper-shaped bread (*ciabatta* means "slipper" in Italian) filled with irregular holes—all the better to trap drizzles of olive oil—did not arise from the ovens of long-ago Sicily or the bakeries of Renaissance Rome. In fact, *ciabatta* has a prosaically recent history (like the carpet slipper it was named for); it was created in the early '80s in what is thought to have been a competitive response to the popularity of French baguettes. Hugely better than the sandwich wrap of today, but still very much a business lunch bread.

Many regions have their own local recipe variations. The *ciabatta* from the north has a crisp crust, is soft and porous, and is light to the touch. The *ciabatta* found in Tuscany, Umbria, and Marche is often firmer and denser. The more open-spongy type, most often found in America, is made from a very wet oozing dough (hard to manipulate if you are a home baker) and requires a *biga* (a natural leavener), or starter—as is used for sourdough bread—to produce a light fermentation along with an inviting aroma, distinctive flavor, and that special combination of crunchiness and porosity. Curiously, the *biga* is referred to as *la madre*, meaning "the mother" in northern Italy, while it is referred to as *il babbo*, "the father" in Tuscany and to the south.

Ciabatta is not to be confused with *foccacia*, which has a far more distinguished provenance; it was not created as a competitive business response, but seems to have arisen from ancient times in response to the peninsula's most basic needs. *Focaccia* was around before the founding of Rome, and uses the same basic recipe for flatbreads that originated with the ancient Greeks and Etruscans. In Roman times is was called *panis focacius* derived from the Latin *focus* meaning "hearth," or place for baking with a central flame.

Be it ancient or modern, "our daily *pane*" has always been a focal point of Italian culinary tradition.

♦ COSIMO, A CAESAR OF THE RENAISSANCE

Florence may have been a republic during the Renaissance, but nonetheless one man posthumously received the imperial title of *Pater Patriae* (Father of His Country), previously reserved for the Caesars: businessman, statesman, foreign minister, and patron of the arts Cosimo de Medici. He was the creator of one of the most peaceful and prosperous periods in any Renaissance city's history, and the greatest subsidizer of Florence's amazing generation of geniuses—his  keen insight and discriminating taste in art, architecture, and literature helped bring into being works that would become immortal.

Cosimo's father, Giovanni di Bicci, in securing the papal account, made the Medicis the most powerful banking family, and put them right at the hub of the affairs of Florence. In a city-state where the parliament basically functioned to anchor the leadership of a mercantile oligarchy of powerful families and guilds, to be first among those equals was a hotly contested prize: when it became clear Cosimo would succeed his father, his enemies intrigued to throw him into prison and then exile him to Venice.

But he would return a year later when a pro-Medici government took over. Technically he ran a banking business and during a rule of thirty years he only allowed himself to be *gonfaloniere,* or visible head of the state, for six years, taking that and other ceremonial posts mainly to run the city's finances. But he was also the mastermind of foreign affairs. He maintained a most welcome peace throughout his reign by clever manipulation of Florence's friends and potential enemies, building alliances against the growing power of the Doges of Venice.

Cosimo's moderate, humane leadership, as well as his generous support of the arts and letters, ignited the Florentine Renaissance, and it was Cosimo, not his grandson Lorenzo, who really made Florence the artistic and intellectual capital of Europe. His reign began with the completion of Brunelleschi's soaring cupola at Santa Maria del Fiore, at which a council of Latin and Greek Orthodox churches was supposed to celebrate an eternal reunion...which didn't last a week.

But not only would the dome itself prove far more important, so would Cosimo's meetings with Greek scholars who would inspire in him a lifelong love of Plato. He would ultimately found a Platonic academy and under his patronage the great scholar Marsilio Ficino would translate all of Plato's dialogues, a cornerstone of humanism's rediscovery of classical thought. To house such works he would create Renaissance Europe's first public library in the Dominican convent of San Marco. Cosimo's Platonic academy would also foster doctrines of neo-Platonic spirituality and mystic love—a fusion of classical and Christian thought—which would inspire Sandro Botticelli and lead him toward the painting of his greatest works, the *Primavera* and *Birth of Venus,* which would be completed during the reign of Cosimo's grandson Lorenzo the Magnificent.

Cosimo's beneficence would continue with the reconstruction of San Marco, above all its delicately luminous frescoes by Fra Angelico; his private chapel of the Magi in the Medici palace painted by Benozzo Gozzoli; and in all likelihood Donatello's *David.* He also supported Fra Filippo Lippi, who painted a *Madonna Adoring Her Child* for the Magi Chapel and an *Annuciation* for the Medici palace. Lippi's warmly colored, sweetly maternal figures reflected Lippi's own very unfriar-like pursuit of women, and Cosimo not only backed him but tried to protect him from his vice, going so far as to once lock him in his studio to keep him from the chase. (It was one of his few unsuccessful projects; Filippo Lippi wound up eloping with a nun.)

Cosimo also inspired other wealthy families to support the arts as well, an activity buoyed by a belief that such Church-oriented patronage could go into "God's account" and expiate their sins, along with the belief that the Medicis should not get too far ahead of them in this regard. All this would further Florence's growth and glory. Before his death Cosimo would declare correctly that the art and architecture he stimulated and supported, along with his philanthropy (he gave away twice as much as he left to his heirs) would be his legacy. He was not so confident in his family, gravely fearing for their future.

Little did Cosimo know that not only would his grandson carry on his legacy well enough to be dubbed Lorenzo the Magnificent, but his great-grandson and great-grand-nephew would become Popes Leo X and Clement VII, and that the name Medici would come to symbolize the glories of Italy as much as the Caesars themselves.

◆ CANTICLE OF THE CREATURES

Perhaps no other figure in all of Christendom is more closely associated with the natural world than Italy's patron saint, Francis of Assisi. (Thousands of bird baths and garden statues can't be wrong!) And the best way to tap into his natural spirit may well be to visit his namesake town.

A good place to start in Assisi is the great basilica erected in Francis's honor during the decades following his death in 1226. The great edifice has three tiers. One has barely entered the upper level before witnessing the most reproduced panel in Giotto's famous fresco cycle on the life of Francis: "Preaching to the Birds." Here the future saint has stopped beside a road in the Spoleto Valley to deliver a sermon to a flock of assembled birds, much to the evident surprise of one of his traveling companions. For their own part, the avian creatures show no trepidation; indeed, they appear receptive and positively rapt. This was no ordinary mortal.

In other episodes during his storied career, Francis recruited barnyard animals for the first staged Nativity, and he negotiated a peace settlement with the menacing Wolf of Gubbio, though neither of those made it into Giotto's fresco cycle.

About two miles above and outside the walls of Assisi, Francis and his fellow monks established the Eremo delle Carceri as a refuge and place of prayer and contemplation. I like to imagine that this is where he composed the first immortal Italian poem written in the Umbrian dialect: "Canticle of the Creatures." (It may have once been set to music, but its score has not survived the centuries.) You may be familiar with the verse if you have ever brought your pet to a "Blessing of the Animals," an increasingly popular ceremony in local churches across the world.

Here's an excerpt from Francis's lovely and moving canticle:

Praised be You, my Lord, with all Your creatures,
Especially Sir Brother Sun
Who is the day and through whom You give us light.

And he is beautiful and radiant with great splendor;
And bears a likeness of You, Most High One.
Praised be You, my Lord, through Sister Moon and the stars,
In heaven You formed them clear and precious and beautiful.

Praised be You, my Lord, through Brother Wind,
And through the air, cloudy and serene, and every kind of weather,
Through whom You give sustenance to Your creatures.

Praised be You, my Lord, through Sister Water,
Who is very useful and humble and precious and chaste.
Praised be You, my Lord, through Brother Fire,
Through whom You light the night.

And he is beautiful and playful and robust and strong.
Praised be You, my Lord, through our Sister Mother Earth,
Who sustains and governs us,
And who produces various fruit with colored flowers and herbs.

✦ CAVE CANEM

Dogs have served as human companions and protectors for millennia. Ample evidence of canine presence in Roman times has been unearthed at Pompeii where the exhortation *cave canem* ("beware of dog") has been preserved in mosaic form for all eternity. Two instances and two very different breeds were depicted.

The first mosaic *canem*, poised with bared teeth, appears to be a Molossian breed, a forebear of today's mastiff or Rottweiler. Common in Greco-Roman antiquity, this breed was the ultimate guard dog, ferocious and trained to kill; they were even pressed into service to fight lions, tigers, and even elephants in the sporting arenas. This mosaic was found in the House of the Tragic Poet.

The second mosaic *canem*, with leash and extended tongue, appears to be an Italian greyhound, a much smaller breed than the one familiar to modern societies. This particular mosaic was found in the entrance to the House of Vesonius

Primus. (The Italian greyhound actually originated in Egypt; in 48 BCE, Cleopatra presented a pair of puppies to the conquering Caesar.) In this instance, the warning might have been for the perky little pooch's benefit as this *canem* could have been easily trod upon.

Either way, *cave canem* could have been interpreted to mean "Watch Your Step!" Little did the residents of Pompeii realize on the morning of August 24th in 79 CE that the far greater imminent danger lurked elsewhere.

✦ THE CASTRATI

No one living today has heard the live song of a dodo, a great auk, or a *castrato*. The first two were natural species that eventually succumbed to the cruel fate of extinction. The third was a cruelly modified species of human that eventually succumbed to changes in musical taste.

Castrati (singular *castrato*) is the Italian term for male singers who were castrated before puberty in order to preserve their high vocal range. Although this practice may have existed as early as the 5th century in Byzantium, it reached its apex in 17th- and 18th-century Italy where as many as four thousand eight- to eleven-year-old boys underwent the procedure *in a given year*. 'Orchiectomy' is the medical term for castration, but this usually clandestine procedure in baroque Italy was anything but medical in the modern sense: it was often administered by barbers or actual butchers. An untold number of boys never made it off the "operating table," receiving lethal doses of opium or other narcotics to counteract the otherwise excruciating pain.

What circumstances would give rise to such a widespread practice? The answer involves an unholy alliance of artistic fashion, religious sanction, and economic pressures.

In the second half of the 16th century, the Sistine Chapel Choir, then populated by Spanish *falsettisti* (men who could simulate high notes), began to also include *castrati*. In 1599 Pope Clement VIII officially sanctioned the presence of those *castrati* by citing St. Paul's dictum "let women keep silent in church" (I Corinthians). Although young boys could achieve the higher vocal range so revered at that time, they would need to be continually replaced as their voices naturally "broke" with the onset of puberty; and besides, a well-trained *castrato* could not just deliver those very same notes but could do so with the full lung capacity of an adult male.

Some commentators of that time considered *castrati* to have "more natural" high voices than the *falsettisti*. Others cherished *castrati* voices for their otherworldly, even "angelic," sound. (In fact, young *castrati* sometimes performed at wakes or funerals dressed as cherubs.) In any event, all the sopranos in the Sistine Chapel Choir were *castrati* by 1625, and *castrati* could be found in church choirs throughout Italy by 1640.

A new art form in the early 17th century, Italian opera, also employed the services of *castrati* from the very beginning. The essential role of *castrati* in opera was all but sealed by a papal bull of 1686 banning women from appearing on stage at any opera house. For the next century, any Italian opera that did not offer an acclaimed *castrato* in a leading role would invariably fail. After years of grueling training, such singers were capable of remarkable feats of vocal range (sometimes up to four octaves), endurance (holding a single note up to a minute), and virtuosic special effects, making them the pop idols of their day.

Accomplished *castrati* earned at least twice the pay of the leading tenors and basses, and some such as Senesino, Caffarelli, and the legendary Farinelli (born Carlo Broschi) amassed great wealth. This is the simple fact that drove so many impoverished families to do what we (and even some of their contemporaries) could scarcely contemplate: to subject their young boys with singing talent to the knife. Only for a "fortunate" few did this gambit pay off; most *castrati* performed in minor choirs and otherwise enjoyed little normality in their lives.

Once musical tastes began to change in the late 18th and early 19th centuries, male tenors supplanted *castrati* in audience favor and leading roles. Fewer and fewer audiences would hear those most sublime "angelic" voices but also fewer families would feel tempted to play the devil's game of "Italian roulette" with their male offspring.

+THE DAVIDS

+DANTE'S COMMEDIA

+DOME-ESTIC PRIDE

+DUOMO, NOT A DOME BUT A HOME

+DOLOMITI AND THE VIA FERRATA

+IL DOGE AND HIS PALACE

+DIVORCE ITALIAN STYLE

+DOG DAYS OF SUMMER

◆ THE DAVIDS

Will the real David please stand up?

Certain Biblical and mythological stories were popular subjects for Italian art in the Renaissance and beyond. Those depicting the triumph of 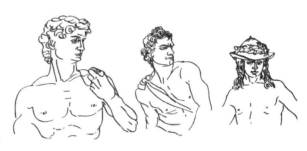 virtue and righteousness over tyranny and oppression proved particular favorites among civic and ecclesiastical patrons who sought to associate those qualities with their own institutions. One such story was the Old Testament tale of Judith and Holofernes. Another one—also from the Old Testament—was that of the shepherd David and the Philistine giant Goliath. In fact, the hero of this second story inspired three amazing statues from three of the greatest sculptors of all time: Donatello in the 15th century, Michelangelo in the 16th century, and Bernini in the 17th century. Their works could hardly have been more different.

The first recorded free-standing nude statue since antiquity, Donatello's bronze David (c. 1440s) showed the young man in a triumphant pose after he had slain the giant. Perhaps the most notable and incongruous aspect of Donatello's bonnet-clad hero is his effeminate bearing, evidently a source of comment if not bewilderment from the time of its creation.

Michelangelo's marble David (1501–1504) cuts a giant figure himself at seventeen feet; it is also the most classical and iconic representation of the Old Testament hero, for many the very epitome of male beauty. Most scholars believe that this David is depicted in a moment of contemplation before his fateful encounter with Goliath.

Although both Donatello's and Michelangelo's David display *contrapposto*—a naturalistic shift of weight to one leg with an offsetting upper body alignment—they both appear to pose in a set, if not static, fashion. In stark contrast, the marble David (1623–1624) of Baroque sculptor Gian Lorenzo Bernini is clearly shown in action, at the very instant he's about to fling the rock which will topple his adversary. This David's extreme body compression and intense facial expression make him the most psychologically evocative of the three.

Perhaps our quest for the "real" David is a fool's errand: regardless of its ostensible subject, a great work of art can offer, in some larger sense, a glimpse of its creator and the very circumstances of its creation.

✦ DANTE'S COMMEDIA

Dante Alighieri's *Divina Commedia* (Divine Comedy) stands tall among the masterworks of world literature, a fitting companion to the greatest creations of Shakespeare and Homer, any single one of which it easily surpasses in both its scope and complexity. Inarguably the very finest work—and in some sense, the *charter* work—in all of Italian literature, Dante's epic poem qualifies as a grand adventure, a gothic thriller, a unique travelogue (to the afterlife, for *heaven's* sake!), a morality tale, and a love story all wrapped up in one magnificent package.

Dante was idolized for his crowning literary and humanitarian achievement not just by luminaries like Boccaccio and Michelangelo from centuries ago but also by William Butler Yeats and the great modernists James Joyce, Ezra Pound, and T.S. Eliot.

The circumstances leading to its creation are well-known. Not only an esteemed poet but also a politically active Florentine, Dante was banished from his city upon penalty of death while away on a diplomatic mission when his White Guelph ruling party was violently toppled by the opposing Black Guelphs. At age 35, Dante was suddenly deprived of not only his political and social standing but also of all his assets and even his family: he was broke and alone. Understandably his spirits were also very nearly broken. Out of the trauma of Dante's exile and consequent spiritual crisis arose phoenix-like his defining work, a genuinely heroic feat of recovery and response. It begins, appropriately enough, with this stanza: *Midway upon the journey of our life / I found myself within a forest dark / For the straightforward pathway had been lost.*

Dante's masterwork is accomplished in too many ways to render justice to here, but let that not prevent us from noting just a few. As already mentioned, it's a genre-bender: an unprecedented amalgam of adventure, gothic thriller, "travelogue," morality tale, and love story. It's astonishingly "modern" in its treatment of the human psyche: both Dante the pilgrim's, as he evolves during the course of his journey into the afterlife, and those of the numerous "spirits" he encounters along the way. It's a miracle of compositional structure, both on the macro basis of the epic's grand design and on a micro basis with the invention and use of *terza rima*, an interlocking rhyme scheme which creates a phonic daisy chain that propels the narrative, and us, headlong though Dante the pilgrim's journey while also reinforcing the work's unity.

Dante's *Commedia* is also an aural wonder, an exemplar of the *dolce stil nuovo* (sweet new style) that was meant for the ears rather than just the eyes. Dante the poet wanted the experience and lessons of Dante the pilgrim's journey to be shared with ordinary folks who happened to be illiterate and not just the upper classes, so he deliberately, and audaciously, chose to craft his masterwork in language close to the vernacular of his native Tuscany rather than the classical Latin read only by the elites of his day. The instant popularity of Dante's *Commedia* as a spoken work not only led in due course to higher rates of literacy but also to the institutionalization of the work's Tuscan variant as the official Italian language. No other work in the history of world literature could make a comparable claim.

Dante's *Commedia* remains as fresh and vital today as when it was conceived. It has become a part of the Italian collective consciousness; every

Italian can recite as least a few stanzas. As but one testament to its standing as an abiding source of inspiration and pride in its native land, fully sixty percent of Italy's population tuned in to a recent broadcast reading of the *Commedia* by actor and comedian Roberto Benigni. (For years Benigni has starred in a one-man show called *Tutto Dante*, invariably sold out.) For most Italians Dante is revered as more than a literary giant: he's a national hero.

Sadly, Dante's hope of returning from exile never came to pass; after twenty years of wandering exile he died in Ravenna. But the bane of his exile was transformed into a literary boon for generations to follow. James Joyce, in his semi-autobiographic 1916 novel *Portrait of the Artist as a Young Man*, aspired to "forge in the smithy of my soul the uncreated conscience of my race." Arguably Dante got there six hundred years sooner.

♦ DOME-ESTIC PRIDE

Art, sculpture, and architecture have always been very important expressions of civic pride and allegiance. But during the Renaissance, stimulated by discoveries of classical frescoes and buildings and the invention of new techniques like perspective, these creations became so dazzling that they fueled passion and loyalty similar to how people today feel about their cities' sports teams. And in Florence, one of the most important cities of the western world and the leading city-state in Italy during the early Renaissance, the devotion to the city's buildings and art approached World Series fever.

Nothing fired that up more than Florence's construction of the first great dome built in Europe in more than a thousand years. The Duomo in Florence, erected on the east end of the cathedral of Santa Maria del Fiore, marked the start of an architectural revolution that later inspired great buildings from the dome of St. Peter's cathedral in the Vatican to the American Capitol. Two of the greatest figures in Florence combined to create the Duomo. Cosimo de Medici was wise enough to choose as the architect Filippo Brunelleschi, a former sculptor turned architect who became, with his work on the Duomo, the first engineer of the modern age.

The immense dome—taller than a football field is long—rose slowly and steadily in rings. First, Brunelleschi would build part of the big white "ribs" that braced the dome, then begin to fill in the space with circles of interlocking bricks. When one ring was complete and self-supporting, he'd move the scaffolding up and build another.

For sixteen years Florentines watched the dome ascend; to describe it they quoted a phrase from Dante's *Paradiso*, "*de giro in giro*," circle by circle. The Florentines clearly loved the clarity and beauty of simple forms like the circle and the square, where their curiosity and intelligence were free to roam without being overwhelmed by Gothic architecture, where they could lift both their eyes and their minds toward the heavens.

With the dome complete, Cosimo de Medici invited the Pope himself to consecrate the finished Cathedral on Easter Sunday in 1436. Weighing 37,000 tons and using more than 4 *million* bricks, the Duomo towered majestically over the city of Florence, a triumph for the Florentine people and the city's most powerful family.

Once finished, the dome was recognized as a marvel of the age, and Florentines would introduce themselves to visitors to the city with the proud words "*io so fiorentino del cupolone*" which means "I am a Florentine of the big dome!" And Florentine Italian love and pride was extended to Brunelleschi; when he died in 1446, he was buried beneath his towering achievement.

◆ DUOMO, NOT A DOME BUT A HOME

When you drive through any village or hilltown, there are signs that direct you to "Centro" and signs to "Duomo," which refers to the town's largest cathedral. The term "Duomo" has been mistakenly conflated with the common architectural "dome" feature of certain styles of cathedrals, as in the iconic "Il Duomo": Santa Maria del Fiore in Florence, whose dome is its defining feature and is known to the whole world.

But the Italian word for "dome" is *cupola*. The term "duomo" is actually derived from the Latin *domus,* which in Roman times referred to the home (think "domicile") of patricians with power and privilege. The most famous, or more aptly infamous, *domus* back in ancient Rome was the Domus Aurea, or "Golden House," a huge landscaped villa built by the Emperor Nero that served as more of a pleasure palace than imperial residence. With the fall of the Empire and ascendancy of Christianity, the term *domus Dei* began to be used, meaning "house of God," to refer to churches in general. So Italian, being a multileveled language alive to such imagery and metaphors, combined home, God, and cathedral into one word.

When it comes to such duomos, one of the only ones in Italy to rival the Duomo of Florence or the incredible St. Peter's is the famed Duomo of Milan, the second largest church in Italy and fourth largest in the world—and that one is dome-less. But it's most certainly a *domus Dei*, a house of God, and a spiritual, artistic, and historical center. With its soaring Gothic spires and more exterior statues than any other building in the world—over 3,000—it was a work in progress for six centuries and it was only considered completed about fifty years ago. Its Baroque marble façade was finished by none other than Napoleon (a Corsican who spoke French with an Italian accent) and he received his coronation as King of Italy (referring to only the northern regions of Lombardy and Emiglia Romano) in the cathedral in May of 1805.

Milan's Duomo, like Florence's, is a symbol of the city. Italians truly care about their duomos. Due to pollution, the cathedral must be cleaned regularly, which is expensive and budgets are tight, and so the recent cleaning and restoration that began in 2012 was funded by a clever "Adopt a Gargoyle" program: for 100,000 euro you can have your name engraved under your favorite grotesque creature (135 were up for adoption) on the facade of the cathedral. The cathedral's management said it wanted "to encourage the Milanese and citizens of the world as a whole to be protagonists in the history of the cathedral … a priceless treasure that belongs to all of humanity."

That kind of love and support is not just reserved for a beautiful architectural feature, but a beloved home for Italian culture and spirit.

♦ DOLOMITI AND VIA FERRATA

Located in the northeast corner of the Italy are the dramatic Dolomites, considered by many to be the most beautiful mountain range in the world. They are part of the northern Alps and are therefore "younger mountains" with soaring jagged peaks resembling gothic spires, often crowned with snow. Some of the rock cliffs rise more than 5,000 feet and are among the highest limestone walls found anywhere in the world. While in some places the peaks are isolated, in others they form spectacular panoramas:

pinnacles and towers with clashing hori-
zontal striations on their rock faces, ledges,
crags that rise abruptly above gentle foothills.
There's a stunning diversity of color with pale
bare rock surfaces contrasted with forests and
meadows below.

(These are not to be confused with the
Dolomiti Lucane, also called "Piccoli Dolomiti," a mountain range in the province of
Basilicata located in the Southern Apennines, so-called because their sharp
craggy peaks resemble those of the Alpine Dolomites—which obviously
makes them worth visiting in their own right.)

The Dolomites are a mountaineering paradise with one of the greatest
thrills a hiker can have: to walk or climb the Via Ferrata. The "iron way"
is a route with fixed "protection" and assistance in the form of handholds,
cables, ropes, rungs, pegs, and metal ladders. These allow otherwise dangerous routes to be undertaken without special equipment used by moun-
taineers, minimizing the risk associated with unprotected climbing and
scrambling so that a hiker in sufficiently good shape can enjoy staggering
views normally accessible only to a serious mountaineer.

The Via Ferrata was not built for sightseeing or adventurous recreation
but for war. During World War I the Dolomites were still a part of the
Austro-Hungarian Empire and therefore a front in the battle between the
Allies (or the Entente Powers) of Western Europe, which included Italy,
and the Central Powers. There were two battles going on in the Dolomites:
the brutal battles of the men fighting each other and trying to gain control
of peaks for artillery sight line advantages, and the battle against the sheer
danger posed by the mountains and their fearsome winters. Aside from
the enormous casualties from the fighting, thousands of Italians were also
lost to falls from the sheer vertical rock faces, exposure to the cold, and
avalanches. Italian troops began to fix permanent lines to rock faces and
to install ladders; this enabled them to move both troops and equipment
through the mountains more quickly and safely.

Once the war ended the local residents began to use and care for the Via
Ferrata. In the 1930's the Italian Alpine Club (Club Alpino Italiano) began
to restore this wartime network, add many new routes to attract hikers to

the area, and provide longer more difficult routes to access the major rock climbing and mountaineering challenges. Tourism, including the popular Via Ferrata, is now the largest part of the economy in the Dolomites. Still, hikers or climbers pass scars of battle that remain recognizable as trenches, dugouts, and other relics of World War I, a reminder of the sacrifices made by the Italian people to keep and to preserve this remarkable mountain range.

◆ IL DOGE AND HIS PALACE

The Venetian Republic had a remarkable run: eleven centuries of independent rule up to the time of its bloodless conquest by Napoleon in 1797, making it the most enduring political entity in world history. During those eleven centuries the position of *Doge*—the leader (from the Latin *dux*) and chief magistrate for life—was filled by a succession of 120 men from the Republic's aristocratic families.

To hold the title of *Il Doge* was almost always a good news / bad news proposition. In the Republic's first three or four centuries, the reigning Doge wielded tremendous power, but he also served at considerable risk if Venetian citizens or elites perceived any abuse of that power. The statistics would make an actuary shudder: six of the first twenty-eight Doges were killed in office (one in a riot, one in battle, four at the hand of assassins) and another seven were deposed, with three of those blinded and exiled for good measure.

From the 12th century on, the position of Doge gained in prestige with that of the Republic while also losing a considerable share of its power to the Great Council of Venice numbering in the hundreds, a more exclusive part of that body called the Committee of Forty, and an even more influential cadre named the Council of Ten.

Wary of corruption, abuse of power, and such practices as nepotism (common elsewhere on the Italian peninsula), the Council undertook an elaborate process to essentially "shuffle the deck" of electors at successive stages in order to avoid collusion in the selection of each new Doge. Once elected to serve, the Doge was subject to constant surveillance: others had to open official correspondence; he could not conduct any personal business; he could not accept any gifts; his ability to travel (or even attend a performance) without Council permission was limited; and the activities and mobility of immediate family members were similarly constrained.

On the other hand, the Doge was the only person who could attend any governmental meeting, and he had exclusive access to all of the Republic's secret files.

The Doge also got to live in the most impressive palace in the city—the Doge's Palace, Palazzo Ducale—with its ethereal, gravity-defying structure; breathtaking "rooms with a view" (of the Canale Grande); and guest entrance for waterborne dignitaries at the very "front door" of Venice. Although the Doge received an annual stipend for living expenses, it was woefully inadequate to support such a monumental residence; nor was the Doge exempt from Venetian taxes. He was to expected tap his own personal wealth for such expenditures.

From the 14th century on, the official garb of the Doge included golden robes and slippers, a scepter for ceremonial duties, and the distinctive gemmed brocade or cloth-of-gold horn-like headdress known as the *corno ducale*. Perhaps the Doge's most noteworthy ceremonial function was to preside over the Marriage of the Sea (*Sposalizio del Mare*), an annual ritual that symbolized the inextricable ties between the Republic and its maritime adventures, both commercial and imperial.

The rite evolved from a ceremony originally marking the conquest of Dalmatia in 1000 by Doge Pietro Orseolo. In 1177 Pope Alexander III visited Venice to offer his thanks to the Republic for its support against the Holy Roman Emperor Frederick I. On Ascension Day he accompanied the current Doge aboard the Doge's state barge, the *Bucentaur,* as it made its way out of the Venetian Lagoon and into the Adriatic. Once at sea he offered the Doge one of his rings to toss into, and "wed," the Adriatic, along with the prayer that "for us and all who sail thereon the sea may be calm and quiet."

The ceremony continued down through the centuries of the Republic, and the grandeur of the event—with scores of watercraft greeting the returning *Bucentaur*—can be witnessed in multiple paintings by Canaletto and others; one such scene by Canaletto, *The Bucentaur at the Molo on Ascension Day*, recently sold at Christies auction house in London for £11.43 million. (Today in post-Republic Venice this hallowed ritual is conducted by the mayor of the city.)

The death of each Doge would also be an occasion of great pomp, with lavish feasts, three days of viewing, a grand procession from the Basilica of

San Marco to that of Santi Giovani e Paolo, and an elaborate funeral service at that final location. (The Doge's family was expected to pay for the entire occasion.)

The elaborate checks and balances on the Doge's power and activities from the 12th century on led to an unprecedented period of overall stability in the Republic's governance, an absolutely necessary condition to maintain its commercial interests and to act upon its extraterritorial ambitions. One notable challenge to that stability materialized with Doge Marino Faliero, a former soldier, provincial governor, ambassador, and member of the Council of Ten who, in spite of his career accomplishments, had the reputation of being thin-skinned. After he assumed the position of Doge he took offense at the disrespectful behavior of certain young Venetian nobles and he formulated a plot against the entire patrician class

that would make him the absolute ruler of Venice. Word of the plot leaked out to the Council of Ten, and ten of Faliero's conspirators were summarily hanged in a row from the windows of the Doge's Palace. After confessing his role in the foiled plan, Faliero himself was beheaded at the top of a staircase in the palace's inner courtyard. There is no record of whether he was still wearing the *corno ducale* at the time.

✦ DIVORCE ITALIAN STYLE

In 1961 director Pietro Germi's satiric farce *Divorce Italian Style* became an international box office bonanza. Sexy and irresistibly funny in the darkest possible way, it told the story of a Sicilian baron so exasperated with boredom by his marriage and filled with lust for his young cousin (played by Stefania Sandrelli) that he plots to steer his wife into an adulterous affair so he can honorably shoot her and then marry his 16-year-old relative.

The outrageous and outrageously successful comedy gave birth to a genre soon dubbed *"la commedia all'Italiana"* (comedy Italian style) and began the international career of Marcello Mastroianni, who somehow managed to sympathetically blend aristocrat and criminal, Latin lover and everyman. American audiences so enjoyed his performance that some fans would greet him imitating the mouth tic he used in the film.

But the film's fanciful black comedy actually satirized a dark truth about Italian life and culture. During the '60s, even at the height of the sexual revolution, Italy was still in the grip of the Catholic Church's prohibition of divorce, according to centuries of tradition and one of the provisions of the 1929 Lateran Treaty between the Holy See and Italy. While Italians pushed back against the repression and especially the treaty—it was signed by Mussolini after all—divorce was not allowed legally in Italy until December 1, 1970.

So *Divorce Italian Style* expressed the raging frustration of a country still in the grip of a medieval morality, where a bad marriage was legally inescapable, to be countered only with patience or, very frequently, a hefty dose of infidelity: sexual *arrangiarsi,* so to speak. But as always Italians and their filmmakers found the comedy in that frustration, both sexual and otherwise, and Mastroianni's beguiling portrayal of the would-be wife-murderer, coupled with the absurd humor of the story, helped in the country's liberation from non-divorce Italian style. If as Marx says history is sometimes tragedy repeated as farce, in Italy sometimes farce can change history.

✦ DOG DAYS OF SUMMER

This popular expression has exactly nothing to do with the effects of intense summer heat on our canine friends. Its actual origin is far more intriguing and is linked with (surprise) Rome and Italy.

Both ancient and celestial in origin, the phrase was translated from Latin to English about five hundred years ago and since has morphed in its meaning—a common tendency when people don't know the origin of a phrase and seek to come up with plausible explanations. Perhaps it comes from a day when the weather is so hot that dogs lie around panting and acting lifeless and lazy, or it's not even fit for a dog, or even mad dogs and Englishmen hate it. The phrase lives on but the original meaning has been lost.

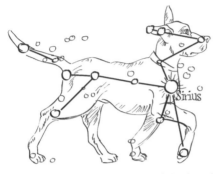

During the time of the Roman Empire (and back to the time of the Greeks as well) there was a period when the Dog Star Sirius (in the constellation Canis Major) rose and set concurrent with the sun. This phenomenon occurred for about forty days between early July and mid-August. The Romans thought the combination of the brightest light of the day, the sun, and what was normally the brightest star at night, Sirius, was responsible for the extreme heat of the summertime; the star is sometimes seen to glow with other colors, and they believed its reddish glow augmented the heat of the sun.

Geminus, a Greek astronomer from Rhodes, in 70 BCE had a more accurate view: "It is generally believed that Sirius produces the heat of the 'dog days' but this is an error, for the star merely marks a season of the year when the sun's heat is the greatest"(July 3–August 11).

There is in fact an Italian weather idiom which refers to man's best friend, but it refers to days of bitter cold versus sultry hot: "*Fa un freddo cane!*" The exclamation literally means 'it's dog cold' or idiomatically, "it's really really really cold."

◆EMPIRE

◆THE ECSTASY OF SAINT TERESA

◆EXPLOSION OF THE CART

◆THE EXCLAMATION POINT!

◆EBRU, THE ART OF MARBLED PAPER

◆ESPRESSO, CAPPUCCINO, AND
ITALIAN COFFEE CULTURE

◆THE ENORMOUS EMPEROR

♦ EMPIRE

Rome, with its magnificent works of art and architecture, gardens and parks, restaurants, and glittering Via Veneto, is not just the eternal but the eternally fabulous city. But with all that beauty and festiveness comes an overwhelming sense of majesty and power. Obelisks everywhere you look, triumphal arches, the Forum, the Colosseum: this was the seat of The Empire, Ancient Rome. One stops and wonders how so much power originated in the country that "owns" pleasure in the collective imagination.

Such is the incredible balance in the Italian heritage and character. If we tend to think of Italians as a very successful "right-brain" culture, so full of art and passion and improvisation, that may be in part because of the anchor of the incredible "left brain" organizational heritage of this greatest of all empires. And they proudly know it too; it's not just history to the average Italian, and certainly not to the average Roman, but a part of the life of the culture.

The Empire at its heyday spread from present-day Iraq to Great Britain. Alexander the Great may have conquered the same immense spread of territory, but with his death that empire fell apart. So how did the Roman Empire literally hold it together?

First came Roman law, which unified the world. Soldiers would conquer, but then the state would build a new society, using law to stand by promises of citizenship and protection. The Romans were the first people for whom authority was a real and legal concept, which would prove vital to stable societies for the rest of Europe's history.

The law protected safety and above all property (which, in those times, included slaves), but also trade; *peregrini* (foreigners, as conquests grew); rights of citizens; and even women's rights, though only against rape. The law became a unifier of humankind, and *ratio scripta*, "written reason." So revolutionarily thorough was Rome's jurisprudence that the Emperor Justinian's codex of the Byzantine Empire in 534 ACE, codifying thirteen hundred years of Roman law, would ultimately span three million lines of text in two thousand treatises of its *Corpus Iuris Civilis*. Roman law in all its magisterial might and precision was the basis for medieval church law and later constitutional law, from the Magna Carta to the Constitution of the United States.

And indeed, the Roman Republic's checks and balances served as the basis for American government. The powerful Senate balanced the role of the magistrates and the *imperium*, led by two consuls, one of whom eventually came from the plebeians, the people, who also had their popular assemblies. This system would ultimately fall to the seizure of power by Julius Caesar, for which Caesar would pay with his life and Rome with civil war. But until then, and even after in a more centralized way, the Roman system sheltered and protected its population, and the emblem of that power—SPQR, SENATUS POPULUSQUE ROMANUS, the Senate and the Roman People—truly meant something, uniting the largest citizenry that had ever appeared on the planet.

When the Republic became an Empire under Julius Caesar and Augustus, leading to a *Pax Romana* that would last two hundred years, during that time the Romans also organized. . . time itself. The Roman calendar had first sprung from the need to know when and how to farm, starting in March, when the ground was prepared for planting. But it wasn't whipped into shape until Julius Caesar—not just a military genius but a man of authorial and scientific curiosity—learned during his Alexandria campaign about the Egyptian solar calendar. He would later regularize Rome's in order to be able to track the sun on his military campaigns after he became dictator, giving us the purely solar calendar we have now. With the addition of two months, Caesar would ironically get his name on the calendar he created to celebrate his planned next round of immortal campaigns only by dying; the month of July would be named after him, as August would be for his successor Octavian, who became the emperor Augustus.

With that mental infrastructure of law and time came a physical infrastructure that has in many ways never been equaled: the achievement of the Roman engineers and architects, also masterful city planners, in unifying the vast sprawling empire through roads, bridges, aqueducts, theaters, forums, walls, colosseums, and monuments. They cared far more for the surveyor's precision and engineer's solidity than the architect's esthetics. Yet

they achieved that too, through mastering two basic innovations: the arch and a recipe for concrete. Arches were developed into barrel vaults, cross vaults, and domes to create the most lasting buildings and bridges the world had ever seen. And utilizing plentiful dark red volcanic ash on the peninsula called *pozzolana* and
adding it to lime and water instead of sand, they made a far stronger form of concrete that made their enormous structures possible. Nero's Domus Aurea, the Colosseum that replaced it and gave the mobs their pacifying "bread and circuses," the Arch of Constantine: all came from this simple discovery.

They also built 50,000 miles of paved roads, which gave birth to the statement "all roads lead to Rome." That stayed true through the rise of Christianity, the darkness of the Middle Ages, and the light of the Renaissance, when the words and the architecture of the Empire infused a revolution in thinking and building and art. Ancient Rome proved to be an inheritance that gives Italy's beloved passion and creativity a foundation as strong as Roman concrete and old as the Western world.

◆ THE ECSTASY OF SAINT TERESA

Tucked away in the small Cornaro Chapel in the Baroque church of Santa Maria della Vittoria, in an off-the-tourist-track neighborhood in the Eternal City, you will find the jaw-dropping *Ecstasy of Saint Teresa* by sculptor and master of stagecraft, Gian Lorenzo Bernini, who might as well have subtitled the work, "This Magic Moment."

Here Bernini takes drama, emotion, and theatricality to heights previously unimagined, bringing to life Carmelite nun Saint Teresa's most mystical vision in accord with her own account. She felt "on fire with a great love of God" so intense it seemed physical. She said "the pain is so severe it makes me utter several moans," yet "the sweetness caused me by this intense pain is so extreme one cannot possibly wish it to cease."

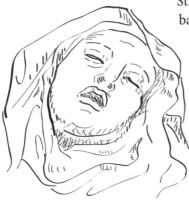

St. Teresa, struck in the heart by a beautiful bare-chested Angel's flaming golden spear, swoons with passion and love for God suffused with the light of the Holy Dove and is lifted upon a floating cloud. In a seeming other reality, eight male members of the Cornaro family and other churchmen are sculpted witnessing (authenticating) the miraculous event from balconied theatre boxes on either side of the chapel, giving the sculptural ensemble both a dramatic stage set and a daring voyeuristic impression. Yet its intent is religious and in service of the Church and the glory of God. Saint Teresa is certainly not nude, but piously covered so that you only see her blissful face, half open eyes, limp hands, and feet peeping out from her heavy draperies, as Bernini captures so convincingly the exact moment of piercing ecstasy.

This work, perhaps more appropriately characterized as an installation (also featuring a frescoed ceiling with a hidden source of natural "god" light) was commissioned as the burial chapel of Cardinal Cornaro at a time when Bernini was already famous but down in his luck. However, things took a decidedly better turn and Bernini received what had been an unheard-of sum at the time of 12,000 scudi (about $120,000) for what many consider his greatest masterpiece.

♦ EXPLOSION OF THE CART

Pyrotechnics are nothing new to celebrations in both the West and East, but nothing quite compares to the Easter spectacle known as the *Scoppio de Carro*—explosion of the cart—a nearly four-hundred-year-old tradition in Florence.

Its origins trace to 1099 and the First Crusade in the Holy Land five hundred years before that. There an intrepid young Florentine by the name of Pazzino Pazzi was first to scale the walls of Jerusalem to hoist the Christian banner. For his courage Pazzino was awarded three flints from the walls of the Holy Sepulchre which he donated to the Church of Santi Apostoli; they reside there to this day. It soon become an Easter tradition to use the flints to light a fire (symbolic of purification) in the church. Florentines would bring their torches and carry back the "holy fire" to their homes as a prayer and blessing for the coming harvest.

Over the years, the ritual became more and more elaborate with drummers, flag throwers, and fireworks thrown into the mix. The sacred flints now light a candle which in turn fires coals transported by an ornate ox-driven cart in a procession to the Duomo. Brought to the altar inside, the coals await a critical moment in the Easter mass when they are used to launch a dove-shaped "missle" which traverses a wire to ignite fireworks from an explosive-laden cart waiting outside... Rube Goldberg would be duly impressed!

As it happens, two of Pazzino's distant descendents (also with the surname Pazzi) staged a failed coup against the powerful Lorenzo de'Medici in the 15th century. Impulsive behavior must have been in the family genes. Some speculate that the slang expression for a hot-tempered fool—*pazzo*—began with this daring and ultimately foolhardy act. In this case, fortunately for Western culture, the historical fireworks fizzled—but the original still lights up the Florentine spring.

❖ THE EXCLAMATION POINT!

Given how exclamatory or even rhapsodic Italian sometimes seems, it makes sense that the roots of the language gave us the punctuation to convey that spirited energy in writing.

In Latin, the word for "joy" or "hurray" is *io,* which medieval copyists used to write at the end of a sentence to indicate such a moment of exaltation. Over time and to save space, the *i* moved above the *o,* and the *o* became smaller, becoming a point. Since all their letters were written as capitals, an I with an O below it looked a lot like an exclamation point.

The mark based on that medieval graphic was first introduced into English printing in the 15th century to show emphasis. It was called the "sign of admiration or exclamation" or the "note of admiration"—referring to that word's Latin meaning, "wonderment"—until the mid-17th century, when it was shortened to make the "point" better.

In Italian today, harking back to its Latinate Italian roots, the word for exclamation point is *punto esclamativo* expressing joy, love, and surprise. Which makes the exclamation point truly the original emoji.

♦ EBRU, THE ART OF MARBLED PAPER

Marbled papers are stunning. To create them is to strike a perfect balance between control and chance.

They originated in Japan at the end of the ninth century. The technique was picked up in China and ultimately traveled down the silk road through Iran to Turkey, where its production soared. As an Islamic craft, it gained patterns that resembled the non-figurative art of arabesques, and came to be known as *"ebru,"* possibly derived from *abrî,* meaning "clouded paper" in Persian, or *abr-o-bâd* meaning "cloud and wind" (other possible origins of the term include the Turkish *abreh,* "colorful" or "variegated," or *abru,* from the water in which it was created). Venetian merchants in Constantinople didn't hesitate to take the marvelous colored papers to Venice, where the technique was appreciated and exquisitely adapted. The craftsmanship ultimately involved lots of secret techniques that would go on to distinguish marbled paper made in Italy, especially Venice and Florence, from the early 17th century on.

To marble involves floating paints on the surface of a water bath and mixing them by physical means (e.g., a comb or the dragging of a fine brush) to create a marbled pattern. A sheet of paper is gently placed on the pattern on the surface of the water and then removed, forming a monotype print. It's a complex process involving myriad interactions and delicate manipulations with even the ambient temperature and humidity affecting the outcome. The technique can produce an infinite variety of no-two-alike patterns.

Marbling became an essential part of bookbinding, with marbled papers being placed on the inside covers of fine books (as is still the case today). The marbled patterns were used to cover the folds, strings, and glue marks of the bindings, and also to serve as an aesthetic transition from the dark leather covers to the parchment-colored pages inside.

Ebru and its secrets were closely guarded aspects of Italian artisanship. There were marblers' guilds separate from the bookbinders' guilds, and the bookbinders would spy on the marblers, trying to discover their techniques to avoid the high cost of their papers. Marblers often had to do their work at night in secret; hardly anyone could hope to learn the art unless they were born into a marbling family. Even then, most apprentices weren't trusted with all the marbling formulas until they were in their 30s or 40s. The *ebru* world would always have an air of Venetian conspiracy and intrigue.

By the 1800's books were being printed more cheaply and in large quantities, which meant fine bindings and marbled endpapers would soon become a thing of the past. However, in this new age of individual artisanship the marbling tradition has revived. As a hobby, visitors to Italy can take a class in paper marbling when visiting Florence or Venice, and make their own *ebru* papers. Small entrepreneurs produce beautiful papers, note cards, desk accessories, journals, folios, frames, and keepsake boxes. These creations boast intricate and delicate patterns and colors that conjure up Byzantine marble slabs, damask fabrics, Turkish arabesques, and peacock tails, as well as flickering waves and shimmering light on the lagoon.

In Turkey the art, still known as *ebru*, never died. In Italy, which likes its renaissances, the lost art has been found.

◆ ESPRESSO, CAPPUCCINO, AND ITALIAN COFFEE CULTURE

Italians are so passionate about espresso, you'd think they discovered it. But what they have done is created a coffee culture, with their own ways of serving and enjoying the brew, that's unparalleled anywhere in the world.

Coffee houses were first established in Constantinople (modern-day Istanbul) in the 15th century, but their popularity was severely limited at first because Islamic preachers considered the stimulating liquid as sinful as alcohol. By the time its consumption was accepted in Turkey, coffee had entered Italy through Venice in the 16th century and created an immediate sensation. At first, since its supply was very limited, it became a luxury item, but as coffee plantations became established in European colonies in South America the price decreased and coffee gradually went from part of the cult of the upper classes to the culture of all Italians. From Venice across the north to Verona, then Milan and Turin, and finally to Rome and all the way to Sicily, elegant coffeehouses were built, some which still operate today.

The Starbucks coffee "experience" was supposedly modeled on and inspired by these coffeehouses in Italy. But besides the fact that, except for the original Starbucks in Seattle, these down-to-earth stores don't pretend to Italian elegance or special décor of any kind, both the coffee product and the experience are vastly different.

For one thing, there are no Lattes or Frappuccinos or caramel-flavored Macchiatos or most of our flavor varieties in Italy. No "Grandes" or "Ventis," just one size for cappuccino and espresso. No "to go" and paper cups, and no special seasonal lattes—in fact, no distinction between a latte and cappuccino—it's all just a cappuccino. And finally, Italians do not tend to sit around and hang out at their coffee bars for hours with their mobile devices.

In Italy the coffee culture is stripped of the proliferation of our for-all-occasions coffees-snacks-and-pastries franchises. It's about the essence of the uniquely Italian cappuccino and espresso, far simpler and purer than what is known in America, and there are salient differences to how Italian coffee is drunk and served. Cappuccino has been called the "Breakfast of Italians." Milk is almost a meal in itself, so having a cappuccino at a bar in the morning requires no other food, especially since the body absorbs lactose from milk, which is a sugar, and that quick release of carbohydrate energy along with the caffeine kick is all you need to wake up; for something more, one might add a small pastry but not necessarily. It's sensible science, but the real reason for the custom is that Italians believe drinking milk after ANY meal will mess up your ability to digest food properly. That means having a cappuccino anytime after lunch or dinner is incomprehensible. You'd be hard pressed to find a restaurant that serves cappuccino after dinner, and if you order it after 11 am, while you will probably be graciously accommodated, you might as well be wearing a "tourist" sign around your neck.

The true go-to anytime-pick-me-up in Italy is an espresso, although one never asks for it by name: one simply requests "un caffe," especially after lunch or dinner. We generally assume espresso has far more caffeine than regular American-style brewed coffee. This is both true and false: true, because espresso is highly concentrated, but false because a shot, even a *doppio*, is far less volume than a cup of regular coffee. So, an after-dinner espresso might keep you up at night, but not as much as you think, which is good because in Italy decaf is pretty hard to find, as it defeats that pick-me-up purpose of "un caffe."

Finally, while flavoring and sugaring up coffee is definitely an American thing, there are a few regional specialties: in the north, there's Cappuccino Viennese, which has chocolate and cinnamon, and in the Marche region the aniseed-flavored espresso Caffe Anisette. And there is one quintessentially Italian (as in with a wink and a smile) variety called *Caffe Corretto*, literally "corrected coffee": you will be served espresso with its "correction," always something boozy like a shot of grappa, Sambuca, or brandy. The two arrive separately, allowing the drinkers to "correct" the coffee their own way and upend the alcohol into their demitasse slugs in one or two sips with a "*Salute!*" ("To your health!"). Perhaps it was inevitable that the "stimulating liquids" of Italy would meet.

◆ THE ENORMOUS EMPEROR

In a time when the Roman Empire was divided, Flavius Valerius Aurelius Constantinus, later to be named Constantine, was about to battle the established Western Roman Emperor, Maxentius, for control of the Western Empire at the Tiber River's Mulvian Bridge in 312 CE.

Fourth-century historian and bishop Eusebius of Caesarea reported that before the great battle Constantine, a pagan and worshiper of Sol, the sun god, dreamed that Jesus Christ told him to inscribe the letter XP on the shields of his soldiers (XP being the first two letters of the Greek word for Christos, XPISTOS); when he awakened the next morning he saw the cross superimposed on the sun with the words "with this sign thou shalt conquer." Constantine did rout and kill his enemy, and on that day the times began a-changing not only for Constantine but the entire course of Western history.

Like any emperor before him, he erected a triumphal arch, the world-famous Arch of Constantine on the Palatine Hill between the Coliseum and the Forum. But unlike all previous emperors, in 313 CE he issued the Edict of Milan ending the persecution of Christians. The agreement granted freedom of worship to all, regardless of their deity, and brought an end to the Age of Martyrs, which had begun after Jesus' death. Christians were also given specific legal rights, above all the right to organize dedicated churches.

Historians have long debated the true nature of his faith, even though he eventually converted. But the genius of Constantine, in this last phase of the Roman Empire, was to grasp the unifying potential of the spreading faith, which had already swept through the Empire's eastern half. There would henceforth be two great powers in the Roman Empire, the state and the Church, with the bishops accepting Constantine's patronage, enforcing his rules on military service, but very much a world apart. The civil and the ecclesiastical would now have a sometimes productive, sometimes destructive, often uneasy coexistence for centuries, no more so than on the Italian peninsula.

Once Constantine defeated his eastern rival Licinius to become sole ruler of both halves of the Empire in 324, he also reigned over the Council of Nicea, held in 324, which began to the codify Christian monotheistic belief with the resulting Nicean Creed which begins with " I believe in one God …" but also established belief in the Resurrection and the Trinity. Constantine, preferring not to "swim upstream," did not ban celebration of pagan rituals and festivals. Rather, almost as part of that complex Trinitarian mode, which shared its belief in a divine resurrection with other eastern religions, the law would allow pagan elements to gradually blend and morph into Christian celebrations with Christian symbolism (for example, choosing Sunday as the day of worship coincided with the day of worship of Sol, the sun god he formerly worshiped). Saturnalia, a major Roman feast celebrating the winter solstice and the return of the sun, quite possibly became our Christmas, as there are no records as to the actual birth date of the historical Jesus.

Constantine sent his mother Helen (who was later canonized) on a mission to the Holy Land in search of the true cross (the cross of his dream and the cross on which Jesus had been crucified). She ultimately found it, and there he erected the Church of the Holy Sepulcher in Jerusalem. Constantine then gradually rebuilt his seat of power in largely Christian Byzantium, and the growth of a Christian ruling class under Constantine ensured the faith's increasing and enduring prominence through the Roman, and later Byzantine, Empire.

But, this being still the world of Rome, there was always a political goal to Constantine's moving closer to the Holy Land. Many of the structures of the Empire's western half were decaying and were under constant pressure from the Gauls and other barbarians. The power and trading base of the Empire had shifted eastward. Strategically, Constantine also moved the administrative capital to the eastern side of the Bosporus, one of the world's greatest and most defensible harbors, from where he could not only control eastern trade traffic but also protect the outlying regions of the empire and be far removed from the old imperial religion of Rome. He renamed and consecrated the city as Constantinople in May of 330, modeling the city on Rome itself, on and around seven hills.

New Rome would be a rival to the old, but would not last as long, although at a thousand years it didn't have a bad run. It would finally fall to the Ottoman Turks in 1453, led by Mohammed the Conqueror, and be renamed Istanbul. Buried among the heaps of the slain would be the body of the last of the Roman emperors Constantine XI, whose body was never recovered.

A similar fate would await the last monument of the first Constantine; while his Arch of Constantine would remain forever glorious, his Colossus of Constantine, a seated monumental sculpture 37 ½ feet high, would, like Constantinople, be pillaged and broken up sometime in late antiquity, most likely for its bronze body portions. This sculpture had loomed over the west apse of the Basilica of Maxentius on the northern boundary of the Roman Forum (for perspective, the head alone was eight feet high). As part of the Renaissance's recovery of the Greco-Roman heritage, the marble portions of the statue were excavated in 1487 and the surviving body parts placed by Michelangelo himself in the nearby Palazzo dei Conservatori Courtyard (now the Capitoline Museum), one of the three *palazzi* of the Piazza Del Campidoglio which he was building at the time. The fragments include the right arm (with elbow), the right kneecap, a right hand, left shin, right foot, left kneecap and left foot, and the head.

His eyes are eerily distant, almost abstract, and the head is more the image of authority and spirituality than a realistic depiction of the man. Constantine's colossal but broken head is a strange testimony to historical transformation: a far-seeing bodiless visage of an emperor who glimpsed and furthered a new empire without realizing what it would do to the one he inherited.

+FERRO

+FARRO

+FICHI FANTASTICI

+FLOWERING IN FIORENZA

+"FLORENCE SYNDROME"

+FIREWATER

+FRA ANGELICO AND FRANGELICO

+FELLINIESQUE

♦ FERRO

Nothing expresses the enchantment of Venice more than the gondola. And that allure is Venice's alone: by law only the Venetian-born can become gondoliers and only several hundred practice the craft today. The gondola's elegant silhouette and *ferro,* the curved comb-like row of metal teeth adorning the prow, is universally recognized. The six teeth of the *ferro* denote the city's six neighborhoods (San Marco, Castello, Dorsoduro, Cannaregio, Santa Croce, and San Polo); the single tooth opposite represents the island of Guidecca; and the semicircular break between the curved top and the six teeth is said to signify the Rialto Bridge.

The word "ferro" is derived from the Latin *ferrum,* which refers to the iron the comb is made from (and Fe, the symbol for iron in the periodic table of elements). And so the gondola is replete with metaphor and history; how fitting that this graceful and languid craft should have come to symbolize *La Serenissima,* "the most serene republic."

♦ FARRO, FUEL OF THE EMPIRE

Farro is a grain of choice for today's ingredient-driven chefs, but long before its current popularity as a foodie artisanal ingredient, it was a staple of the Roman legions and helped fuel the Empire's expansion throughout the Western world.

When Sicily is referred to as "the breadbasket of Rome," the grain referred to is not the one that goes into crusty Italian bread, but *grano farro*, the oldest cultivated grain in the world. It not only nourished the legionnaires but fed the masses. Farro ground into a paste and cooked was the primary ingredient in *puls,* the polenta eaten for centuries by the Roman poor.

Its cultivation fell out of favor after the fall of the Empire as it was later supplanted by higher-yielding modern wheat varieties. But farro—strong, feisty and naturally resistant to fungus—still grows wild and is cultivated throughout Italy. Farro contains a significant seven grams of protein per serving, greater than brown rice if not quite as much as quinoa, and although not gluten-free, it has significantly less gluten than wheat. Enjoyed for its great nutty flavor, and a chewy texture similar to spelt, it can be a tasty alternative to oatmeal; or added to soup, stew, or salads; or even as a side dish. Sometime, to really eat like an Italian gourmet, you should eat like a farmer or a soldier, and conquer new food frontiers.

✦ FICHI FANTASTICI

If you've ever tasted figs and murmured about how divine they were, you were merely echoing centuries of global culture.

The ancient Hebrews looked upon the fig tree as a symbol of peace and plenty, while Buddhists know it as a tree of life and knowledge. Mohammed's followers called it the "Tree of Heaven." The Egyptians considered figs sacred and commonly buried their dead with baskets of figs to aid in the soul's journey into the afterlife, and as for Cleopatra, she made sure the asp that sent her into the next world came in a basket of figs. Plato called figs the food of athletes and they were commonly presented with laurels to winners of the Athenian games.

Figs may have been the earliest domesticated crop, dating back 11,000 years to the Jordan and Euphrates Valley. Later, especially through the Phoenicians, they spread to China and India, and relatively recently were introduced to America and South Africa.

You can track Roman and Italian culture's evolution through its embrace of the fig. The old Romans sacrificed the milky sap of the wild fig tree to

Juno, and came to believe that figs were sacred to their culture. Pliny the Elder (Roman naturalist and philosopher) asserted that a sacred fig tree grew in the Roman Forum and that the tree was known as "Ruminalis" because the legendary she-wolf that suckled the founding twins Romulus and Remus was discovered resting with them under that fig tree.

And when Cato advocated the conquest of Carthage to the Roman Senate, he used as his crowning argument the advantage of acquiring fruits as glorious as North African figs, specimens of which he pulled from his toga as exhibits to the other Senators. So in the Punic Wars, the army not only traveled on its stomach, but for it.

Figs epitomize Italy and the Mediterranean, its climate, its food, its way of life. The fig is a fruit to be eaten slowly and savored, from the luscious mouthfuls of soft, pink flesh to the tiniest edible seeds.

And it doesn't hurt that they are high in fiber and rich in calcium, iron, phosphorus, and potassium, as well as vitamin C and B. Figs have the highest overall mineral content of all common fruits; a half cup of figs has the same amount of calcium as a half cup of milk. Figs can provide up to a 50 percent concentration of immediately accessible sugar, a more natural alternative to an energy bar.

The fig's first commercial appearance was in 1892. But as far as its appearance in America goes, even today most Americans would likely not be able to recognize a fresh fig. They most commonly associate "fig" with the Fig Newton, which is more about the town of Newton, Massachusetts, a town near the cookie manufacturing plant, than it is about the fig itself. And that's too bad, because the inclusion of figs makes everything not just more nutritious but more voluptuous—on salads; in risotto; marmalades stuffed into pork or chicken; or simply baked into tarts, cakes, and cookies, as in a scrumptious toasted fig and ginger pound cake with lemon mascarpone or just gelato *limone*.

Have you ever noticed that fig trees never seem to bloom? Fig blossoms are inside the fruit—the crunchy edible seeds within that give the fig its unique texture are actually tiny flowers. In the same granular and delicious way the fig has bloomed throughout human history, and nowhere more beautifully than in the culture that was willing to invade another over its bounty.

◆ FLOWERING IN FIORENZA

Call it seredipity, synchronicity, even a miracle.

There are times when nations progress tremendously in a very short time in a certain arena of intellectual and cultural achievement: for instance the writings of the French Enlightenment on law and morality, or the chain of scientific and industrial discoveries in England leading to modern astrophysics and the Industrial Revolution.

But in one small city on the Italian peninsula, during (for the most part) one century, the classical Greco-Roman world was rediscovered and integrated into a revolution of Western thought by scholars like Leon Battista Alberti and Pico della Mirandola; modern scientific curiosity made its debut in the notebooks of Leonardo da Vinci; and the art of that great genius, along with the art of Michelangelo, Raphael, Donatello, Botticelli, Masaccio, Fra Angelico, and Fra Lippi, not to mention the architecture of Brunelleschi, flowered before the world.

And why not, given that the very name of the city, Florence, means "flowering" and "in bloom". How even more historically synchronicitous that this city with the symbol of springtime in its very name would be the main center of the "rebirth," the Renaissance, the greatest cultural transformation in the Western world, and a period which shaped our entire modern view of life.

There is some hard logic to this synchronicity: the logic of money. During the 14th century Florence had already bloomed financially, having grown rich in the wool trade and banking. The foundation for our modern banking system—the invention of the letter of credit, a financial *arrangiarsi* to circumvent Church edicts regarding the sin of moneylending—had been invented, along with rudimentary insurance policies, further spurring the growth of the banks centered in Florence. So the city, by the end of the 14th century, was one of the largest cities in Europe, capable of spending the kind of sums needed to enhance its prestige through works of art and architecture.

But here's where some of that mysterious serendipity again comes in: living contemporaneously with the great geniuses of the Renaissance was a family, the Medici, that not only had the skills and the moxie to become the leading family and political power in Florence, but also the intellectual inclination, taste, and judgment to recognize such genius and foster it whenever possible.

As Douglas Preston wrote, "as the fifteenth century dawned, Florence hosted the kind of inexplicable flowering of intellectual and artistic genius that has occurred fewer than half a dozen times in the course of human history." And thus ended the long darkness of the mirthless Middle Ages. Between the birth of Masaccio in 1401 and the death of Galileo in 1642, Florentines largely catalyzed the modern world, revolutionizing art, architecture, astronomy, and mathematics. The gold florin, with the Florentine lily on one side, became the coin of the realm. Landlocked Florence produced brilliant navigators like Amerigo Vespucci who mapped the New World and gave America its name.

Above all, by declaring allegiance to concepts like those of the Greek philosopher and mathematician Protagoras, who proclaimed "Man is the measure of all things," Florentines threw off the dreary cloak of medievalism, where human existence was considered nothing more than a short (often dark) passage to a more glorious afterlife to come, and established this earthly life as the main event. They celebrated the individual, the city, humanity at the center of the universe.

So you could even say that in the Quattrocento, Florence invented the idea of what it is to be modern. The course of Western civilization was changed forever.

♦ "FLORENCE SYNDROME"

It's actually described in Segen's Medical Dictionary:

> A psychosomatic response—tachycardia, vertigo, fainting, confusion and even hallucinations—when the "victim" is exposed to particularly beautiful or large amounts of art in a single place (e.g., Florence, Italy); the response can also occur when a person is overwhelmed by breathtaking natural beauty.

The term "Florence Syndrome" (also referred to as hyperkulturemia and colloquially as "art sickness") is synonymous with the Stendhal Syndrome named for the 19th-century French author Stendhal, who described his experience of this phenomenon during his visit to Florence. At the Basilica of Santa Croce, where he viewed Giotto's frescoes and altarpiece in the Peruzzi and Bardi chapels and saw where Michelangelo, Galileo, and Machiavelli were buried, he was overcome with emotion and feelings of rapture tinged with anxiety. He wrote in his book *A Journey from Milan to Reggio*:

> I was in a sort of ecstasy, from the idea of being in Florence, close to the great men whose tombs I had seen. Absorbed in the contemplation of sublime beauty . . . I reached the point where one encounters celestial sensations . . . Everything spoke so vividly to my soul. Ah, if I could only forget. I had palpitations of the heart, what in Berlin they call "nerves." Life was drained from me. I walked with the fear of falling.

Psychiatrists have debated whether "Florence Syndrome" really exists—but its rapturous effects are serious enough for some of its "victims" to require medical treatment. The staff at Florence's Santa Maria Nuova hospital regularly treats tourists suffering from dizzy spells and disorientation after viewing the masterpieces of the Uffizi Gallery or Michelangelo's statue of David and the city's numerous other treasures. Even though there are many descriptions, going back to the early 19th century, of people suffering vertigo and fainting spells while taking in Florentine artwork, especially at the Uffizi Gallery, the condition was only named in 1979 by Italian psychiatrist Graziella Magherini, who observed and documented over one hundred similar cases among tourists in Florence.

And while there are no studies to define or better quantify Florence Syndrome as a specific psychiatric disorder, there is evidence that the same cerebral areas involved in emotional reactions are activated during the exposure to beautiful works of art. Is this then, unlike love, the fever for which the beloved isn't the cure? Hard to say for sure, but perhaps when in Florence you might want to occasionally grab "un caffe" and a book, perhaps a copy of Dante's *Commedia*, to get your eyes off the Donatellos and Fra Angelicos and Botticellis and Giottos for just a little while.

• FIREWATER

From firewater to aqua vitae ("water of life"), rocket fuel to "hair of the dog," grappa has been called a variety of things and, aside from inducing raging intoxication, the distillate (70 to 120 proof) has been credited for restoring vitality; relaxing the brain; sharpening the mind; improving memory; easing rheumatism, toothaches, and indigestion; prolonging life; and, on a good day back in the day, curing the plague, not to mention nowadays curing the common cold. Of course, given how potent it is, its drinkers would probably believe it capable of curing anything.

Grappa is a pomace brandy like cognac but it doesn't have that same illustrious history of being the drink of a monarch. Instead its story is rustic and humble and comes from the northern peasant farmers of Trentino—Alto Adige, Friuli, and Val d'Aosta—trying to, basically, anesthetize themselves against the winter cold. In a fine example of no-waste recycling they ingeniously made from winemaking's leftovers, the pressed grape skins, the pomace which was then fermented and distilled.

Not named originally for Bassano del Grappa and or even Monte Grappa, where today lots of grappa is produced, the word grappa is thought to derive from *graspa*, which is dialect for "vine shoot." Grappa is not specific to any grape but, like a fine wine, the better the grape, the better the grappa.

By the 1960's grappa was in decline except as an old-fashioned folk remedy, but all this changed largely on account of one woman, Giannola Nonino, who was determined to transform what many considered "moonshine" into a sophisticated spirit to rival the great *eaux-de-vies* of France. Her husband's family distillery, Nonino Distillery in Percoto, Italy in Friuli, had been producing grappa since 1897. Her revolutionary idea was not to brew it out of a mishmash of harvest leftovers but cultivate vines for the purpose of making grappa, and so she began by making a single varietal grappa (now known as Monovitigno) from the rarest and most prestigious vine of Friuli, the Picolit, in 1973. They sold very little of it at first, but as a charismatic and astute marketer undaunted in her vision of the transformation of this drink, she offered her grappa free to journalists and restaurateurs, and asked that it be served at important commercial and government dinners. Slowly it became a success born of passion, vision, and devotion to detail and quality—plus she also understood she needed more elegant packaging and commissioned distinctive bottles by Venini, renowned Murano glassmaker, and Baccarat to showcase her reborn grappa.

Twenty-five years later Giannola Bulfoni Nonino, the mother of post-modern grappa, was awarded the "Cavaliere del Lavoro" (Order of Merit for Labor) by the President of the Italian Republic for her efforts to preserve and enhance Italy's cultural heritage. In 2003 she was awarded the "Leonardo Prize for Italian Quality" (Giannola is among the only twenty-five women to have been thus honored) and has received numerous other awards. And the story of Ms. Giannolo and her artisanal grappas made the *How It's Made* Discovery Channel documentary series.

Today grappa has protected status: it can only be called grappa if made in Italy, the Italian part of Switzerland, or San Marino, through a process of steam distillation. You can experience many different single varietals of grappa as well as blended ones, and some are aged one to two years (often in oak, which results in a golden tint) and labeled "Riserva," or "Stravecchia." The transformation of this peasant drink became truly complete with the creation of a glass designed to fully reveal the sensory pleasures of grappa, featuring a very narrow neck providing a limited evaporation surface.

When sipping from that glass, as with a fine wine, inhale first; a good grappa might have some delicate floral aromas reminiscent of a summer meadow. The rim of the glass is narrow too, to limit the flow to the tip of the tongue so the taste buds there can discern fruit and mineral notes, as well as the high alcohol content in the aftertaste, but in harmony with the other flavors. It can be pungent and even taste harsh but is immediately warming and unquestionably potent.

You can thus sample the best of grappa, enjoy it as a postprandial *digestivo*, and experience part of Italian gastronomic culture. Or, like those freezing peasant farmers of northern Italy, you can knock some back and say in whatever your language is: more grappa.

♦ FRA ANGELICO AND FRANGELICO

Devotion meets decoction...only by chance, it seems . . . and "only in Italy" as the name of perhaps the most religious of Renaissance artists is nowadays found on one of the world's tastiest liqueurs.

As the noted art critic John Ruskin described him, Fra Angelo (meaning *angelic brother*), an early Renaissance artist and Dominican friar, was not only a great artist but a genuine saint. Fra Angelo has long been called "Beato Angelico" (the Blessed Angelico) because, a deeply conservative rustic who became a monk, he believed his talent was a blessing given to him by God, and his painting should be purely devoted to God and the goodness of God's works.

Angelico was a true transition figure of Renaissance art, medieval in his exclusive focus on religious subjects—the stories of the Gospels, the enthroned Madonna and child surrounded by saints and angels—but an early adopter of perspective and volumetric figures, whose paintings depart from flat iconic depictions and come alive with beautifully observed details. His delicate, lustrous colors seem to have a remarkable inner glow, and are embellished with jewel-like tints and accents of gold leaf.

Somehow Angelico managed to combine a monk's life with the career of a highly professional artist, who was in touch with the most advanced developments in contemporary Florentine art, and in later life traveled to Rome for prestigious commissions. He resided in Fiesole and then later lived in the monastery of San Marco in Florence. Thankfully Cosimo de Medici knew of this "painter-brother," and when it came time to reconstruct the dilapidated Dominican monastery, he charged Angelico with its decoration, making sure there was a large cell reserved for him so he could escape any intrigues of political life and remain in a state of contemplation. The result, now a museum, is one of the most beautiful shrines to art and devotion in all of Italy, with luminous and moving frescoes on every wall, on the lunettes over the cloister doors, and in the rows of monastic cells, radiating reverence and the eternal peace promised to the faithful.

Ruskin's depiction of Fra Angelico may have contained a bit of hyperbole, but the artist-monk was recently beatified (the third of four steps required for sainthood) by the Vatican, and in 1982 was named the patron of artists by Pope John Paul II.

So how does this most sanctified of artists find his name on an alcoholic beverage? The eponymous Frangelico is a pale gold-colored liqueur rich in texture, made from an infusion of roasted hazelnuts, cocoa, and vanilla. Its origins are said to go back over three hundred years to a monastery in the Piedmonte area of Italy. According to Gruppo Campari, the owner of the brand, the name Frangelico is based on legend of a hermit named Friar Angelico who "created unique recipes for liqueurs . . . ," apparently an activity carried on by certain monasteries.

But what are the odds of such a hermit distiller having not just the same name but in effect the same title as the great artist? Fra Angelico the painter is the liqueur's more likely namesake, although it is true that the bottle itself resembles the habit of a Franciscan friar (brown in color with a rope belt), while Fra Angelico was a Dominican, whose robe would have been white and without the cincture. Whatever its origin, the drink has been known to inspire a devotion all its own.

◆ FELLINIESQUE

"Life is a combination of magic and pasta." —Federico Fellini

Conjure up a fantastical world where dreamscapes and human landscapes become one; a world of sensual enjoyment and extravagant vitality that sometimes seems all a pageant or a circus parade; a world of lost boys and playboys and film maestros and their ample-breasted seductresses; and the flamboyant lyricism of that world can only belong to one filmmaker.

80

Originally a neorealist director, Federico Fellini moved into more poetic territory in *La Strada* and *Nights of Cabiria*, tales of loving and long-suffering women, a circus strongman's wife and a prostitute, played by his wife and muse, Giulietta Masina. Subsequent films featured dreams and surreal fantasies that celebrated life and love or symbolized its most grotesque nightmares; in masterpieces like *La Dolce Vita, 8 ½*, and *Amarcord*—with operatic brio and passages of visionary cinema—Fellini told stories of romance and spiritual desolation, the struggle to create art, and the vagaries of memory.

Fellini's cinematic and actual home was Rome, and in *Fellini's Roma* he finally made it his protagonist. Not just a glorified travelogue as some have suggested, this is a portrait of the eternal city as equally carnal and sacred, and in its series of vignettes, sometimes the two seem interchangeable.

The prostitute, a symbol of transient pleasures of the flesh, becomes eternal; and the Church, symbol of the eternal, becomes temporal. In *Roma*'s most audacious sequence (preceded by a parade of prostitutes), Fellini presents a "Vatican fashion show," with roller-skating priests and bishops whose robes are festooned with blinking neon lights. And to the question one onlooker poses—should the world follow the Church or the Church the world?—Fellini's satire suggests the Church, with its pomp and splendor and worship of a "Holy Father" whose word is absolute, entered the world a long time ago; why not also advertise its garments as fashionwear and tart up the holy vestments?

What's the boundary between reality and unreality, the sacred and the profane? Fellini doesn't draw it, and he seems to believe that Rome can't either. For in Felliniesque cinema, as much as in Shakespeare's *The Tempest*, "we are such stuff as dreams are made of."

- GRAFFITI

- THE GRAND TOUR

- GELATO, AMBROSIA OF THE BOOT

- GIANDUIA, GROWN-UP NUTELLA

- GREEK SOUL OF SICILY

- GIOTTO, MASTER OF EMOTIONS

- GIRASOLE

G

♦ GRAFFITI

Graffiti has been part of the urban landscape for many millennia and the word itself derives from the Latin *graphium* and Greek *graphein* meaning "to scratch, write, or draw." The graffiti of the ancients range from simple written words to more elaborate wall drawings, going back to ancient Egypt, Greece, and Rome.

The first example of what is considered "modern style" graffiti survives in the Greek city of Ephesus (in modern day Turkey). Local guides will tell you it's an advertisement for— surprise—a prostitute.

The eruption of Mount Vesuvius in 79 CE preserved in amazing detail the city of Pompeii, including the graffiti of Pompeii and Herculaneum, and there was quite a bit. Subject matter generally dealt with sex, wine, money, and politics, all providing insight into Roman street life. Pompeii was the Las Vegas of the Roman Empire. When Vesuvius blew it left not a shred of evidence that Christianity had in any way insinuated itself into the life of this bacchanalian port city.

Most of the graffiti that has come down to us through the ages and the ashes is crude in nature and includes words and pictures. Pompeiians liked to paint and draw—exquisite portraits, dogs and horses, donkeys too—but they especially liked to draw phalluses and all that entailed. Erotic frescoes have been found on what were the walls of many upper-class homes, even on the walls of brothels as guides to just what services could be performed.

And at what archaeologists consider a Pompeii bar there's an extremely graphic representation of a man and woman semi-naked making love while balancing on a tightrope and drinking huge glasses of wine.

Here are some samples of the graffiti that has been found and their translations.

"Lucius Pinxit."
"Lucius wrote this."

"Epaphra, glaber es."
"Epaphra, you are bald."

"Apollinaris, medicus Titi Imperatoris hic cacavit bene."
"Apollinaris, doctor to the emperor Titus, had a good crap here."

"Oppi, emboliari, fur, furuncle."
"Oppius, you're a clown, a thief, and a cheap crook."

"Talia te fallant utinam medacia, copo: tu vedes aquam et bibes ipse merum."
"If only similar swindling would dupe you, innkeeper: you sell water, and drink the undiluted wine yourself."

"Phileros spado."
"Phileros is a eunuch."

"Vatuan aediles furunculi rog."
"The petty thieves request the election of Vatia as adele."
("Adele" refers to an elected official who supervised markets and local police.)

"Virgula Tertio su: Indecens es."
"Virgula to Teritus: You are a nasty boy."

"Suspirium puellam Celadus thraex."
"Celadus makes the girls moan"

As the old expression goes "the more things change the more things stay the same."

• THE GRAND TOUR

Imagine a male version of an overseas finishing school, debutante ball, and shopping spree all rolled up into one grand adventure. For young men of means from Britain, that was the essential Grand Tour experience from the mid-seventeenth through the mid-nineteenth centuries. (Wealthy young women with chaperones, as well as well-heeled travelers from the Americas, also shared in the Grand Tour during the nineteenth century.)

The Grand Tour was "cultural immersion" travel at its most exclusive. Most popular among young members of the British nobility and scions to British fortunes at the height of the empire, the Grand Tour usually took the form of a months-long itinerary of the cultural capitals of Europe, invariably including the golden triad of Florence, Venice, and Rome. These three destinations fulfilled different but complementary roles in a young man's (or, later, woman's) cultural and social education.

Florence offered exposure to a treasure trove of Renaissance art; it also provided an Anglo-Italian support network for young Englishmen of means and with connections. Rome, of course, offered the monumental artistic achievements of antiquity and its own empire. Venice was a must-experience stop, and the mecca of all Grand Tours for its artistic glories as well as its scenic and decadent charms (as in here's where "debutante ball" attendees wore masks and shed clothes).

All three locales provided the added attraction of weather more congenial than what the British would find at home.

In an era before cameras, few Grand Tour grandees would be satisfied to just bring fond memories home. So was spawned the thriving industry of "view paintings" (*vedute*), especially of Venice from such celebrated artists as Canaletto (Giovanni Antonio Canal, 1697–1768). Today significant numbers of Canaletto *vedute* can still be found in Britain in the Royal Collection, the Wallace Collection, and in Woburn Abbey. A typical piece, *The*

Grand Canal View from Palazzo Baldi toward the Rialto, sold at Sotheby's in London in 2015 for £18,600.600—no mean return for the Grand Tour equivalent of a postcard from the Boot!

♦ GELATO, AMBROSIA OF THE BOOT

The experience of gelato in Italy is a revelation. As in so many of their native products, Italians seem to achieve something bordering on magical with this dessert.

The word "gelato" is derived from the Latin for "frozen," but that does not remotely begin to capture its essence. Those who know both gelato and American ice cream tend to equate the two, but it's truly "different in kind" from its American counterpart.

For starters, in warm weather months gelato is ubiquitous throughout the Boot, which is not necessarily good, but in this case, it is. In every village, town, and city you will find dazzling displays of colorful flavors swirled into creamy peaks garnished artistically with fresh fruit and nuts, which create curiosity and wake up your appetite even if you have none (so often eyes tell the stomach what to think). Most gelato cases are filled with a plethora of flavors, usually no less than twenty, some of which you may have never had before or even imagined. Many proprietors, especially in a busy place, are not much for letting you sample, but you can get multiple flavors in a cup, and you can have gelato more than once a day. Still nothing quite prepares you for that first experience on your palate (and being reminded of "The Ecstasy of Saint Teresa"... or, in other words, "I'll have what she's having").

The differences come down to both texture and flavor. Typical American ice cream is whipped at high speed with air, sometimes containing as much as 60 percent, while gelato contains very little. You'll notice as soon as gelato touches your tongue that it's exceptionally creamy. Fat conscious? Don't fret; creamy richness does *not* equate to fat grams! The intense "true" flavor you experience when you sample well-made gelato is a result of the significantly lower fat content (up to 50 percent). Extra fat serves to coat your tongue and mask your taste buds' ability to more directly experience the true flavors from the finest ingredients. So in the case of gelato less fat means more flavor (for many of us, this is perhaps the most important food fact we will ever learn). And much of the gelato served in Italy is held at higher temperatures, softening it and further amplifying the flavor.

Cool refreshing indulgences similar to gelato have a long history dating back to biblical times. Isaac served Abraham a yummy concoction of snow, honey, and goat's milk: this was referenced as "sherbet." Around 3000 BCE, Chinese emperors began enjoying frozen treats made from snow, fruit, wine, and honey. Later the Chinese introduced their delicacy to Arab traders who then shared their delicious discovery with the Romans and Venetians. Something similar to *sorbetto* was a favorite of Emperor Nero who sent an army of slaves into the Apennines each year to gather snow that could be stored in caves so that he could enjoy his favorite cool fruity indulgence throughout the year.

It was in late Renaissance Florence that the revolutionary idea of using cow's milk was first conceived by one of the personal chefs of Caterina de Medici. When Caterina married Henry II of France, she was accompanied by her chefs, who were included as part of her dowry along with their recipes and many other ingredients of modern cuisine. A century later a Sicilian opened a wildly successful café serving gelato on the Left Bank of Paris that is still in business today—Café Procope, at 330 years of age the oldest restaurant in continuous operation in Paris. Remaining more a delicacy of the noble class, these frozen delights spread to England and then made their way to America, where they evolved (devolved?) into ice cream. Gelato, meanwhile, never waned in its hold on Europe and especially Italy.

You can find outstanding gelati everywhere on the peninsula (however quality does vary and there is more and more mass production; look for "*artiginale*" and beware of colors that are too bright and peaks that look too uniform). If you are in search of the Holy Grail of gelato, many suggest Sicily, where most gelateria still make gelato by hand in small batches. In the modest yet dazzling baroque city of Noto on Sicily's southeastern coast, legions of visitors come to Caffè Sicilia on the Corso Vittorio Emanuele in search of its artfully made marmalades, honeys, nougats, pas-

coppa o cono?

tries, and, above all, gelati. Aficionados describe the store's fourth-generation owner and chef as a (mad) genius and an alchemist of flavors. They say his *fragola sorbetto* tastes like the iced cool essence of luscious, sun-ripened strawberries, freshly picked; the chocolate gelato is so dark and rich it is said to be almost a spiritual experience; and that seismic sensations can be brought on by tasting *gelato di fior di spezia* (spice flower) and *gelato di insalata di arance* (blood orange salad) flavors, fusions of tastes woven from centuries of cultural history combined in the heavenly experience of true gelato.

♦ GIANDUIA, GROWN-UP NUTELLA

Before the Italians invented Nutella (Thank you, God!) they had invented *Gianduia*, sometimes spelled *Gianduja*, its more sophisticated refined older cousin. One of the best places to sample it is Turin, the capital of Piedmonte (derived from *ad pedem montium*, meaning "at the foot of the mountains") where it was originally invented and where nearly 60 percent of Italy's chocolate originates.

Back in the 18th century, Turin was the epicenter of chocolate; even the Swiss came to Turin to learn the trade. Chocolate was big business in Turin and the chocolate makers were producing and exporting 750 pounds a day, importing their raw cacao from the New World. Then, in 1806, Napoleon set up a naval blockade, which limited supplies and and made their availability unpredictable. Economic necessity, local agriculture, and ingenuity were the mother of invention—the ingenious Piedmontese turned to their abundant groves of hazelnuts from the Lange, a lush hilly area south of Turin, for a delectable solution: hazelnuts of Piedmonte (these nuts are prized the world over, known as *tonda gentile delle Lange* which means sweet round nut of the Lange). They roasted, ground, and mixed the buttery rich hazelnuts with the then scarce, expensive cacao to create the delectable dessert paste. It was later named after a Piedmontese comic character, Gioan d'la Duja (meaning "John who loves wine," with the *duja* referring to the flask he carried his wine in).

♦ GREEK SOUL OF SICILY

Many assume that the further south you go in Italy, the more "Italian" the country becomes in the stereotypical "mama mia" sense—red sauce, garlic, old ladies in black, and dark-haired, dark-eyed, dark-skinned beauties like Michael Corleone's lovely Appolonia. But in Sicily, the island that's the most southern part of the country, you will also be surprised to find fair-skinned, blue-eyed, and red-haired beauties, and cuisine that surprises the palate by blending sweet and savory non-Italian ingredients like complex North African spices.

Geography is destiny. One can't sail the Mediterranean without bumping into Sicily, and in the ancient world, that meant seafarers from Carthage (modern Tunisia), Phoenicia (the Middle East), and Greece were bound to encounter its shores. Exploration would not have been time-consuming by ancient standards, given that Sicily, while the largest island in Mediterranean, is still fairly small: east to west is a 3 ½ hour drive, and north to south, a 2 ½ hour drive. Sicily, being closer to Tunisia than to Rome (on a clear day you can see North Africa) and smack in the middle of the Straits of Gibraltar and the Middle East, was also a perfect crossroads location of great strategic, trade, and economic importance with its fertile soil for the cultivation of grains, fruit trees, other crops, and the breeding of livestock for two millennia.

But since it couldn't raise its own standing army or navy, control of Sicily has been in play since the beginning of Western civilization, as this summary timeline shows:

Greek Sicily 750 BCE (Magna Graecia)

Romans 212 BCE (Sicily becomes ancient Rome's first province outside the peninsula as a result of the Punic Wars with Carthage)

Byzantines 535

Saracens / Arabs 827

Normans 1061 (Count Roger de Hauteville, Roger II, Frederick II)

Spanish 1282

Bourbons 1713 (Kingdom of the Two Sicilys)

Italy's Unification 1860

Imprints of the Greeks, Carthaginians, Romans, Byzantines, Arabs, Normans, Spanish, and the Bourbons are still evident, for example, in agriculture and cuisine. The Greeks planted olive trees and grape vines, while the Arabs vastly improved Sicily's agriculture by introducing advanced methods of fishing, irrigation, and farming; they also brought lemon trees, orange trees, almond and pistachio trees, date palms, sugar cane, jasmine, sumac, and saffron. Much later, the Spanish brought tomatoes, potatoes, chocolate, and prickly pears.

The melting pot aspect of Sicily has led not only to delightfully changeable and varied dishes, but cultural richness in archaeology; art and architecture from a variety of traditions; prosperity and protection (they were the breadbasket of Rome); and pleasures including, during its Norman-Arab period, Persian silks and harem girls. But the downside is that Sicily has been overrun and governed by foreign invaders for over two thousand years. That's inevitably led to a bit of identity confusion: Sicily has been a granary of Rome, an outpost of the Eastern Church, and the possession of all the abovementioned conquerors, while also being coveted by Crusaders and Italian city-states of every kind.

But since language, literature, and centuries-old beliefs perhaps have the most lasting effects on a people's character and vision, deep down the soul of Sicily is Greek. The Greek language was the common tongue of Sicily well into the early Middle Ages; even under the Romans, while Latin became the "official" language, most Sicilians continued to speak Greek. As early as 800 BCE the Greeks began their colonization of Sicily and southern peninsular Italy—the area became known as Magna Graecia and eventually became home to more Greeks than Greece itself. Within a few centuries of its foundation, the city of Syracuse was considered the one of the most beautiful cities of ancient Greece, rivaling Athens in power and prestige. Sicily was not a conquered people ruled by a provincial government; it was a Greek island no different than Crete or Rhodes and a far more integral part of the ancient Grecian world.

This core legacy manifests itself in some of the world's best preserved Greek temples and amphitheatres—from the Temple of Concordia in the Valle dei Templi at Agrigento to the Teatro Greco-Romano at Taormina and Parco Archeologico della Neapolis at Siracusa (Syracuse). And as these structures suggest, Greek gods and heroes had a place in Sicily; that's confirmed by the Sicilian locations of many Greek myths.

For example, the province of Enna is considered the home ground of the cult of Demeter, goddess of agriculture, fertility, and the harvest. Demeter's daughter Persephone was abducted by Hades into the Underworld at Lake Pergusa near Enna, as dramatized in Bernini's sculpture *The Rape of Proserpina*; as a compromise Demeter was forced to share Persephone with Hades four months a year, which saddened her so greatly it led to the season of winter. The gods apparently had a preference for Sicilian real estate, both residential and business: Aeolios, King of the Winds, lived on the Aeolian Islands, while Hephaestus (Vulcan), son of Zeus and the blacksmith god of fire, lived on Mount Etna, where he forged his father's lightning bolts with the flames from the fiery volcano.

Odysseus, hero of Homer's epic the *Odyssey* and legendary King of Ithaca, journeyed the Mediterranean for ten years trying to get home, and many of his adventures took place on the island of Sicily. The heinous sea monsters Scylla and Charybdis, who terrorized sailors, dwelled around the Straits of Messina; Scylla was a six-headed sea monster and Charybdis the water-sucking daughter of Poseidon who created deadly whirlpools. Odysseus was forced to choose between these two awful alternatives —between "the devil and the deep blue sea"—while sailing through the Straits of Messina; he opted for Scylla and the loss of only a few sailors rather than risking the loss of his entire crew and ship through Charybdis.

Meanwhile the god Dionysus came across a strange, unknown plant during his voyage to Sicily. Curious, he took an example with him and on his arrival home planted it, and the plant was of course a vine! Once he sipped its fruit, being (apparently) no fool, he knew he had such a fantastic going concern that he made himself the god of wine, which also led him to become the god of divine inspiration. So the next time you sip some vino, spare a thought for Dionysus and the once-Greek land of Sicily.

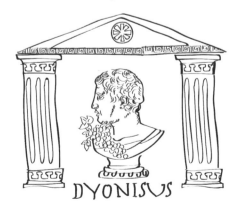

DYONISVS

♦ GIOTTO, MASTER OF EMOTION

Giotto di Bondone was, quite literally, a pivotal figure in Western art history. His body of work stands as a turning point from the highly stylized lifeless medieval forms to the fully inhabited expressive human subjects in religious narrative art. Gone are the flat and clone-like assemblages of sinners and saints. In their place Giotto breathes life into his living subjects, endowing them with physical bulk, individual facial and gestural expression, and palpable emotion—in other words, with humanity. More than any other single artist, Giotto ushered in the Renaissance.

One of many examples of his humanistic touch can be seen in the second panel of Giotto's cycle on the life of Joachim—father of the Virgin—in the Scrovegni Chapel. Here we see Joachim making his way back to the company of his fellow shepherds after his expulsion from the temple on account of his childless marriage. An acute sense of personal shame is manifest in his rounded shoulders, downward gaze, and "closed" body language. Echoing and amplifying Joachim's despair is the clear sense of embarrassment felt on his behalf by the two shepherds he encounters: they divert their gazes from Joachim and from each other. These emotions resound against the backdrop of a barren rock face.

But perhaps the most poignant expression of feeling in this powerful vignette comes not from the three humans depicted but from Joachim's small dog. As if frozen in time by a stop-action camera, our protagonist's canine friend is seen to simultaneously leap up in greeting and pull back slightly in apparent apprehension at his master's disconsolate bearing. It's the ultimate grace note in this stunning narrative composition, and just one more demonstration of Giotto's timeless genius.

♦ GIRASOLE

Fields of happy faces seem to joyfully greet you throughout Tuscany, Marche, and parts south, as tourists seek out summer's sunflowers like New England leaf peepers seek out autumn foliage. Rows upon rows of them—needless to say, a highly coveted photo op, and a sheer delight to the senses (so put that smartphone back in your pocket for awhile).

Called "sun-turner" in Italian, Spanish, and French (*girasole, girasol,* and *tournesol*) for their heliotropism—following the path of the sun throughout the day—sunflowers actually only do this as young buds; once their full yellow faces appear they figure it out and their movement stops and they face east, toward the morning sun. This gives fields of sunflowers their uniform orientation; even at twilight, when the Sun is in the west, the sunflowers will still be facing east.

Like the tomato and zucchini, sunflowers come from the New World and have only been cultivated in Italy the past several hundred years; yet it seems unimaginable that they weren't always part of the landscape. Their warm glow just seems a part of the Italian scene.

And there's more to the cheerful sunflower that meets the eye, which speaks to pre-New-World Italian history. Like so much of the natural world, sunflowers manifest an uncanny mathematical architecture and consistent patterning that borders on the mystical. Which brings us to Fibonacci (naturally another brilliant Italian), considered the greatest European mathematician of the middle ages.

His full name was Leonardo Pisano, born in Pisa around 1175 CE, right in the depth of the medieval darkness. However, Leonardo grew up and was educated in North Africa and learned the Moors' system of doing arithmetic. He recognized the advantages of the "Hindu-Arabic" system based on ten digits with its decimal point and a symbol for zero: your basic 1–9 and 0 instead of Roman numerals. His book on how to do arithmetic in the decimal system, called *Liber abbaci* (meaning "Book of the Abacus" or "Book of Calculating"), completed in 1202, persuaded many European mathematicians to use this "new" system. The book, written in Latin, sets forth the rules we all now use to add, subtract, multiply, and divide, together with many problems to illustrate the methods. So, what does this have to do with the perky girasole?

Leonardo (his nickname was Fibonacci, possibly from *filius Bonacci*, "the son of Bonaccio") is most famous for a series of numbers he included in his book which are now referred to as Fibonacci numbers: 1, 2, 3, 5, 8, 13, 21, 34, 55, 89, 144, 233, 377 and so on. It's a series in which each number is obtained from the sum of the two preceding. It turns out this pattern occurs throughout nature in various ways: most flowers' petals are a Fibonacci number and their seed heads grow in efficient spirals, such as the pattern of seeds in the head of the beautiful sunflower.

Look at any such plant and you notice two series of curves for the seed heads, one winding in one direction and one in another, the number of spirals not being the same in each direction. The number of spirals in each direction, going from the center to the edge (where naturally there are more of them) is generally either 21 and 34, 34 and 55, 55 and 89, or 89 and 144. This is seen in pinecones and the diagonals of a pineapple. No matter how large or small the flower heads are, in order that (it's theorized) the seeds are uniformly packed along the seed head, the numbers all belong to the Fibonacci sequence—1, 2, 3, 5, 8, 13, 21, 34, 55, 89, 144, etc.—and express a related concept called the golden mean. You can look at many plants to see this phenomenon, but the sunflower is where it's most brilliantly on display.

And you thought the sunflower was just another pretty face...

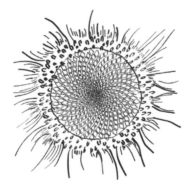

◆HUMAN CHESS GAME

◆HAND GESTURES

◆HIGH HEELS

◆THE HARRY BEHIND HARRY'S BAR

◆THE FOUR HORSES OF THE BASILICA

◆HALL OF THE HUNT

◆HEAD OF THE MOOR

H

♦ HUMAN CHESS GAME

In a country that still celebrates any number of wildly colorful traditional festivals, the human chess game of Marostica is one of the most extravagant and romantic.

An old town framed by castles just a half-hour's drive from Venice, Marostica literally packs them in—as in horses, costumed chessmen and court retainers, and avid spectators— every September on the second weekend every even-numbered year (worth remembering). The  chess game goes back to 1454 when, according to legend, two noblemen, Rinaldo D'Angarano and Vieri da Vallonara, fell in love with the beautiful Lionora, daughter of Taddeo Parisio, at the Lord of Marostica's castle (yes, it is a troubadorial song come to life). They challenged each other to a duel, but the ruler, fearing loss of life (and valuable alliances in the Venetian Republic which at the time ruled the town) created a substitute battle for them: a human chess game. In so doing he proved himself not only a classically skillful Italian diplomat—for he also decided that the loser would get Olrada, the younger sister—but something of an eccentric artist.

And so on a 20x20 meter chess board at the Piazza Castello (now known as Piazza Degli Scacchi or "Plaza of Chess") actual mini-armies of Whites and Blacks on horseback played the game on the central square, *la partita a scacchi con personaggi viventi* (chess with live personages), with the suitors calling the moves. The entire court and population were present, and the contest was accompanied by fireworks and dances.

Once it was decided, the pawns trudged away, the king and queen marched away, and the knights rode away on their horses, but the spectacle so seized the imagination of the town that it never ended, moving from glory in the Renaissance to marketability in the 21st century. It's a beautiful, astoundingly long-lived spectacle and respectful of tradition: the costumes, multicolored banners, and martial parades are the same, the courteous ritual of the game continues, and the moves are still called in Venetian dialect. Pure history meets pure fantasy in ways that evoke everything from Renaissance pageantry to Fellini, preserving for all time a tribute to brain-over-brawn and non-bloody civility as rare in its time as it is today.

✦ HAND GESTURES

Those who love Italian culture and language know that Italians have cultivated a whole other form of communication: the language of gestures. Whether through the lift of an eyebrow, shrug of a shoulder, or mere flip of a wrist they are able to express themselves with clarity, subtlety, and wit.

Italians start talking with their hands about the same time they start to vocalize. Some even joke that gesturing begins in the womb. Is this yet another endearing manifestation of an expressive and passionate people, or does it go deeper? Is the seemingly natural impulse for gestural embellishment and theatrical punctuation a cultural hardwire? It appears that way, as one can only marvel as Italians multitask with gracefully choreographed gestures while chatting animatedly on their cell phones, weaving their Vespas through rush hour traffic, or simply smoking cigarettes. Some gestures are very simple—I'm hungry, he's crazy, hurry up, be quiet—while others are far more subtle and nuanced, conveying shame, pride, resignation, supplication, or fatalism. About 250 gestures used in everyday conversation have been catalogued according to Isabella Poggi, professor of psychology at Roma Tre University and an expert on gestures.

Hypotheses abound as to why Italians developed this gestural vocabulary as a supplemental form of communication. Italy's geography and natural topography offer some clues. Italy is surrounded by water, smack in the middle of the Mediterranean Sea, and at the crossroads of Asia, North Africa, and the Middle East. The city-states had a long history of trading with other countries, most famously the merchant ports of Venice, Genoa, Naples, Amalfi, and Pisa. In all these cosmopolitan port cities foreign visitors mixed it up with local populations (think of the original *Star Wars* "cantina scene," or better yet, the bigger and even more confusing entrepot in *The Force Awakens*). To be able to communicate past different spoken languages was a smart commercial and political strategy.

So the Italian people have always needed to communicate with non-Italian speakers to do business and thrive in a world where, especially back in the ducal days, they weren't the largest and most powerful country. Gestures can complement spoken language and can even replace words. But of course, there's another piece of this puzzle: what Diane Halles, author of *La Bella Lingua*, calls "the Babel of dialects." A standard Italian language is a modern phenomenon: Italy has only been a unified country for a little more than 150 years (since 1861) and even to this day numerous local dialects are still spoken that are so different from each other that they're practically different languages.

Why so many dialects? No it's not exuberance and creativity, although there's some of that in speakers' cherishing of their local word forms. In speaking of his beloved country Petrarch said: *Il bel paese ch'Appennin parte, e 'l mar circonda e l'Alpe* ("The beautiful country that the Apennines divide, and the sea and Alps surround.") One in ten Italians lives on an island and mainland Italians are often separated by rocky barriers; about 75 percent of Italy is mountainous. Even the south, which is considered homogeneous, is extremely varied. The coastal areas of Calabria are typical of a Mediterranean shoreline while Puglia is flat like a rolled-out focaccia with the stunningly majestic Piccolo Dolomiti of Basilicata sandwiched in between.

So topographical divisions of mountains and sea have kept Italians isolated from each other and have contributed greatly to Italy's linguistic, cultural, and gastronomic diversity. In landlocked Umbria, villages less than twenty miles apart as the crow flies—Spoleto and Norcia—even today are only reachable by a circuitous mountain road that takes over forty-five minutes to drive.

But when it comes to gestural language, necessity is not just the mother of invention but also improvisation and even fun. Gestures are a primal, direct means of communicating which, with the Italians, take on more expressive soulful dimensions. It certainly may be true that Italians had to talk with their hands just to talk with each other. But if that happens to be an endearing manifestation of an expressive and passionate people that allows all sorts of sensual and witty and irreverent nuances to enter the act of communication, chalk that up to the enjoyment of *la lingua* and life.

♦ HIGH HEELS

"Give a girl the right shoes and she can conquer the world."
— Marilyn Monroe

High heels made their fashion debut in the fall of 1533.

Just under five feet tall, not a great beauty and a famously great eater, Caterina de Medici was far from a runway model. She did however have quite a taste for the finer things and was a Renaissance trendsetter.

The occasion was her wedding to the Duke of Orleans and Caterina wanted to make a grand entrance and formidable impression on

the Royal Court of France—especially as her betrothed had a tall, stately, beautiful mistress. Her wedding attire was quite sumptuous, a gown of golden brocade with a bodice encrusted with jewels and edged with ermine. To complete the ensemble, and to elevate her stature, a Florentine artisan had been specially commissioned to make her a fine pair of gilded shoes with four-inch heels. These are the first example of the modern high-heeled shoe: the thin heel was atop a solid wooden platform that covered the base of the shoe from heel to toe. Importantly, and as she had desired, wearing these golden slippers caused quite a stir.

An early source of inspiration for high heels is thought to have come from the Near East and male equestrian footwear. Heels helped to straddle the stirrup and create greater stability for the rider in the saddle. Another source was chopines, similar to a clunky elevated clog, which made their appearance in Venice in the 1400s. Chopines had a practical purpose at first, to protect shoes and dresses from mud and dirt in the street, but over time they became a symbolic reference to the social standing of the wearer: the higher the chopine the higher the status. Height and status seemed to naturally go hand-in-hand as the popularity of high heels spread across Europe.

Caterina ultimately became the Queen of France and heels naturally became *de rigueur* in the French court and among the wealthy and well-born. Pumps became status symbols and one of the dividing lines between classes. The phrase "well-heeled" originated to describe this phenomenon.

The trend Caterina and her Florentine shoemaker started never died, especially among royalty. Other monarchs who loved to wear high heels were Mary Tudor (the higher the better) and Marie Antoinette, who famously, or infamously, wore a pair of fancy heels when she met her fate at the guillotine. As Marilyn might have added, if you're going to lose the world, at least keep the shoes.

✦ THE HARRY BEHIND HARRY'S BAR

For any Hemingway enthusiast, no visit to Venice is complete without a stop at Harry's Bar. Hemingway drank and ate there, and he wrote about it. He was so friendly with the establishment that he even went as far as putting its founder, Cipriani, in one of his novels. In fact, Cipriani is the only then-living person to have ever appeared in any of Hemingway's fiction.

The back story of the world's most fabled watering hole aptly begins with a partnership between a Venetian barman named Giuseppe and a boozy Bostonian named Harry.

During Prohibition swank European hotel lounges served as civilized oases for moneyed Americans. Giuseppe Cipriani was a young barman at the posh Europa-Brittania Hotel where he met young Bostonian Harry Pickering in 1929. Pickering had been traveling with his aunt and her male companion to, ironically, dry out in sunny Italy; instead he drank even more vigorously, insulted his aunt, and the offended couple left him lira-less in Venice.

Pickering turned to Cipriani, perhaps his only friend at the time, and asked for a loan of 10,000 lire (about $500 in 1929 dollars and about $8,000 today)—enough to pay his hotel bill and purchase his passage back home. Cipriani gave him the money out of compassion or pity, never expecting to see it or Harry again. But true to his promise, though it took two years, Pickering returned to Venice and repaid the 10,000 lire, and then handed Ciprani another 40,000, proposing the two of them open a small American-style saloon that would be called Harry's Bar. Located just off the Grand Canal but with no real view of the Grand Canal, it was a cramped establishment with low tables and chairs. But when Harry's Bar opened in May of 1931, patronized by Venice-loving European aristocracy, it was greeted with immediate success. Pickering would ultimately lose interest in the hospitality industry and return home to Boston; when he died he left the establishment entirely to Cipriani.

WWII came to Venice and Cipriani, at first quietly and cleverly noncompliant under the occupation (see *Arrangiarsi*), displayed impressive courage in 1943. A group of Fascists entered Harry's Bar and ordered him to put up a sign saying, "We do not want Jews in this establishment." When they returned a few days later, no sign was in evidence; they demanded to see it, and Cipriani took then back to the kitchen, where it was displayed on the kitchen door. The infuriated Fascists proceeded to destroy the place. A few days later the German consul proclaimed that Harry's Bar was a hangout for "unacceptable non-Aryans." Rather than relent, Cipriani closed the doors of Harry's Bar in defiance.

Several weeks after the liberation of Venice in April 1945, Cipriani was summoned by the US Commander of the Allied forces. "You are not a good Italian," he told Cipriani.

"Why?"

"Because you have not reopened Harry's Bar."

As Cipriani recounts it, "For probably the first time in my life, I did not feel inclined to quibble with the authorities."

In the decades after the war, thanks in part to Hemingway, the tables would be filled with artists and writers like Georges Braque and Truman

Capote, Peggy Guggenheim, business magnates, and Hollywood stars from Orson Welles to Rita Hayworth to Woody Allen. Although unlike any other bar-restaurant in Italy, yet never a true club, Harry's Bar was the place where everyone seemed to know everyone else.

But more than a "Cheers" for the *cognoscenti*, Harry's Bar is one of the few places in the world that created both a classic cocktail, the Bellini, and a classic dish, Carpaccio, each named in honor of an illustrious Venetian artist.

Harry's Bar received two prized Michelin stars at a time when there were no three-star restaurants in Italy. American food writer James Beard was once asked to describe the food at Harry's Bar and he answered, "Well, he doesn't serve Italian food; he serves Cipriani food."

Over the years, Harry's Bar in Venice has maintained its aura and status as a first-rate restaurant and was even declared a National Landmark in 2001 (which means that they cannot move or even change the furniture or décor). Numerous Harry's Bars around the world—and they are legion—have no relation to the Cipriani original and are related only tenuously, if at all, to each other. However, the Cipriani family owns the casual Harry's Dolci on the Venetian island of Giudecca; a restaurant in Dubai and one in Mexico City; and several restaurants and banquet spaces in Manhattan, Miami, and Los Angeles: the living legacy of a modest man with firm principles, a flair for branding, and making the best out of the bad, the ugly, and the very good indeed.

♦ THE FOUR HORSES OF THE BASILICA

Four magnificent copper horses prance in place on the loggia above the central portal of St. Mark's Basilica in Venice. But the originals of these fine equine specimens, located *inside* the basilica for protection from the elements just yards from their weather-exposed replicas, traveled far and wide in both the ancient and modern worlds.

One theory has it that the statues originated with Lysippos, one of the three greatest sculptors of classical Greece in the 4th century BCE, and that the emperor Nero brought them to Rome. Sometime after the burning of that city they surfaced in Byzantium where the emperor Constantine installed them on the Hippodrome, his magnificent new chariot racing arena. (The sculptural grouping is thought at that time to have included such a conveyance.) There they remained for nine hundred years.

The Fourth Crusade provided the Venetian Republic with a splendid strategic opportunity. When knights of the crusade were stalled in Venice for lack of funding and ships, the Venetian Doge, Enrico Dandolo, provided both in exchange for those crusaders' support *en route* in settling some old scores: first by capturing the eastern Adriatic port city of Zadar, then under Hungarian rule; and later as the expedition unfolded, by installing a new regime in Constantinople. (Three decades earlier the Byzantine government had imprisoned Venetians living in its territories and confiscated their property.) Although into his nineties and completely blind, the remarkably vigorous doge personally joined, accompanied, and, at times, directed the knights.

In 1204 the blind doge and his fellow crusaders sacked Constantinople. Although Dandolo never returned to Venice—he died the following year and his remains abide in the Hagia Sophia—most of the spoils of that looting, the horses included, did make it back. The horses' heads were separated to facilitate their transport (eerily presaging a famous scene from *The Godfather, Part I*); the collars that now appear around their necks were added to disguise that act.

The four horses took their place on the loggia of St. Mark's in 1254 and remained there until 1797 when Venice surrendered to Napoleon after more than a thousand years as a Republic. Napoleon brought the horses—along with many other artistic treasures from the Italian peninsula—to Paris, but less than twenty years later they were returned to Venice in accordance with the Congress of Vienna. In the twentieth century they were removed for safekeeping during both World Wars and then taken on tour to European capitals and the New World (New York and Mexico City) before returning to their current location in the Basilica's museum.

Over two millennia these stately creatures were coveted by three emperors and they captured the imagination of countless imperial subjects, foreign travelers, and modern tourists. Now that's horsepower!

◆ HALL OF THE HUNT

It could be a movie scene out of a fantasy of antiquity, beginning with what seems to be a panorama of ancient Egypt, with boats and barges and fishermen, and then progressing to images of hunters who capture the ferocious animals of the world's most exotic locales, using only spears and traps and their own courage and inventiveness. They hunt tigers with the help of a glass sphere that causes them to pounce on their own reflections. All sorts of (then) exotic animals, like bears and elephants and rhinoceroses, are seized and then sent out to sea from the ancient city of Carthage many scenes later.

Only this isn't a movie: it's 3500 square meters (that's over eleven thousand square feet) of the largest, richest, most complex and most vividly preserved floor of mosaics in the world, crossed on elevated walkways so that no visitor can mar its beauty. And its scenes are no fantasy, but instead a record of actual hunts for animals later displayed in the *venationes* (beast spectacles) of the Roman Empire—only part of a series of mosaics that amounts to a guided tour of ancient Rome.

This historical treasure trove can be found at the 2000-year-old Villa della Casale in the town of Piazza Armerina in Sicily. The presence of this enormous and continuous floor of mosaics—miraculously not destroyed but preserved by 12th-century mudslides—has earned the villa and the town designation as a UNESCO World Heritage Site. The Villa also owes that honor to a number of other historical features. In its sheer size—it includes not only the Hall of the Hunt, but continues to a marble basilica and then a *palestra*, or gymnasium, and baths—it shows how such a residence could also be used for public functions, and so indicates (along with adjacent storehouses used for grain) the importance of the villa and Sicily as an administrative center and as a fertile breadbasket for Rome. In fact, in what was by then a four-quadrant empire, Sicily was no outpost but a vital ruling province, and the Villa was probably at its center.

And the motifs of the Hunt's mosaics show the profound historical influence of North Africa on Sicilian life. As Pliny the Elder said in a remarkably modern-seeming statement, "there is always something new out of Africa," and the Hunt's mosaics, quite possibly created by a North African artist with firsthand knowledge of such expeditions, show the incredible pull of Africa on Sicily—the capture of leopards, for example, a big cat symbolic of the region.

Such images had to be wildly exotic back then, and tremendously impressive to visitors. They were indeed created to in part enhance the prestige of the owner, who, historical hints tantalizingly  suggest, was possibly a consul, a prefect/landlord, or even Maximianus Herculis, considered a co-emperor with Diocletian. If we have an image of that owner, it may not be in the hunt, but in a figure in the Villa's successive astonishing series of mosaics depicting Bacchic rites and the Labors of Hercules (no, the owner wasn't exactly modest).

There are still more mosaics in this window on upper-class Roman life: details as large as, in the *palestra,* a widescreen view of the original Circus Maximus complete with chariot racers, and as intimate as a very erotically specific illustration of (the owner of the villa's?) paramour. Most remarkable of all—and prompting a sensation when the villa was rediscovered one hundred years ago—are the mosaics of scantily clad women exercising in what seem to be bikinis (see the previous "Barbells and Bikinis"), but what were actually the sportswear of patrician women of the era.

The Villa della Casale is truly an archaeological and cultural wonder, and was no doubt as dazzling in the days of ancient Rome as it is for visitors today. When the Roman hunters and horsemen, at ceremonial occasions at the Villa, saw themselves depicted in the Hall of the Hunt mosaics, they almost certainly puffed their chests with pride—and had a lot to tell the young women in bikinis (see "Barbells and Bikinis").

◆ HEAD OF THE MOOR

Italian ceramic styles differ region to region (like dialects and pasta shapes) and in Sicily everywhere you go you see "the head of Moor" motif, especially in the decoration of planters. There's quite a startling and macabre legend behind this, a folktale that's got it all—seduction, conquest, love, jealousy, revenge—passions that can deeply affect the souls of Sicilians! And it's so bloody strange (not in the Brit sense but in the literal sense, as you'll see) that the more south you go and the hotter it gets, in Italy but just about anywhere, the more the stories get "out there" and filled with ghosts and gore and all sorts of macabre and crazy elements, from "creation mythology" to family histories to little romantic snafus like this one.

The story is set in the old Arabic neighborhood of the Kalsa in Palermo, which at its height during the Norman Arab period rivaled Constantinople and was the second largest city in the Muslim empire. According to oral legend, during this period of Islamic domination there lived a beautiful girl who mainly spent her days at home, taking care of the flowers and plants on her balcony in the Kalsa. The girl had a lovely singing voice which both enchanted and enflamed the curiosity, hopes, and hearts of male suitors. But the girl resisted them all and focused ever more diligently on caring for her plants and flowers.

One day, a mysterious and handsome young Saracen passed by her balcony and fell head over heels for her. He immediately declared his passion to her; she was bowled over by him and taken by his boldness, and succumbed to his charms.

Unfortunately, the Moor was already married and even had *bambini*—kids. When she learned of this she was in no mood to be forgiving. She waited until nightfall when he returned to her and then killed him in his sleep by cutting his head off. Tormented by her impulsive and passionate gesture she memorialized his head into a planter, which she displayed on her balcony and in which she planted rosemary (the herb of remembrance). Each morning the girl watered the plant with her tears, and it thrived.

In this way, her lover remained with her, and her gesture became a Sicilian symbol of love lost and crossed but somehow lasting—not to mention (it seems) a kind of good luck charm for plants by transmuting bloodiness into beauty.

♦ "INNER ITALIAN"

♦ ILLUSIONIST MAGIC

♦ ISABELLA D

♦ IPPOLITO'S GOLDEN APPLE

♦ IGNUDI, NOT GNUDI

◇◇ ◇J

♦ INNER ITALIAN

The "Inner Italian"—a concept that will have resonance for anyone read-ing this book regardless of inherited ethnicity—is that part of our nature that most easily falls in love, dreams, and revels in the senses. It is our most expressive, exuberant, spontaneous self—there inside just waiting to be set free.

We associate Italians with being con-vivial and festive. We're used to visiting sunny Italy and encountering a host of garrulous, gregarious, and ebullient people. But it's worth remembering that we also love Italy for its centuries of monumental (especially in Rome) achievements in art, architecture, music, clothing, glassware, not to mention, of course, the cuisine . . . and the list goes on and on.

Still there seems to be a lightness of spirit that's gone along with these centuries of struggle and labor, and a feeling of celebration of life as the embodiment of the Dionysian (Bacchus in Roman mythology) archetype. Demeter, it was said, put Dionysius, the god of wine, on earth to "lift the care of mortals." And not just with drunkenness. Dionysius is also the god of divine inspiration, releasing the best in us.

For part of his spell is an acute, passionate experience of life in the pres-ent moment, being at one's most receptive and responsive. Perhaps that, and not just the tendency to speak more honestly when not so inhibited, was what Pliny the Elder meant when he so aptly said *"In vino veritas"*—in wine, truth.

To be truly in the moment, open to life, enraptured by it. . . that was captured by another lesser-known Italian sage, Domenico Modugno, in his very Italian song "Volare." He sang about flying in an endless "blue painted blue" sky of love and art (Marc Chagall's, to be specific) to "the heights of the sun" as a soft music played just for him.

Letting yourself go, flying free, as one beautifully arranges words, and art, and life.

We all love and need to travel to Italy, with or without a plane ticket.

♦ ILLUSIONIST MAGIC

When Ludovico Gozaga, Duke of Mantua, decided the plain, closed-in, featureless greeting room of his ducal palace needed a renovation, he had it utterly transformed with busts of Roman emperors, lunettes with mythological themes, representations of his family's life, and two walls of views overlooking lovely scenery, not to mention an oculus dome in the ceiling open to the heavens.

And he did all that by commissioning artist Andrea Mantegna to create that new room with nothing but paint, along with a genius perspective on...perspective.

Amid all the achievements of the Quattrocento, mostly located in Florence and Rome, this Mantuan masterwork, known as both the *camera picta* (picture room) and *camera degli sposi,* holds it own. Mantegna transformed an interior room into an expansive and transportive visual experience both in terms of physical space (scale, depth, architectural elements, indoors and outdoors) and time.

Eons before 3D movies, there had been examples of *trompe l'oiel,* pictures that fool the eye, from Greece, Rome, and Pompeii, generally depicting a window, door, or hallway hinting at a larger room. But in the early Italian renaissance, Mantegna, brother-in-law and student of Jacopo Bellini, took that art to a whole new level in Mantua. It's a triumph of the form that anticipated not only his contemporary Antonio da Correggio's (1489–1534) Assumption of the Virgin in the Duomo of Parma, but the flourishing of illusionistic painting in the Baroque period.

The *Camera degli Sposi* not only has views with an illusion of depth opening up on a garden-like world, with faux windows that appear to cast light, but architectural elements, all painted, that frame or foreground them. And the family greets you perched on a space on a wall, painted in one of art's first life-size group portraits just as they'd appear if you were looking up at them as they gathered on, say, a balcony: we see a dog, the family's favorite little person (apparently an accoutrement of such a courtly home), and a reception for their smiling daughter in a carefully and beautifully composed assemblage.

The work, which took nearly ten years to complete (1465–1474), is painted in fifteenth-century fresco style and shows a mastery of lifelike color and various ranges of perspective, none more so than in the dramatically foreshortened views of cherubs and other onlookers peering down from the oculus in an early  example of *sotto in su* (from above to below) painting. In one humorous touch a mischief-maker seems about to drop a potted plant down on unsuspecting guests beneath.

Camera degli Sposi is also very much a characteristic work of patronage from a non-republican Italian city state, in this case a duchy, where the support of the well-born and well-educated was absolutely essential to the continuation of the arts. The Marchese and his consort, Barbara of Brandenburg, and their children, friends, courtiers, and animals are grouped along various spaces engaged in pursuits that celebrate their present successes and future ambitions. On the north wall, in a meeting scene, Ludovico Gonzaga is shown in the midst of an impressive group that not only includes his son the cardinal, but the Holy Roman Emperor Frederick III and Christian I of Denmark. And the progression of their activities suggests a chronology of the activities of their reign.

The room presents an illusion of Roman Empire classical antiquity as captured in the governance of, basically, a local Italian marquis. As the

Gonzagas no doubt hoped, people can happily accept that illusion when it comes so splendidly framed by the illusions of a master painter.

♦ ISABELLA D

Author Matteo Bandello wrote she was "supreme among women" and diplomat Niccolo da Correggio called her "The First Lady of the World." Isabella D'Este Gongaza, a woman of destiny and the Marchessa of Mantua, was related to nearly every ruler in Europe by birth or by marriage, including her namesake, the queen who sent Christopher Columbus on his voyages. She was a patroness of the arts, collector of antiquities, skilled diplomat, founder of a school for girls, and a great beauty painted by Titian and da Vinci, whose fashion sense was emulated by women throughout the courts of Italy and France.

The comings and goings of Isabella's eventful life are known in some detail as she was a voluminous letter writer, as were others in her circle. Over two thousand of her letters survive and offer unique insights into the Renaissance art world and the role of women during the period.

From a very young age, no woman was better prepared to be one of the leading women of the era. Isabella was the firstborn of six children of the ruling family of Ferrara, who believed in educating their daughters and sons equally; as a consequence she received a classical and musical education unparalleled for women of her time, and at the time of her marriage (at age sixteen) she well versed in the politics of the day, to the point of being able to debate with ambassadors. Betrothed since age six to Francesco Gonzaga the Marquis of Mantua (and grandson of Ludovico III, who commissioned the *Camera degli Sposi*—see "Illusionist Magic") she married him in 1490. Francesco has been described as "short, pop-eyed, snub-nosed and exceptionally brave." He was regarded as a formidable *condottiero*—a paid military professional aka Renaissance warlord and mercenary—who was more keenly interested in horses and sports than art and literature, and seemingly not the best match for the precociously cultured Isabella.

Still their marriage was happy at first. Isabella was very popular and following their nuptials rode through the streets of Ferrara astride a horse draped in gems and gold. Under their reign, and Isabella's orchestration, the cultural life of the Mantuan court flourished. Isabella was a fashion avatar known for her signature plunging décolletage which was widely imitated, and for her penchant for furs, perfumes, and decorative turban-like head dress.

Together she and Francesco had eight children (six survived). But their marriage fell under the shadow of the Borgias when Isabella discovered love letters between Lucrezia and her husband. In 1509 Francesco was captured by King Charles VII of France and held prisoner for three years in Venice. In her husband's absence Isabella came into her own, serving as Regent, defending Mantua as commander of the city, and managing to negotiate a peace treaty providing for her husband's safe return. It didn't help their relationship that her diplomatic skills and political acumen eclipsed those of Frances-co, but ultimately that didn't matter, as he'd contracted syphilis (either from his very public affairs before his imprisonment or Venetian courtesans afterwards) and died in 1519.

Isabella continued to serve as Regent to their eldest son Frederico who, unlike his father, recognized his mother's skill and great popularity and kept her in a prominent governing role. She proved a master of Italian politics of the time, positioning Mantua as a Duchy (a sovereign territory), which advanced her son's title to Duke. Eight years later, she returned to Rome to purchase a 40,000-ducat Cardinalate for her second son Ercole from Pope Clement VII. Before her death at age sixty, she also supported many Renaissance painters, poets, and musicians. She converted the Ducal Apartment into a museum, collected many artworks and antiquities over her lifetime, and is associated with Bellini, Giorgione, Raphael, and Perugino, as well as Bartolomeo, Montagna, Titian, and Leonardo da Vinci, who were all commissioned to paint her portrait.

She's remained a sensation even in our era. The preliminary sketch of Isabella by Leonardo hangs in the Louvre, but it has always been a mystery where the finished portrait might be; some wonder if that portrait is in fact the enigmatic *Mona Lisa*, as there are strong compositional similarities. In October 2013 the art world went into a fever of excitement when the missing da Vinci portrait of Isabella apparently reappeared in a private collection held by an Italian family in a Swiss bank vault. Whether it will join the twenty-three fully accepted Leonardo da Vinci paintings in the world, or be attributed to one of his pupils, is still being debated and investigated in Italy (while the painting is nonetheless valued at ninety million pounds).

Isabella also lives on at the Brooklyn Museum of Art (along with Artemisia Gentileschi) where she was given her well-deserved place at the table in Judy Chicago's "The Dinner Party," a symbolic gathering of feminist icons. In every sense of the word, Isabella ruled.

♦ IPPOLITO'S GOLDEN APPLE

Cardinal Ippolito II d'Este, raised to an ecclesiastical career, never was elected to the papacy. His mother, Lucrezia Borgia, and his grandfather, the licentious Borgia pope Alexander VI, were roundly condemned—and his colleagues frowned upon his raw, unseemly ambition. Five times he tried and failed at the papal conclaves. Finally Pope Julius III, sensing a way to blunt the danger of a born campaigner and intriguer, awarded him the governorship of Tivoli, away from Rome, as a consolation prize.

Little did Julius know just how much Ippolito would console himself. From 1550 until his death in 1572, Ippolito built in Tivoli his Villa d'Este on an almost Vatican scale of art, architecture, and horticulture, envisioning the estate as a new Gardens of the Hesperides. In fact his painter-architect-archeologist Pirro Ligorio ingeniously flattered his patron by linking the myth of Hippolitus, the symbol of restraint that figured in his name "Ippolito," with that of Hercules. Ligorio proclaimed that the demigod Hercules managed to restrain anger, greed, and lust by using philosophy (somehow represented by his club), and so his killing of the sleepless dragon and stealing of the golden apples of Hesperides symbolized reason's victory over lust. It was a pretty outrageous Renaissance version of spin, given that lust for self-aggrandizement, not to mention the sin of pride in comparing himself to Hippolitus and Hercules, certainly figured into Ippolito's Villa d'Este.

Fortunately, over four centuries later, the result is a stunning symbiosis of nature (the long cypress-shaded approach walkway, the *Giardino delle meraviglie,* or gardens of wonder) and manmade spectacle. Tivoli Villa d'Este is part of the UNESCO World Heritage Site list, thanks to its innovative landscaping—a model for European estates of the period—but above all for its five hundred fountains, water jets, and water plays (*giochi d'acqua*) and cascades.

The combined sound of the sheer profusion of fountains has the splashing and rumbling of a waterfall. The giant hydraulic column that is the Fontana dei Draghi (Fountain of Dragons) rises from a four-headed stone monster symbolizing the dragon Hercules conquered when he stole the Golden Apples, and as such is the symbolic centerpiece of the Villa.

But then there's the Fontana di Tivoli, which flows into the Viale delle 100 Fontane (Avenue of the 100 Fountains), three tiers high and over four hundred feet long. The Fontana di Nettuno has a design vision drawn from the Villa Hadriana and was later rebuilt to incorporate concepts from Bernini's design for the enormous faux waterfall of the Reggia di Caserta. Two towering jets of water are flanked by six smaller ones and seven cascades that plunge down mountainous stone ramparts.

And then there are the delightful Water Organ and Owl fountains, which produce hydraulic-pneumatic water music and movement among mechanical birds from the flow of their water systems. The Organ Fountain, designed by Claude Vernard, is so beautifully sculpted with Greek gods and goddesses and so ingenious that it was a wonder of its era, and it still dazzles and delights crowds today.

To provide all the water for his fountains, Ippolito indulged in his own Herculean labor, very much at the expense of Rome: building an aqueduct and diverting part of the Aniene River, a principal water source for the city. Since then, especially in the past fifty years, there's been much restoration and planting. With the addition of luxuriant rose gardens, the Villa, especially in the spring, has a beauty it didn't have in Ippolito's day. This is especially true of the rose-covered walls that surround Diana of Ephesus, the Roman Goddess of Nature and Abundance, whose multiple breasts spill streams of water; Ippolito, apparently remembering (briefly) that he was a churchman, decided to modestly place her in a secluded part of the gardens.

The final consolatory touch for Ippolito, given that in effect he was banished from Rome (Julius III cleverly wrote into his contract that he could not own property there), was to build the Fontana di Rometta, or little Rome: replicas of the Tiber River and some of the major statues of the Imperial City. Many of those have since been stolen and destroyed, but the she-wolf suckling Romulus and Remus—the legendary founders of Rome—and Minerva, the Roman Goddess of wisdom, still remain.

Given the taxes and water theft that went into it, you could easily replace "little Rome" with "stolen Rome." But what else do you expect from a man whose self-image was based on Hercules thieving the Golden Apples? And in its sheer architectural appeal and breathtaking scale, the Villa D'Este has become more a symbol of the generosity, beauty, and Diana of Ephesus-like abundance of its country—paradoxically, given the boundless acquisitiveness of its patron, a gift rather than a theft.

♦ IGNUDI, NOT GNUDI

"The Ignudi" is a phrase coined by Michelangelo to collectively describe the twenty seated sculpturally-embodied male nudes (sometimes called the "athletes") on his Sistine Chapel ceiling, and is derived from from *nudo*, meaning "naked," giving the word a new art-historical context.

To some extent they function purely as decorative elements, and with their dramatic gestures and contorted postures they support large painted medallions while sitting on pedestals of *trompe l'oeil* archi-

tecture. But their prominent position, contiguous to the nine prophetic visions, makes them similar in importance to the attendants painted for the sibyls and prophets. Michelangelo showed these nudes in many poses and expressions, as if they are reacting to the adjacent scenes, and they form almost a silent Greek chorus, a guide to the emotions governing the scenes. They exude earthly power in the midst of the divinity, and as Charles de Tolnay has suggested they may have been meant to serve as "intermediary spirits between men and the Godhead."

♦ I ♦

Although the poses of the nudes were drawn from pagan sources, there was a well-established tradition supporting nudity in Christian art, in that all souls were believed to be naked in the presence of God. However, since they were not directly relevant to the themes of the ceiling, the *ignudi* outraged many within the ecceliscal ranks. Still, an even larger controversy was to come when Michelangelo painted the Last Judgment twenty-four years later; the sheer overwhelming presence of *ignudi*, even among the saints, would prove too much for ecclesiastical viewers. Michelangelo would be caught between the centuries-old Italian conflict of art and religion, and many figures would be ultimately covered by draperies.

On the other hand, and very much so, *gnudi* (pronounced "nu-dee") are also "naked" ravioli made from ricotta cheese, seasonings and a little bit of flour. These pasta-less dumplings that hail from Tuscany—exceptionally, light, fluffy, and creamy—are loved by serious foodies and anyone who loves gnocchi. When served, *gnudi* are often topped with fresh herbs, sometimes prosciutto, as well as shavings of cheese such as Pecorino Romano. But this little dumpling's name is derived—surprise—from the Italian word meaning *nude*, so it has no problem being served like the name implies. And unlike Michelangelo's *ignudi*, there's not a lot of protest when they appear in abundance.

♦JAZZ

♦JEANS OF GENOA

♦SANGIOVESE BY JOVE

♦JEWEL BOX OF THE ADRIATIC

♦ ♦ ♦

♦KABBALAH AND THE POPE'S CEILING

♦ JAZZ

Italy has given us many gifts, not the least of which is pizza, appreciated by most everyone everywhere. Jazz has been America's gift to Italy. No European country has embraced it more (as any fan of the film *The Talented Mr. Ripley* can remember), and Italy's great love affair with jazz is still going strong today. No town, not even a really small one, is without a jazz club.

Jazz and its syncopated rhythms found its way into the ears and hearts of Italians during World War I with the presence of American musicians in military bands. The improvisational nature of jazz with its spontaneous riffs, runs, and vamps, connects perfectly with the Italian "way." That and its ensemble aspect mirrors the Italian tradition of energetically and cheerfully making do with your friends with whatever is there in the moment, from *arrangiarsi* to all the ways recipes have been accidentally-on-purpose concocted over the centuries.

Arturo Agazzi and his syncopated orchestra was one of Italy's first jazz acts and was met with immediate success in the 1920's. The power and appeal of the musical genre prevailed despite anti-American sentiment during Benito Mussolini's fascist 1930s and Hitler's hatred of such "Negro music." Even Mussolini's son, Romano, was not only a huge fan but also a talented and prominent jazz pianist. Louie Armstrong toured Italy in 1935 with great success, which along with Jesse Owen's success in the Berlin Olympics, must really have left *der Fuhrer* furious.

Jazz really took off post-WWII with all the popular American styles, as bebop, Free Jazz and Fusion all had their Italian equivalents. Jazz clubs are now everywhere on the Boot. Like a language with accents and dialects, jazz takes on the character of the culture of the musicians and has done so in Italy. Italian musicians have shaped their own brand of jazz, improvising on European song forms, classical composition techniques, and distinct regional folk music (for example, Enzo Rao and his group Shamal have added their native Sicilian and Arab influences) bringing their own flavor to the musical jambalaya we call jazz.

The Umbria Jazz Festival is one of the most important international jazz festivals—held annually since 1973, usually July 1—in Perugia, Italy. And now there is also the Umbria Jazz Winter Festival, held annually from late December to early January in the city of Orvieto.

After playing a jazz concert in Milan, Louis Armstrong explained why the Italians treated American jazz musicians with the same reverence afforded a Verdi or Puccini. "The Europeans figure our music's the same," Armstrong said. "We play them both from the heart." The great Satchmo, as always, hit the sweet note of truth.

✦ JEANS OF GENOA

Jeans are the garment *de rigueur* of fashionistas and Boho hipsters. But they're also the ultimate casual or workday clothing the world over, and they had their earliest humble beginnings in Italy long before Levi Strauss and the California Gold Rush. They actually represented an Italian-French collaboration long before there were rival fashion houses in each respective country who would never engage in such a thing.

Genovese sailors needed durable utilitarian trousers that could stand up to the rigors of an ocean voyage; that could be worn wet or dry; that had legs that could be rolled up while swabbing the deck; and that were made of a fabric that could withstand laundering by dragging them in mesh nets behind the ship (where, over time the sea water would bleach them white). Denim fit the bill and the first denim cloth was a cotton serge-like material fabricated in Nîmes, France—hence "de Nimes," which became "denim."

The term "jeans" comes from the dye of the cloth: in French, *bleu de Gênes*, and in Italian, *blu di Genova*, literally the "blue of Genoa," which took the French route to "blue jeans."

If this seems a bit of a stretch, in the Church of Saint Rocco in Venice you will find the painting *St. Roch Curing the Plague* in which Roch is garbed in, believe it or not, rolled up blue jeans. This painting by Tinoretto (c. 1560) ... is proof that jeans, from their earliest days, could indeed stand up to anything!

✦ SANGIOVESE BY JOVE

Jove, or Jupiter, or Zeus in Greek mythology, is god of the sky and thunder who rules all other deities. The Sangiovese grape derives its name from the Latin *sanguis Jovis*, which means "the blood of Jove." It certainly is the ruling grape in Tuscany and the iconic grape of Italy. When it's young, it's mischievous, with fresh flavors of cherries, red berries, and spice. But once mature, it transforms entirely, gaining a distinguished oaky, savory, leathery and (to oenophiles) God-like gravitas.

The Sangiovese is the principal grape used in all Chiantis, from rustic table wines (Chianti "regular") to the aged and mighty Chianti Classico Riserva. Sangiovese is blended with traditional French varietals such as Cabernet and Merlot to create many of the modern "Super Tuscan" wines such as Tignanello, and is the exclusive varietal of the noble and distinguished Brunello di Montalcino.

Like the ancient deity for whom it was named, the Sangiovese grape can be temperamental, high-maintenance, kingly, and quite mercurial. Sangiovese has a thin skin and takes its time to ripen, preferring to bask in the Tuscan sun as long as possible. In times when the weather and the grape cooperate, prestige and honor have come to the Italian winemaking industry. However in 2008, a bad weather year, Sangiovese was at the center of an embarrassing scandal known for several ensuing years as Brunello-gate, in which an undisclosed number of Brunello di Montalcino's producers were investigated for blending unauthorized grapes with Sangiovese. The result was guilty verdicts, fines, declassified wines, and tarnished reputations.

As self-proclaimed "Sangiovesista" winemaker, Carlo Ferrini, states, "No grape brings more joy or more pain."

♦ JEWEL BOX OF THE ADRIATIC

Mae West once famously declared, "Too much of a good thing can be wonderful." She was no doubt referring to the Basilica of St. Mark in Venice.

With over 85,000 square feet of (mostly gilded) mosaics, hundreds of Byzantine columns and capitals, dozens of kaleidoscopic polychrome marble floor patterns and animal designs, and enough ecclesiastical booty to tilt a pirate ship, St. Mark's Basilica served as monument to the Venetian Republic's wealth, power, and magnificence as much as it served as a house of worship. Think of it as civic bling.

Today's multi-domed extravaganza began as a modest chapel to accommodate St. Mark's relics after Venetian merchants smuggled them out of Alexandria, Egypt in 828  ACE. The present structure was completed around 1071 but greatly embellished in the centuries to follow with architectural purchases or plunder. As but one prominent example, during the Fourth Crusade in 1204, the four horse statues above its main entrance (see "The Four Horses of the Basilica") were looted from the Hippodrome in Constantinople where they had pranced unbridled for nine hundred years.

The sheer expanse of interior gilded ceiling mosaics has earned the Basilica the nickname *Chiesa d'Oro* (Church of Gold). But just behind the altar stands the greatest Byzantine gold memento of all: the celebrated Pala d'Oro (cloth of gold) retable. Measuring nearly seven feet high by eleven and a half feet wide, this extraordinary altar screen evolved over a period of centuries. Although most of the present screen was commissioned in Constantinople by Doge Ordelafo Faliero in 1105, it incorporated enamels and other elements from a silver antependium commissioned more than a century earlier in the same city by Doge Pietro Orseolo (976–978). The uppermost third of today's Pala d'Oro was added during the rule of Doge Pietro Ziani (1205–1229) with enamels and other elements "appropriated" from the Monastery of the Pantokrator in Constantinople during the Fourth Crusade. The last major modification of the grand cloth dates to 1342–1345 during the rule of Doge Andrea Dandolo.

Apart from its shimmering gold background and exquisite enamels, the Pala d'Oro is studded with a constellation of pearls (roughly 1,300 of them) and a rainbow of stones: garnets (400), amethysts (90), sapphires (300), emeralds (300), rubies (90), and topaz (4). The overall effect is dazzling. Perhaps its most notable element on close inspection is the book held by the enthroned Christ in center position: text from the Holy Scripture has been replaced by gems signifying, in a quintessentially Venetian material way, the preciousness of the Word. St. Mark's Basilica stands, quite literally, as the greatest jewel box in Christendom.

St. Mark's opulence has not always been confined to the sense of sight: for much of its storied history this jewel box on the Adriatic has also functioned as a spectacular music box. With multiple choir lofts, splendid acoustics and, at the Republic's height, two organists, two choirmasters, and dozens of singers and other musicians, the Basilica offered unsurpassed stereophonic bliss, especially for the most strategically seated high church and state officials.

The Basilica of St. Mark's deservedly ranks at the top of any visitor's list to Venice. At times of *acqua alta* (high water), one struggles to stifle the melancholy thought of so much sunken treasure.

◆ KABBALAH AND THE POPE'S CEILING

The creation of Adam is the most famous section of the Sistine Chapel and, along with the Mona Lisa, is one of the best known images in the world. The composition is highly original; we see Adam freshly formed, eyes open in a languid half-consciousness as he has yet to receive the divine life force through his left hand (traditionally the hand though which we receive all blessings). God is portrayed here in his role as Creator rather than the Almighty. As Creator he is surrounded by many extra figures and angels, surging toward his creation in a scene that is busy in a primordial way: there is a woman under God's left arm and a babe under his left hand and angels behind him, and all of them are surrounded by a big vermillion cape with a blue-green cloth tailing beneath like a kite.

Many questions and debates have ensued through the ages. Who is the woman under God's left arm? Some say it must be the soul of Eve waiting to be embodied while others suggest she's the concept of Sofia, the Greek symbol of wisdom. Most believe the babe under God's left hand is the soul of Adam about to be transmitted and infused into him—but what's the story behind the big purple cape with the tail?

An interesting hypothesis was proposed regarding the "cape" in 1990, by an American physician, Frank Meshberger of St. John's Medical Center in Anderson, Indiana, and published in JAMA—the Journal of the American Medical Association. When viewing the Creation he had a bit of a déjà vu and Eureka moment, recognizing something very familiar but out of context: that the background figures and shapes portrayed behind the figure of God and enveloped by the cape appeared to be an anatomically accurate picture of the cross-section of the human brain, with the borders in the painting correlating with surfaces of the inner and (the outline of the cape) outer brain, as well as the brain stem, the basilar artery, the pituitary gland, and the optic chiasm. A farfetched but remarkable coincidence? Maybe, but then Michelangelo had well-documented expertise in human anatomy and would have had firsthand knowledge of the shape and proportions of the brain (his experience in dissection is documented in *Lives of the Artists*, written by his contemporary and admirer, Giorgio Vasari).

Another theory derives from the notion in the Jewish mystical Kabbalah that man is born out of the consciousness of God. This interpretation derives from the fact that Adam's eyes are already open. Is he already alive and about to receive not the energy of life but a shared consciousness with the divine? Is humankind only truly born with the bestowing of divine intelligence and wisdom? It's very possible that in addition to knowing anatomy, Michelanagelo in his formative years living in Lorenzo de Medici's household had been exposed to Jewish teachings. A sonnet of Michelangelo's suggests that God in the painting is bestowing "intellect" on Adam in a Kabbalistic way. The Medici brought many great scholars and artists to Florence to share their ideas and knowledge, and some of them studied the Zohar, the book at the center of the Kabbalah.

Ultimately what we see in the Sistine Chapel is an artist's vision crystallizing the knowledge and sensibilities of the world around him and a vision of Creation all his own. We may never know Michelangelo's intent, but knowing the great intellectual and mystic traditions that might have inspired it only makes the monumental power of the Sistine ceiling all the more epic.

◆ LEONE

◆ THE LAOCOON

◆ LATIN

◆ LA BELLA LINGUA

◆ LA BELLA FIGURA

◆ LIMONE

◆ LIVIA'S PAINTED GARDEN

◆ LE VITE

◆ LA DOLCE VITA

♦ LEONE

Lions had disappeared from what is now considered Western Europe by the time of Christ, half a millennium before the first settlement formed near what is now considered Venice. One might wonder, then, why lions seem to pop up on buildings, flags and countless other surfaces throughout the city.

It all began with a heist.

The year was 828. Two Venetian merchants, Buono da Malamocco and Rustico da Torcello, made their way to Alexandria, Egypt on a surreptitious mission, their objective to retrieve the remains of St. Mark the Evangelist who had been martyred in that African city seven and a half centuries earlier.

Although Venice possessed the remains of Theodor of Amasea, whom it claimed as its patron saint, the Adriatic city was by then well on its way to becoming a commercial and territorial world power, fully deserving of a patron saint of sufficient status to affirm its rightful standing before God as well as man. In a sense, snagging an evangelist's bones was like securing ecclesiastical plutonium: one instantly became a member of "the nuclear club" (along with, say, Rome, which boasted the primo apostle Peter) in first millennium terms.

127

The two Venetians had willing accomplices: priests from the church of St. Mark in Alexandria who feared for the saint's remains from the ruling Saracens. Thus the heist was in part an inside job. Employing an ingenious gambit, the merchants were able to smuggle Saint Mark's body past Muslim guards at the port of Alexandria and out of the country by wrapping it in a layer of pork and cabbage; the guards recoiled at the porcine cargo and readily let it pass.

When St. Mark's body (*sans* head, as it happens) arrived in Venice, it immediately supplanted the remains of St. Theodor in the doge's private chapel, and work began almost immediately on a sumptious and grand basilica—also a property of the doge, but open to citizens of the Republic—that would serve as a more suitable setting for such a prize possession. (Back in Alexandria, St. Mark's remains had been replaced by a lesser known martyr, St. Claudia, so something of a slow motion "three-saint monte" had just played out across two continents.)

The ubiquitous lion of Venice is in fact the *winged* lion symbol of St. Mark (established in the Apocalypse of St. John 4:7), the patron saint to which the rising Venetian Republic had traded up.

La Serenissima gained a high-octane saint and the ruling caliphate in Alexandria lost a strategic asset, if only for blackmail purposes. Had the Muslim port guards only known of Homer's *Odyssey* they might have been better prepared: *Beware of Venetians importing pork.*

♦ THE LAOCOON

"Beware of Greeks bearing gifts" was the prescient warning Laocoön (pronounced la-oc-o-wan), high priest of Troy, along with his two sons, was trying to deliver to prevent their fellow Trojans from accepting the Greeks' gift of a ginormous wooden horse. As Roman poet Virgil described in his epic *The Aeneid,* Laocoön and his sons died before they could deliver the message, strangled by supernatural serpents sent by the goddess Athena to protect the Greeks and insure the destruction of Troy.

In 1506 a Roman peasant working his vineyard near the Coliseum opened up a hole in the ground and discovered a larger-than-life statue of an older man and two younger ones being strangled by giant snakes. Pope Julius II, a lover and collector of Greek art, immediately sent experts, including Michelangelo, who identified the find as being the long-lost *Laocoön*: the most celebrated statue in pagan Rome, and before that, Hellenistic Greece. This sculpture commemorating the triumph over Troy had been brought back by the Roman legions as spoils of conquest at the close of the Hellenistic Empire. Pliny the Elder, the leading Latin writer on art (among many other things. . .) had described the statue as standing in the palace of Emperor Titus and reverently described it as "superior to all works in painting and bronze."

The Pope paid the peasant handsomely and paraded the cleaned-up *Laocoön* though the streets of Rome, where it was enthusiastically received and created a sensation among the people. Julius decided to place the *Laocoön* with his other ancient works in the Vatican's octagonal courtyard, where it still remains. The statue's popularity led the Pope to consider opening up his private collection of sculptures to the public, thus starting, at least unofficially, the Vatican Museum, which today houses the most important art collection in the world. Its scale is staggering, with over nine miles of art and artifacts housed in over 1,400 rooms, chapels, and galleries.

The unearthing of the *Laocoön* had an enormous impact on Renaissance art and sculpture, and it became the most studied, admired, and copied work of ancient art. Michelangelo was entranced by its dynamic complexity, writhing musculature, and emotionalism. You can readily observe its influence in his sculpture the *Heroic Slave* (located in the Louvre), twisting to break free of his restraints, in his Sistine *Ignudi* whose body postures evoke the sons, and in his Minos, who has a snake provocatively wrapped around him in the *Last Judgment*.

At the time the *Laocoön* was discovered his right arm was missing. Michelangelo was asked to sculpt a replacement but he declined, not feeling worthy. The *Laocoön*'s original arm was found in 1906 and finally verified and reattached in 1960. And so, long after Athena herself has become history, the loyal priest and his sons who tried to keep Troy from its fate have themselves become immortal.

♦ LATIN

"Latin is a language, as dead as dead can be. First it killed the Romans, now it's killing me." So goes the lament of struggling Latin students . . . who have nearly gone extinct themselves.

And that's too bad. Called Latin for where it originated—ancient Latium and today's region of Lazio for which Rome is the capital—the Latin language dominated Western culture for well over 1,000 years. As English is to the Internet today, so Latin was to scholarly writing for centuries regardless of the author's native tongue; and the Catholic Mass, no matter how much it bewildered many believers, was conducted in Latin for centuries.

Contrary to popular belief, Latin is not really a dead language: it's just hidden in all the other Romance languages. Over 80 percent of the English language comes from Latin and Greek roots and over 70 percent of English is derived from strictly Latin roots. "Vulgar" Latin—as in of the people, not crude—developed into the Romance languages (Spanish, French, Romanian, Italian, and Portuguese) which derive as much as 90 precent of their vocabulary from Latin. No surprise, Italian is the Romance language that's the closest.

Rather than irrelevant, Latin can be and is a revelation: a window into the culture of the western world. Language is the lifeblood of a culture, and if you want to really understand a culture, you have to learn its language. (It also can be romantic and fun, as in the poems of Catullus or Horace, and phrases like the schoolboys' favorite, *Illegitimi non carborundum,* or "don't let the bastards get you down.") Especially through its Italian nephew, Latin today can still offer a refreshing and even surprising perspective on our own contemporary culture by telling us where we have come from—which is why the Latin etymology of words is part of the "romance" of so much of La Dolce Vita "U".

♦ LA BELLA LINGUA

Given that Italian is only the nineteenth most-spoken language in the world, it's remarkable that it's the fourth most studied. And it's probably not because people loved Latin so much that they raced to study its descendant, or because they figured they'd save time, given Italian only has 200,000 words.

No, it probably has something to do with the fact that Italian has an enduring reputation as the language of love and romance. It's fun and sexy. As Diane Halles wrote, Italian is "as bawdy as it is beautiful, a zesty linguistic stew as peppery as the *puttanesca* sauce named after Italy's notorious ladies of the night." It's melodic and emotionally expressive, both in delicate and dramatic ways, and its liveliness and exuberance appeal to the body and the soul. And everything just sounds better in Italian.

With so many fewer words Italian glides on its musicality (all those vowels) and its sensuality. You can feel and understand the words from the sounds—and in fact, for that very reason, there's no specific Italian word for "spelling." And if that's not enough to make the language vivid and alive in the moment, so many expressions are visual analogies—the word for coward, *coniglio*, means rabbit, and to flirt is "to make like and owl." It's not as if the language of Galileo and Enrico Fermi is incapable of handling scientific abstraction. But so much of it is luxurious, voluptuous, even sybaritic.

Most languages evolve over time, and Italian evolved from vulgar Latin. That's not as in "crude"; it simply means that classical Latin was a literary language, while regular citizens spoke the earthy *vulgare*, which evolved into local languages like French and Italian, and with its more colorful directness gradually displaced its sternly remote elder. For example, *caballus*, the vernacular for "nag," replaced the Latin *equus* (as in equine) and became the root of both the Italian *cavallo* and the English "cavalry."

But Italian was ultimately shaped very powerfully by a single man— Dante Alighieri. Much of what Italian is today is inextricably linked to his *Divina Commedia* which was written in the Tuscan dialect that eventually became standard Italian. When he wrote it, as a poet he picked and chose what he liked best from 36 different dialects, very much shaping the language that is Italian today. Since he wanted his greatest work to be read by the people and even listened to, he was writing for the ear as well as the eye. So he laid down like a composer the basic musical rhythms and lyrical resources of the modern tongue. How can a language not be poetic when it was shaped by perhaps the greatest poet who ever lived?

Dante's *Commedia* engendered modern Italian because it was so embraced by the people through the ages, providing the glue when Italy had no national identity. The *Commedia*, long before Italian unification, was Italy's tradition and oral history; recently Roberto Benigni read it on the radio and sixty percent of Italy tuned in. All schoolchildren study at least the *Inferno*. Dante's work has bestowed its poetry on Italian life and speech. (see "Dante's Commedia" and "Mapping Eternity")

Poetic compression is part of what makes Italian so appealing to the ear, and not just the big vowels, the lyrical twirls, and the "thrilling" twilling. English may have three times more words than Italian, but with all Italian's prefixes and suffixes, shades of meaning are created that rival the *sfumature* of Leonardo's brushstrokes. *Vento* is wind while *venticello* is a gentle breeze. *Baci* is a kiss, *bacino* a little peck. *Caldo* is hot, hot, hot, while *calduccio* is nice and warm.

And Italian makes little necklaces of words into unique turns of phrase, metaphors, or idioms that convey the things we have a single word for, that are intensely visual or appeal to all the senses, and are full of native Italian wit and a sense of fun. There's that phrase for flirting, *fare la civetta*, to make like an owl, that conveys "come-hither" seductiveness. Similarly, to form a line is to *fare la coda* (make a tail); we'd all agree there's no more tail-end feeling than being on a long line. An unwelcome guest, *un cane in chiesa*, is a dog in a church. Makeup is *trucco*, a trick.

But perhaps the key to Italian's appeal is its musicality. *Imparadisata*, lifted into heaven, has in the swelling chords of its intonation that very meaning. Dante created a word to describe how he wrote: *sovramagnifi-centissimante*. Do you even need to be told that means in a very very very magnificent way? And if some words suggest the depth and breadth of op-era, certainly an expression of the Italian soul, other words and metaphors suggest the improvising on a riff that belongs to jazz. Take these expressions using *bianco*, white: *settimana bianca*, a ski week; *matrimonio in bianca*, an unconsummated or unhappy marriage rendered as colorless; *voce bianca*, the voice of a castrato, a young (virginally white) innocent voice that did not ripen to maturity.

La bella lingua is mainly that for visitors; the newspaper La Repub-blica stated Americans saw it as *"coma una lingua polisenorialecapace de aprire le porte al bello"* ("a multisensory language able to open the gates to beauty"). That's certainly true in that it has the capacity to find art and delight in so many aspects of life. In the words of one unnamed Italian, "Things don't have to be exactly what they look like, reality doesn't have to be dull and ugly."

But for Italians it's even more than that: in such a relatively new country, the language is in many ways their fatherland and community. Italian is also lacking in words for privacy and loneliness, perhaps because it's so much a language of togetherness and empathy. We all want to express what we feel in the moment and have others be *simpatico* with that, and that's where the inner Italian and *la bella lingua* meet.

◆ LA BELLA FIGURA

In his book *Il libro del cortegiano (The Book of the Courtier)*, published in 1528, Count Baldassare Castiglione blended medieval and Renaissance ideals of conduct, highborn chivalry and the new aims of humanist education, and crystallized a conception of the perfect gentleman for centuries to come.

His book came out of nostalgia for what he considered his personal Camelot, the court of Urbino, and is cast in the form of a series of dialogues about how to form the ideal courtier of virtue and reason who can, basically, keep his prince on such a path. Castiglione combined an incredible number of abilities in his vision of that ideal: not just refined manners, loyalty, modesty, integrity, good looks with a *simpatico* nature, but also a mastery of horsemanship, jousting, and various martial arts. Not to mention a liberal education including drawing, music, poetry, and the languages Latin, French, Spanish, and the Italian of Dante.

But Castiglione's key quality to aspire to is *grazia*, gracefulness, brought about by *sprezzatura*, concealing art in such a way as if everything appears to be brought about without any hard work or thought. It combines our concept of grace under pressure and "don't let them see you sweat" with a uniquely Italian idea of manifesting one's actions and deeds with the goal of beauty and even perfection. This ideal of effortless mastery and nonchalance reflects in part the old Latin saying *ars est celare artem* (the art is the concealment of art) and also Ovid's *ars casum simulat* (art producing the illusion of spontaneity, of just happening).

So the ideal gentleman is in effect a piece of seemingly effortless art himself, striving to *far un bella figura*: cut a fine figure and make a good impression. That essence of refinement pervades the book, so much so that Castiglione envisions a ladder of love that becomes, with the courtier's age, progressively more refined, from sensual to Platonic love to the love of God.

In the Italian High Renaissance, *sprezzatura* was the highest aspiration: aristocrats desired to possess it and artists strove to depict it. But how practical is this code of conduct for those Italians then and now for whom stabling horses is not financially doable and dueling impossible? The more attainable ideal is *la bella figura*, a fit aspiration, and remains for any and all classes of people in Italy.

Much more than the ability to look good and use the right utensil, *la bella figura* is a uniquely Italian concept—an awareness that certain circumstances of one's public life require certain behavior. It's shown by the housewife who makes sure her neighbors know she washes her floors daily or a laborer who never goes out without his shoes polished. It's in the habit of never going to visit someone without a gift, even if it's just a small potted plant. It has to do with grace and dignity regardless of how much or little money you have; you can be poor and still have this essence of character, conducting yourself a certain way, generously and well.

Sprezzatura and Castiglione's concept of the gentleman, as developed in *The Book of the Courtier,* would be spread through sixty editions in Italy

in the sixteenth and seventeenth centuries alone and would continue to be published throughout the Western world, influencing great artists from (in different ways) John Milton to W.B. Yeats to James Joyce. Castiglione's portrait by Raphael hangs in the Louvre. But *la bella figura,* as cherished by all Italians, would become culturally hardwired, more fundamental than *sprezzatura,* and just as much an ideal of personal grace.

◆ LIMONE

*Amalfi sunrise
a cluster of lemons free
of the bird netting*

When life hands you a *limone* … Rejoice!

In America lemons may be associated with life's bitter disappointments, not to mention cars that don't work. But in Italy the *limone*, with its color and fullness, adds vitality, a bright twist, a zing to one's existence. It's the color of happy, and the embodiment of endless summer. And its acidic and acerbic quality is bracing, just as a little bittersweetness can enhance one's appreciation of life.

Maybe that's because, on the Amalfi Coast, where everything seems to be coming up lemons, the fruit is not the hard yellow rocks many are used to, but large and plump, heavy with juicy sunshine. . .which is why they should from now on be called *limone*. There's no sight quite like terraced groves of *limone* climbing high up the steep cliffs, their bright yellow fruit and deep green leaves somewhere between the mountains and the blue sky.

Limone have been growing along the Amalfi coast since Roman times, celebrated in mosaics and frescoes of Ercolano and Pompeii as well as on pottery up to the present day. Initially they were grown as ornamental plants and prized for their aesthetic and aromatic qualities. So you can see how different they were and are from the lemons so many are used to.

The two main varieties of *limone* are those grown around the Sorrento coast and those grown on the Amalfi Coast. The Limone Costa d'Amalfi are also called Sfusato Amalfitano for their elongated and pointed shape, while the Sorrento ones, Limone di Sorrento, are rounder, but both are exceptionally fragrant and juicy. They're harvested more than once a year, but the best *limone* are harvested from March to late July.

The skins are rich in oil and brightly colored, ideal for creating the famous liqueur Limoncello, made by soaking lemon zests (scrapings from the skin) in grain alcohol or vodka for a month or more. The result

135

is a thick, sweet dessert cordial with an intense lemon flavor, best stored in the freezer and served well chilled; it's become just about the national drink of Italy. Locals attest that Limoncello tastes very different depending on whether the *limone* are from Amalfi or Sorrento. Wherever they're from, an afternoon and/or evening can disappear very nicely and easily when a bottle of Limoncello is around.

The *limone* are also used for preparing many seafood dishes and making other regional specialties, such as Pasta al Limone. For desserts they really shine, putting their glow on Torta al Limone (lemon cake) and the Delizia al Limone dessert created in Sorrento. And don't miss a cool refreshing Granita di Limone. Whether in ice or on ice, sour or sweet, *limone* add zests and zest to life.

✦ LIVIA'S PAINTED GARDEN

More than any other city in the world, Rome is home to the most extraordinary and well-preserved ancient art and artifacts; and therefore a bit lost in that incredible shuffle of antiquity is probably the least well-known and least visited, but one of the most sublimely beautiful: the summer dining room of Livia, wife of the Emperor Augustus.

The room was discovered at the Villa of Livia in 1863 just after the well-known statue of her husband Augustus had been found nearby. The Villa's existence and location had been well-documented by Pliny the Elder and numerous others, but the *triclinium* (dining room) was an astonishing and immediately imperiled discovery. As stated in the report by the Pontifical Ministry of Public Works, though it had *"painted walls in good condition representing fruit trees and flowers with various birds, (t)he ceiling had entirely collapsed and the stucco decoration which once decorated the vault was found among the rubble which filled the room."* Due to the state of disrepair, much worse by the end of this century, a drastic decision was made: save the frescos which had been painted *c.* 30-20 BCE and were still in good condition by detaching them from the rock walls. In 1998 they were installed in Palazzo Massimo, Rome's Archeological Museum, in a room built to the dimensions of the original at Villa Livia.

The Romans knew how to stay cool during the dog days of summer. Livia's dining room was semi-subterranean, dug into rock, a common setting for rooms which were to be used in the scorching summer months. In lieu of dining alfresco, a serene summer garden of the imagination was painted.

One can feel the sensation of coolness, not just from being underground but by the mood created by the stunning illusionist garden spreading out all around (though there is a low painted fence, which helps to render a sense of perspective) removing all sense of enclosure or confinement; the walls seem to dissolve into a serene, open, airy vista. Wonderful atmospheric light, refreshing and relaxing, simulates the cool blues of early evening. And of course there is the variety of nature, far more bounteous than in a real garden: fruiting pomegranates and quinces, flowering poppies, roses, irises, chamomile, palms, pines, and oaks, and all sorts of birds—partridges, doves, and goldfinches, taking flight or feasting on fruit and resting on branches. The details are so well-rendered that in certain trees you can see both the silvery underside of some  leaves and darker top side of others and so almost feel the breeze and hear the soft rustling of the leaves and branches.

There's an amazing feeling in the painted garden of open space and of being in the moment, along with an interesting touch: enclosed in a golden cage resting on the low wall is the one bird unable to fly free . . . perhaps to remind us we are inside too, in a realm of art that captures nature and puts us under its spell.

✦ LE VITE

Giorgio Vasari (1511–1574) was a dynamo of the Medici era. He was employed by the Medici both in Rome and in Florence after the family's return to power in the sixteenth century as their go-to guy and the equivalent of a "Minister of Culture." City planner, architect, decorator, and general contractor, he remodeled and spruced up the beautiful center of Florence inside and out until it looked much the way we know it today. He renovated churches and designed and built the famous Uffizi Gallery with its "secret" Vasari corridor (*see* "Ponte Vecchio") which provided a private passage for the Medici from the Palazzo Vecchio to their residence across the river at the Palazzo Pitti. He was a painter as well (and so a very hands-on culture minister), painting the frescos inside Brunelleschi's engineering marvel, the cupola atop Santa Maria Di Fiore, and the wall and ceiling frescos of the grand Sala di Cosimo I that decorate the Palazzo Vecchio.

But far more than an architect, painter, or even an impresario (which he most certainly was) Vasari was a gifted communicator. He had a preternatural knack for branding and was the person who coined the term "Renaissance." And he's most remembered as the writer of the book *The Lives of the Most Excellent Painters, Sculptors, and Architects*, referred to as "*Le Vite*" in Italiano for short, his most enduring legacy, making him the father of modern art history. *Le Vite* puts two hundred years of Renaissance art in historical perspective but, more than that, it brings the artists to life, not just hailing their work but evoking them as individuals with unique talents and personalities.

A work of this scale and breadth had never been attempted, let alone conceived of, before him. Dedicated to his patron Cosimo I (grandson of Lorenzo and great-great-grandson of Cosimo the Elder), *Lives* was first published in Florence 1550, with an expanded second edition in 1568.

Today the book is taken with a certain number of grains of *sale*, for while it's a very good narrative work, and very reader-friendly, it's part history, part criticism, part biography, and—as is generally agreed—part fiction, with a lot of gossip thrown in. For the readers of the Renaissance, there was far less separation between these elements, and so the book mingles the real with imaginary almost like a Shakespeare history play, but dicier. Famous artist and randy friar Fra Filippo Lippi runs off with a nun and gets her pregnant; another artist delights in young men with curly hair (Leonardo), while another seduces a woman in Venice by playing his lute (Giorgone), and another dies of sexual excess (see "Rockstar of the Renaissance").

To be fair, it has more gravitas than a Renaissance *People* or *Us* Magazine. Vasari's stories are borne out by firsthand sources, even if, when facts were sketchy, the blanks still had to be filled. Yet what he writes always reveals the ideas and attitudes of the time, and the way the artists come to life as personalities reflects the new individualism where, for the first time, artists weren't anonymous craftsmen but separate and charismatic talents.

Lives did have a notorious bias toward Italian artists, Tuscan in particular, which means Vasari neglected Venice and mostly ignored other parts of Europe (though, in his defense, he wrote about what he was most familiar with). Between the first and second editions, he visited Venice and included some material on Titian but completely left out masters such as Veronese, expressing the opinion that the Venetian school placed too much emphasis on color and not enough on composition. So there are only 14 pages for Titian compared to 24 for Raphael and 28 for . . . Vasari himself.

But on the other hand, we can be grateful for his 76 pages on Michelangelo. Vasari was his friend, great champion, and the designer of his tomb in Santa Croce with a monument including allegorical figures of Sculpture, Architecture and Painting (although it is probably not what Michelangelo would have had in mind). And *Lives* is still read today by art history students and others interested in art. It has been a great help in the attribution of paintings and despite some of its factual shortcomings has proved the basis for many biographies of artists such as Leonardo.

And given how he credits the Medici for the many artistic "fruits" of the Renaissance and sings their praises for their prescience and philanthropy, in addition to everything else, Vasari was an avatar of the modern day spin doctor. Scrupulous and objective not so much, but always colorful and enlightening.

• LA DOLCE VITA

One of the great subjects of Italian filmmaking has been Rome itself: from the tenacious *Open City* of World War II to the indolently sensual and sophisticated *Great Beauty* of today—and between those portraits is Federico Fellini's landmark *La Dolce Vita*, one of his most sensational and successful films, set in the glamorous and hectic Rome of the 1960s.

The title has come to symbolize all that's desirable about Italy, but perhaps the film's original title says more of what the film is really about: "life is brutal and terrible but you can always find a few wonderful moments of sensuality and sweetness." For any filmgoer (or Italian), Fellini's shortened title will inevitably be said with a knowing intimation of the longer title, but also a memory of the delights the short title suggests.

From its opening shot of a statue of Christ being carried by helicopter across a landscape both too ancient and too modern for the Savior, *La Dolce Vita* paints a picture of Rome in a volatile but always exciting period of transformation. Through it all wanders gossip columnist Marcello, played, of course, by Marcello Mastroianni, the classic image of the "Latin lover," this time in chic suits and shades on the Via Veneto in a new freewheeling and sometimes unnerving city.

But the film also showcases—and its fans always remember—the Rome the world loves, never more so than in the Trevi Fountain sequence, when the exuberantly sexy Anita Ekberg, playing a Hollywood starlet, teases Marcello by wading into the fountain's basin. It's the highlight of the film's typically felliniesque circus of party scenes and sexual temptations in its hero's week of wanderlust in the Eternal City.

Over the film's seven days and nights, Marcello is also called to experience one trial after another that tests him to his core. But that rollercoaster aspect of the movie is part of what Fellini intended with his long title—the film ends with a sequence that combines a view of what seems like a sea monster on a beach, a blob of dark chaos, but also a girl's beatific smile. And it's that smile of promise and hope on which the movie ends.

- MAPPING ETERNITY

- MAGI CHAPEL

- MEZZOGIORNO

- MARGHERITA,
QUEEN OF PEARLS AND PIZZA

- MARINARA

- MURANO, ISLANDS OF GLASS

- THE MANY FACES OF VENICE

- MARCELLO

✦ MAPPING ETERNITY

One of Dante Alighieri's particularly audacious achievements in his Divine Comedy (*La Divina Commedia*) was to bring the afterlife to life—to "map eternity" in ways that were both highly imaginative and highly relatable. But Dante's map of the afterlife was no mere creative exercise: his objective was to chart the right course for himself and his fellow humans from one of sin and everlasting punishment to one of self-awareness, repentance, and ultimate salvation. No small undertaking!

The protagonist of Dante's masterwork is none other than Dante himself in the role of spiritual pilgrim. This seeming audacity on the poet's part is instantly offset by the humbling experiences to which he subjects his namesake pilgrim and alter ego. Accompanied by the classical poet Virgil, Dante the pilgrim must navigate a gauntlet of horrors in *Inferno*, which he enters on Good Friday; on Easter Sunday he emerges into the light of day at the base of *Purgatorio*, where he endures additional trials and self-revelations; and even in *Paradiso* he is further tested, not just by one but by three separate saints. Although Dante the pilgrim's journey has a happy outcome (hence the work's name, *Commedia*), it is anything but a cakewalk.

Inferno is, quite literally, hell; the inscription on its gate famously reads "Abandon hope, all ye who enter here." The realm of Inferno takes the form of a funnel with nine concentric "circles" tapering down to the center of the earth. Each successive circle houses spirits of the dead who remain unrepentant, and thus eternally damned, for increasingly egregious sins in life: lust, gluttony, greed, anger, heresy, violence, fraud, and betrayal, not to mention their various derivatives. In every case the damned endure punishments ingeniously matched to their principal sin in life (a device known as *contrapasso*): hypocrites stagger under the weight of gilded lead cloaks; the heads of false prophets are twisted around backwards; flatterers paddle about in human excrement; sowers of discord are hacked apart, only to be reconstituted and hacked apart again *ad infinitum*. Often these punishments are meted out at the hands (or claws) of a motley array of gruesome monsters or beasts; a favorite of young readers is the flatulent *Malacoda* ("evil tail"), who summons his fellow devils by making "a trumpet of his ass."

Dante the pilgrim finally encounters Satan in the ninth circle at the frozen nadir of Inferno. A three-headed figure both of horror and misery (sort of an anti-trinity), the fallen angel chomps with his three mouths on the worst of traitors: Judas—traitor of God—and Brutus and Cassius—traitors of Rome. Meanwhile the tears that stream from his six eyes freeze beneath him with the flapping of his wings, keeping him immobile from the waist down.

The Island of Purgatory

Through a neat act of physics, Purgatorio is a seven-tiered ziggurat-shaped mountain island formed by the displacement of the fallen angels' impact on earth—the impact which formed Inferno, its spatial and spiritual mirror image. While Dante's Inferno contains "circles," his Purgatorio features "terraces." At each terrace or level, the souls found there are in the process of purging themselves of one or another sin of successively lesser consequence: pride, envy, wrath, sloth, covetousness, gluttony, and lust. And while Inferno was all about punishment, Dante the pilgrim's observation and personal experience of Purgatorio reveals more of a "stick *and* carrot" ethos. For instance, penitent spirits in the second terrace, associated with the sin of envy, find themselves clad in gray cloaks and their eyes temporarily sewn shut with iron wire—but they can also hear voices telling stories of generosity, the virtue opposite to the sin of envy. In the sixth terrace, associated with the sin of gluttony, the penitents are forced to fast in the presence of fruit trees just beyond reach, but those same trees have voices telling tales of temperance, again the opposite virtue. Once the penitents experience their final purgation—passing through a wall of flames on the seventh terrace—they enter the Garden of Eden at the very top of the mountain. Here Dante walks through fire to once again see his beloved Beatrice, who acts as his guide for the next stage of his journey.

Paradiso, third realm of the afterlife and the pilgrim Dante's "destination," also has its own special configuration: nine concentric spheres, each associated with specific heavenly bodies and derived from the Ptolemaic astronomy practiced in Dante's time. Although this is heaven, the first three spheres each represent a *deficiency* in one of three virtues: the first sphere (the moon) stands for inconstancy, a deficiency in fortitude; the second sphere (Mercury) stands for ambition, a deficiency in justice; and the third sphere (Venus) stands for unbridled passion, a deficiency in temperance. Then, however, we move on to spheres representing the four cardinal virtues (prudence, justice, temperance, and fortitude), the three theological virtues (faith, hope, and love) and the angels. Beyond the spheres, and perhaps all form and categorization, our pilgrim enters the Empyrean, the ultimate abode of God—more than a physical place, a state of grace suffused with light. Here Dante experiences his last, "Beatific" vision of his beloved Beatrice. Dante's pilgrim enters, at the end, a sense of union with the divine, joining with "the Love that moves the sun and the other stars." T.S. Eliot called the last canto of Paradiso "the highest point poetry has ever reached or can reach."

Like all great literary journeys, Dante the pilgrim's adventure is ultimately a journey within. One of the marks of genius of Dante the poet was his ability to create such an imaginative metaphorical itinerary for his pilgrim's road to salvation.

◆ MAGI CHAPEL

You enter a small chamber lit by candles. Even before your eyes have become accustomed to the low flickering light you can discern a constellation of reflected glints from the surrounding walls. These glints originate, you come to realize, from delicately applied gold leaf and silver. Patches of white now seem to protrude: the flanks and haunches of horses. You begin to notice velvet garments in beautiful hues with fine brocade; profusions of encrusted jewels; exotic flora and fauna; a fairytale landscape. Before and around you slowly unspools a stately procession: a cavalcade of kings and their minions whose members' opulent livery and sumptuous attire you could scarcely have imagined in this life …

If Florence in the Quattrocento had a "Lifestyles of the Rich and Famous" show, the Chapel of the Magi in what is now known as the Palazzo Medici-Riccardi would certainly have been featured as the most fabulous private screening room in the Western world—a wrap-around visual extravaganza that could only have been created by someone with the sweeping vision of a Cecil B. De Mille and the showmanship of a Federico Fellini combined with the delicate sensibility and exquisite craft of a Russian lacquer box miniaturist.

That someone was Benozzo Gozzoli (*c.* 1421—1497), and his spectacular fresco cycle of the procession of the Magi on their way to Bethlehem is one of the true glories of fifteenth-century Florentine art.

Gozzoli could hardly have been better prepared for the task of painting Cosimo de Medici's private chapel in 1459. He began his career as a goldsmith, evident not just in his handling of precious materials in the fresco (gold, silver, lapis lazuli) but also in the precious objects they helped him represent: gifts from the Magi, luxurious fabrics, gilt brocades, bejeweled crowns, and so much more. He assisted Ghiberti with the famous Baptistery doors in Florence, work that would have honed his skills in handling both spatial relations and the visual demands of narrative. He also apprenticed for Fra Angelico, an influence most apparent in the sublime choirs of angels depicted on two walls of the chancel adjoining the chapel's central space.

Cosimo de Medici was to die within five years of the completion of Gozzoli's famous fresco cycle. We cannot know the ultimate disposition of the great patron's soul in the afterlife—but he certainly got to enjoy a piece of paradise in this one.

◆ MEZZOGIORNO

Meaning "land of the midday sun" (from, literally, "midday" in Italian) *mezzogiorno* is a southern dialect rendition of *meridies* (Latin for "noon" and of course the sun's position at midday). Similarly southern France is known as Le Midi referring to "midday" in French.

While of course any land anywhere can be the land of the noon sun, here the term really has a traditional farming connotation: it refers to the blazing midday heat, which changes the farmer's time for working on the land to early in the morning or after sundown.

The term came into vogue around the time of Italian unification and includes the administrative regions of Abruzzo, Apulia, Basilicata, Campania, Calabria, Molise, and Sicily. But political districts notwithstanding, the word has come to have a poetic resonance. When one says "the West" in America, one means a lot more than geography. In that same way *mezzogiorno* evokes a land where everywhere one hears the sound of cicadas; feels warm breezes fragrant with the scent of oranges and almonds; and sees rough landscapes dotted with ancient olive and fig trees and lemon groves, whitewashed houses decorated with dried chili peppers and profusions of flowers . . . the whole earthy, sultry, soulful south of Italy, spoken with fond desire and igniting the imagination.

◆ MARGHERITA, QUEEN OF PEARLS AND PIZZA

Margherita Maria Teresa Giovanna di Savoia was the first queen of united Italy. She was an early modern icon of Italian style and considered a beauty on the order of a Titian or Veronese masterpiece. She had charm and grace and was enormously popular with the Italian people, and her story in some way parallels aspects of the life of Lady Di, though without the tragic ending.

In 1868, 17-year-old Margherita was married to her cousin Umberto, the 24-year-old heir to the Italian throne, at the Royal Palace in Turin (the then capital of Italy). A year after their marriage, Margherita gave birth to the couple's only child, a son, Prince Victor Emmanuel (who would later become King Victor Emmanuel III and Emperor of Ethopia).

Precious gems were of great importance for the image of a sovereign and Queen Margherita loved jewelry and had a magnificently lavish collection, but she was most famous for her vast collection of exquisite pearls; one of her most impressive necklaces contained 684 of them. She was affectionately known as the "Queen of Pearls" and was rarely seen in public or in her portraits without a profusion of them. (The original derivation of "margherita" relates to pearls and purity and today means daisy in Italian.)

Countless tributes were dedicated to Margherita from sweets and streets to schools and towns. Pizza Margherita was also allegedly named for her, though the particulars of that story don't really hold up to careful scrutiny (but, as in so much that's legendary in Italian life, it's a very enjoyable thought).

As recounted by pizza expert Scott Wiener, it just may be a "creation myth," which goes something like this:

In 1878, King Victor Emmanuel II died, and Umberto and Margherita were crowned. Following the coronation, the royal couple made trips throughout Italy to greet their subjects, and Margherita's warmth, charm, and beauty won the hearts of her people everywhere. Here it gets a little shaky, as we'll see later, but for now . . . when they traveled south to Naples they sampled local cuisine which included pizza by Raffaele Esposito, who prepared three different topping combinations for the royal couple: olive oil, whitefish, and mozzarella and crushed tomato. At the last moment Esposito's wife, in a spontaneous display of patriotism, tossed fresh green basil on the pizza topped with crushed tomato and mozzarella to match the colors of the Italian flag. The Queen was positively delighted and the rest, as they say, is history.

It is conceivable that the King and Queen may have visited the pizzeria formerly owned by Esposito, which has been owned and operated by Esposito's nephews, the Brandi brothers, since the 1930's. Today the pizzeria proudly displays a "document" dated June 11, 1889, relating to the "historic" event. The document is vague and only confirms the tasting of the pizzas:

Household of Her Majesty
Capodimonte

11 June 1889

Moth Office Inspectorate

Most Esteemed Raffaele Esposito. I confirm to you that the three kinds of Pizza you prepared for Her Majesty were found to be delicious. Your most devoted servant,

Galli Camillo
Head of Table Services to the Royal Household

One other reason the pizza story doesn't quite pass the sniff test: the Mezzogiorno wasn't exactly thrilled to be annexed by the North in the unification process, and the feisty Neapolitans were unlikely to be celebrating the Queen, even a charming and beautiful one, with the same enthusiasm as the citizens of the North. Perhaps the Brandi Brothers were early branding experts and figured a way to create lasting differentiation in an increasingly competitive marketplace. You might say, in a distaff version of a title of a song by Eric Clapton, that they were riding with the Queen.

♦ MARINARA

Ever wonder why there is no seafood in marinara sauce given that, after all, at its root is the word *mare,* meaning "the sea"?

"Marinara" is derived from the Italian word *marinai* meaning "sailors"; marinara sauce loosely translates to "sauce of the sailors." It originated with the mariners of southern Italy (both Naples and Sicily claim to be its birthplace) in the 16th century, after Christoforo Columbus and his Spanish crew introduced the just-discovered tomato from the "New World." In those days of no refrigeration, the newly concocted sailor sauce was perfect for seafaring because its ingredients—oil, tomato, garlic, and dried herbs—traveled well and did not spoil easily, and pasta with this sauce could be assembled easily for a filling, inexpensive and tasty meal for the men at sea. So too with newly arrived Italian immigrants (by 1920 there were five million who had made their way to America); they took inexpensive

149

beef ground by butchers and transformed it into a dish of meatballs over spaghetti with marinara sauce.

There is no Italian word for gravy, the closest to it being *sugo* and *ragu* which refer to sauces made with meat while *salsa* is used for lighter preparations. Curiously many post–WWII Italian American households, especially in the Northeast, referred to tomato sauce without meat as "gravy," adopting American terminology. As the saying goes, "When in Rome …"

♦ MURANO, ISLANDS OF GLASS

Since ancient times, there has always been something almost mystical about glass: its transparency and translucency; the way it becomes a kaleidoscope for colors, reflections, and illusions; its ability to focus, distort, and refract light into the hues of the rainbow. That makes it seem natural that the most fantastical and magical city in Italy, Venice, became a center of artisanal glassworks.

Glassmaking in the lagoons of Venice probably began as early as the eighth century. By 1291 the glassmakers of Venice had refined their skills and knowledge into proprietary production methods, and that year the government banned glass furnaces from the central lagoons of Venice, restricting them exclusively to the Murano lagoons five to six miles away. Most historians assume the order was due to fear that the fires of the glass furnaces might spark a massive conflagration in the mostly wooden structures of the crowded city. But another reason might have been that the move to Murano was designed to isolate the master glassblowers and prevent the sharing of their valuable knowhow with foreigners. Whatever the reason, Murano at that point became synonymous with an exclusive mastery of artisanal glass.

The glassmakers were important to the economy of the Republic and they were granted special privileges: the right to wear swords and to be immune from prosecution for a variety of offenses by the notoriously high-handed Venetian state. In the late fourteenth century, the daughters of master glassmakers were even allowed to marry into Venice's blue-blooded families. However, there was one pretty big catch: the glassmakers' secrets were so jealously guarded by the doges and mercantile council of Venice that those glassmakers weren't allowed to leave the Republic. If a craftsman decided to set up shop anywhere beyond the Murano lagoons, he risked being assassinated or having his hands cut off.

What made Murano's glassmakers so coveted? They had that brilliant mastery of craft and inventiveness we so associate with Italian fine design. They were the first people in Europe (and only ones for a long time) who knew how to make glass mirrors. They also developed special techniques— glass with threads of gold (*aventurine*), multicolored glass with floral pat terns (*millefiori*), enameled "liquid" mosaic glass (*smalto*)—that made their work even more prized. They had a virtual monopoly on quality glass that lasted for centuries.

To this day Venetian glass maintains a near-mythical allure and appeals year in and year out to souvenir-seekers. Venice's chamber of commerce estimates that five million visitors a year trail down Murano's Fondamenta dei Vetrai (Glassblower Street), where the shop windows are stacked with everything from glass gondoliers and grotesque clowns to the most exquisite goblets, vases, candlesticks, and dazzling chandeliers.

When it comes to art glass and so much more, Venice is a shimmering world unto itself.

◆ THE MANY FACES OF VENICE

Imagine that you live in a city where many if not most of your neighbors are clad in masks and capes. The very idea seems improbable if not downright bizarre—and *creepy!* Yet such was the practice in the Republic of Venice, not just for a once-a-year evening of trick-or-treating or even a fortnight of revelry, but for weeks and eventually months on end over the course of many centuries. How does such a strange custom take root?

Let's first consider a timeline. Occasional mask-wearing may have begun in Venice in the late twelfth century with the annual celebration of a military victory for the still young Republic. The first documented reference to mask-wearing came with a 1268 law responding to a case of masked men throwing "scented eggs" at ladies. Mask-wearing became established during the annual pre-Lenten celebration of *Carnevale* (*see* "Carnevale"), only to expand over the centuries to other times of the year. By the fifteenth century, maskmakers (*mascherari*) were a privileged group with their own guild

151

and laws, and by the eighteenth century—the Republic's last—sanctioned mask-wearing took place for fully half of each year.

While masks can be found in many cultures, their use tends to be only occasional or ceremonial, and then, typically, to project an alternative identity: a totemic animal, perhaps, or departed spirit. In the Venetian Republic, however, nontheatrical masks were for the most part employed to simply *conceal* their wearers' identities. In an Italian world with strict class distinctions and strong religious proscriptions, masks offered a useful sort of ritualistic *arrangiarsi* (see "Arrangiarsi") to allow intercourse—of *all* sorts!—between individuals who would otherwise never be allowed to fraternize. They fulfilled a similar purpose for nobles who wished to communicate with foreigners, an act officially prohibited to guard the Republic's strategic secrets in the mercantile or manufacturing (e.g., glassmaking) spheres. Masks also enabled the elites to gamble in public without compromising their social standing or revealing their financial gains or setbacks (see "Ridotto Royale"). They were used by inquisitors and their witnesses to avoid identification and retribution, respectively. They were also used during public voting events as the equivalent of private polling booths.

In short, the anonymity afforded by masks allowed the Venetians they disguised to, ironically, "be themselves" in matters ranging from the civic to the lascivious—which was very much in evidence in this cosmopolitan pleasure-center of Italy. *Siamo a Venezia*, one would say. We are in Venice. We are constantly being excommunicated by the Pope, which doesn't bother us too much since we have the best courtesans in Europe. As long as one is not a threat to the Republic or your fellow Venetians, what happens in Venice, stays in Venice . . . you get the picture.

While these masks enabled their wearers to be more forward in expressing their true opinions or acting upon their most basic impulses, they may also have allowed their wearers to retreat, when desired, into their own private shells. Only twice the size of New York's Central Park, Venice was once the second most populous city in Europe, after Paris. Wearing a mask in the close confines of the Republic may have served a similar distancing function as the ubiquitous earbuds worn by riders on crowded Manhattan subways today.

The most common mask type was called the *bauta*, a stark white full-faced covering that would flair out at the bottom to allow its wearer to talk, eat, and drink without necessitating its removal. Although mainly worn by men, women would occasionally don the *bauta*. An exclusively feminine mask was the *muta*, little more than a black disk with eyeholes and a slight protrusion for the nose that would leave about an inch of skin to show around its outer edge. Its name, which translates to "mute," derives from

its unique form of attachment: the wearer held it in position by placing a button sewn inside the mask between her teeth, preventing her from being able to speak! (The *muta* was *de rigueur* for upper-class Venetian ladies at one time; in fact, any fashionably dressed woman without one was generally thought to be a courtesan.)

Venice itself is often masked in mist. Perhaps imitation is indeed the sincerest form of flattery.

♦ MARCELLO

In 1960, Marcello Mastrioanni—playing dashing, amoral gossip columnist Marcello Rubini in Fellini's *La Dolce Vita*—became a new Via Veneto-chic image of the classic figure of the Latin lover. But he quickly proved to be much more than an Italian Cary Grant. Over the decades he was sensitive enough, smart enough, funny enough, and moving enough to play everything from a bored aristocrat trying to divorce his wife Italian style (by killing her, see "Divorce Itailian Style") to a brilliantly confused director in *8 ½* to a retired tap dancer in *Ginger and Fred* to a haggard expatriate lord in John Boorman's *Leo The Last*. He ultimately became one of the quintessential actors of Italian cinema.

Perhaps part of his ability to lose himself in his roles came from his humility, learned during an early life marked by the travails of his country in the mid-20th-century. The son of a carpenter, he was at one point forced to work as a draftsman in a northern Italian Nazi labor camp, from which he managed to escape. After the war he struggled in poverty at odd jobs and in the lower ranks of Italian theater, finally breaking through in an Italian production of *Les Miserables* in 1947.

The film that catapulted Marcello Mastrioanni to stardom was Fellini's *La Dolce Vita*. Mastroianni characteristically said that he was cast by Fellini because he had a "terribly ordinary face" (and producer Dino DeLaurentis clearly agreed; he quit the film over Fellini's not casting Paul Newman in the role). But he still inherited the Latin lover tag, not the least because of his ongoing romance with Catherine Deneuve.

He went on to appear in 140 motion pictures, earn three Best Actor Oscar nominations, and win two Best Actor awards at Cannes. *La Dolce Vita* was the beginning of an immortal cinematic partnership with Fellini that included *8 1/2* (1963), *City of Women* (1979), and *Ginger and Fred* (1985).

Many of us have our favorite Mastroianni scenes, often with the beautiful actresses he played off of so well: wistfully chasing Anita Ekberg across Rome in *La Dolce Vita*, struggling with the needs of many women in *8 ½*, reuniting with his ex-partner Giulietta Masina in *Ginger and Fred*, reduced to sheer awestruck lust by Sophia Loren doing a striptease in *Yesterday, Today, and Tomorrow* (along with all the males in the audience, and at least some of the females). Loren and Mastroianni, in particular, were a magically winning screen couple in several films; that intelligent humility of his made him a great co-star as well as a great star.

In his onscreen comic brio, passion, canniness, and world-weariness, Mastroianni was so beloved by all Italy and he so embodied its spirit that

when he passed away, the Trevi Fountain itself was draped in black. Offscreen he explained his success in his autobiography *I Remember Yes I Remember* when he declared "I love life and perhaps for this I have been loved in return by life" (using the word *riamato*, which means "re-loved"). His life, even more than the movie he starred in, embodied the spirit of *la dolce vita*.

- NUTELLA

- NATIVITY SCENES

- THE ITALIAN NAVY

- NORMAN ARAB SICILY

- NEPOTISM'S LEGACY

- NERO'S GOLDEN HOUSE

♪ NUTELLA

Italy's most successful modern entrepreneur made his fortune by staying in touch with his inner child and living as a real life Willy Wonka. Michele Ferrero, creator of the global brand Nutella, was a shy, humble man who died never having given a newspaper interview. His estimated net worth was $26.5 billion and he ranked 22nd on a recent Forbes list of billionaires—his empire built, as the magazine very simply stated, from "chocolates."

His most delectable invention, Nutella, a creamy chocolate hazelnut spread, has been part of the collective memory of Italian children for the past fifty years, as comforting and beloved a mainstay of their world as Oreos and Coca Cola are for American kids. And today this holds true well beyond Italy's borders, as Nutella is an international phenomenon that has truly captivated the world's taste buds: 2014's estimated global sales in 53 countries were 365,000,000 kg. That's 2.2 million pounds a day!

Ferraro's greatest skill was his sense and knowledge of what children want. "Never patronize a child" he is quoted as saying in the 2004 book, *Nutella: An Italian Legend* by Gigi Padovoni.

The story of Nutella begins in the 1940s with Ferrero's father Pietro, a pastry chef from Turin, capital of the hazelnut-rich region of Piedmont and home of the premium chocolate confection *gianduia* (*see* "Gianduia"). He had been observing factory workers eating bread with tomatoes and cheese as a meal and thought they might want something *dolce* to go along with it. His response was a *pastone* (pastry mesh) of chocolate and hazelnuts and cocoa butter shaped into a loaf and wrapped in tinfoil so it could be sliced like a *salumi*. He called it *Pasta Gianduija*. The workers liked it, but its real fans were their children, who ultimately became the target market. And since *Pasta Gianduija* was far less expensive than chocolate, this added greatly to its appeal.

Shortly after World War II Piero died and his son Michele took over the factory. On a very hot day in the summer of 1949 a mishap occurred: the loaves at the warehouse melted and they were forced to transfer the now spreadable product into jars. That mishap soon qualified as a divine accident in every sense of the word, a pivotal transformation, as Ferrero began to sell this softer, creamier, more versatile and convenient *Pasta Gianduija* under the new name *Supercrema Gianduija*.

Then, in another serendipitous event, a 1962 Italian law forbade brand names with superlatives (e.g., "super," "ultra") so another name had to be chosen. The name that emerged had an English word as its root, "nut," combined with the Italian suffix "ella" and all its affectionate connotations (as in mozzarella and tagliatella).

In 1964 the renamed Nutella made its commercial debut with a splash of clever television advertising and branding: a little spreadable joy. . . something "special" without it being a Sunday or holiday or birthday. . . a yummy antidote to small sadnesses and disappointments. Bambini were besotted, and in the '70s Nutella hit it big in Europe and then reached the United States in 1983, where its use exploded (witness the street corner crepe stand).

Michele Ferrero didn't stop there. He oversaw a multinational confectionery empire which included other tasty and whimsical creations like minty and fruity TicTacs, Ferrer Rocher candies, Mon Cheri (cherry liquor filled chocolates), and Kinder Eggs and Kinder snacks. It seems no accident that that last product name can refer to "kindness" or "children."

Ferrero was passionate about product quality, and his secret Nutella recipe has the legendary aura of the original Coke formula. And unlike with Coke, Nutella's imitators have all failed miserably, in part because the public imagination has invested the original with so much love and even

158

national pride— on Nutella's 50th anniversary the Italian government issued a commemorative stamp.

Michele Ferrero died a year later, poetically on Valentine's Day, 2015. Posts on Twitter read "world's flag should be at half mast: Nutella owner has died." For this deeply religious man—he made a pilgrimage to the shrine of the Madonna of Lourdes each year—perhaps an appropriate epitaph would be ". . . and a little child shall lead them" from *Isaiah 11:6*. One likes to imagine a flock of *amorini* and *putti* giving him a happy welcome.

⋆ NATIVITY SCENES

An ecclesiastical jack-of-all-trades, St. Francis of Assisi was an impresario with few equals. If P. T. Barnum cynically believed "there's a sucker born every minute," the quintessentially compassionate Francis doubtless felt that there's a future convert born just as often. Francis saw it as part of his mission to reach out to those future converts on *their* terms rather than his own: to bring the church closer to the people and to bring the Holy Scripture to life.

These impulses led him to create that wonder of holiday stagecraft we now take so much for granted: the Nativity display. Contemporaneous passion plays never dealt with the birth of Jesus, so Francis conceived a virtual reenactment of Christ's birth complete with not just human stand-ins but also barnyard animals. After receiving papal permission, he presented the very first Nativity display in the mouth of a cave near the small town of Greccio.

It proved to be an instant sensation. The popularity of Nativity scenes large and small has never abated in the seven centuries since.

Today virtually every Italian home owns a *presepe* (literally "crib" or "crèche"), or tabletop nativity set, displayed each year from December 8th through the feast of the Epiphany in January. These *presepi* can cost much less than a hundred euros or considerably more: into the thousands for the more elaborate and artful handmade displays.

For Nativity aficionados no trip to Italy is complete without a visit to Via San Gregorio Armeno in Naples—also known as "the street of Nativity workshops" or "Christmas Alley"—the very epicenter of *presepi* production. High above the city, and on the other end of the scale, is the largest Nativity

scene in the world, *Presepe Cusiniello,* housed in the Museo Nazionale di San Martino and showcasing over 160 characters, 80 animals, 28 angels, and more than 400 miniature objects.

If a trip to Napoli isn't in the cards this holiday, try to visit the stunning Neapolitan Baroque Crèche inside the great medieval hall at the Metropolitan Museum of Art in New York City, which draws visitors the world over. Gracefully suspended angels and cherubs adorn a towering tree. The 360-degree theatrical landscape beneath the great spruce depicts the Nativity with humble shepherds and their flocks along with ox and lamb; the three elaborately bedecked Magi in procession with their exotic retinues; and, the most quitensseially Neapolitan touch, colorful peasants and townspeople engaged in their quotidian tasks. Finally, for added drama and stagecraft, there are background pieces of the ruins of a Roman temple and a typical Italian fountain with a lion's-mask waterspout.

The impresario from Assisi would doubltess approve.

♦ THE ITALIAN NAVY

Question: Why does the new Italian navy have glass bottom boats?
Answer: To see the old Italian navy.
— Henny Youngman

How soon we forget! For most of the last millennium the Italian peninsula projected maritime superpower status and produced some of the greatest maritime fighting forces (not to mention navigators, explorers, and traders) in all of history.

Geography is destiny (see "Greek Soul of Sicily"). The Italian boot nearly bisects the Mediterranean, so little wonder that it should develop as a base of maritime power. But that is not how matters began: toward the end of the first millennium the coastal communities of the Italian peninsula found themselves increasingly under attack by bands of pirates, mostly Saracens. Eventually a handful of medieval city-states developed sufficient maritime defenses to repel the incursions and then rid their surrounding waters of the pirates. Those defenses became fleets, and those fleets became the instruments of trade and even colonization around the Mediterranean and beyond.

The four great medieval maritime republics of Italy were Amalfi, Pisa, Genoa, and Venice; today their flags form part of Italy's naval ensign. Amalfi offered the first competition to Arab traders in the Mediterranean; it also introduced a code of maritime law and even established a trading colony in Constantinople. But after a couple of centuries of success at sea Amalfi lost its independence to powers on land: first to the Principality of Salerno and ultimately to the Normans. Amalfi's primacy in the Western Mediterranean was supplanted by that of Pisa, but Pisa too eventually lost its independence to Florence.

The greatest medieval maritime republics of all were Genoa, once part of the Holy Roman Empire, and Venice, once part of the Byzantine Empire, each situated near the top of a sea on either side of the Italian peninsula. Genoa at first allied itself with Pisa in the 11th century to battle the Saracen pirates in the Ligurian and Tyrrhenian Seas. Venice was defeating pirates in the Adriatic at around the same time. With the First Crusade (1096–1099) Genoa established a foothold in the Holy Land and dominance in the eastern Mediterranean that was to last for almost three centuries. With the Fourth Crusade (1202–1204), Venice seized power over the principal seaside outposts of Byzantium. For the next 175 years Genoa and Venice vied for naval supremacy until the balance of power tipped toward Venice in the War of Chioggia (1379).

By the end of the 14th century Venice employed 36,000 seamen in its merchant vessels and warships. The *Arsenale* (which gave us the word "arsenal") in Venice could turn out a fully armed galley in a single day.

In subsequent centuries Genoa supported Spain in its westward adventures while Venice parlayed some of its maritime wealth into land gains on the mainland.

Some of the greatest mariners of all time were products of the Italian peninsula: Amerigo Vespucci of Florence (also a navigator, financier, and cartographer whose name became that of the New World); Giovanni da Verrazzano, also of Florence, whose name now adorns America's longest suspension bridge, in New York City; Giovanni Caboto (John Cabot) of Venice; and, of course, Cristoforo Colombo (Christopher Columbus) of Genoa.

At the start of World War II the Italian Navy (then known as Regina Marina) was the second largest naval force in the world.

A glass-bottom boat excursion would doubtless reveal more wrecks from Italy's historic foes than from its defenders.

(The ensign of the Italian Navy is the Italian tricolor with the coat of arms of the Marina Militare. The quarters refer to the four Medieval Italian or "Maritime Republics" (*Repubbliche Marinare*):

✦   1st quarter: Republic of Venice—winged Lion of St. Mark wielding a sword

✦   2nd quarter: Republic of Genoa—red cross on a white field

✦   3rd quarter: Republic of Amalfi—white Maltese cross on a blue field

✦   4th quarter: Republic of Pisa—white Pisan cross and a red field

✦ NORMAN ARAB SICILY

When Norman conquerors invaded Sicily in 1061, defeating the Muslim Saracens, and seizing the Arab capital Bal'harm (Palermo) and the rest of Sicily over the next thirty years, they encountered a vibrant culture in which Greco-Roman, Byzantine, and North African Muslim ingredients were combined like a deeply rich and flavorful *arancini.* Thankfully for European history, instead of laying to waste that culture, they not only tolerated it but learned from it, even immersing themselves in it for the next two centuries, sowing the seeds for the intellectual and cultural movements that would blossom into the Italian Renaissance.

The "Norman-Arab civilization" lasted until around 1250, bringing to Sicily northern European Catholicism, art and architecture, and exploration of the roots of classical civilization—and that produced a fusion of knowledge, and the arts and an era so rich and strange that one of Sicily's kings, Roger II, wore Persian silks, had a harem, and was called a "baptized sultan." The new kingdom of Sicily for the first time looked toward Italy for future conquest and growth—but those distinctly eastern habits and a whole new level of pan-cultural thinking would be carried on by Roger's grandson Frederic, who would become known as *Stupor Mundi*: The Wonder of the World.

Roger II spoke Arabic perfectly and guided his kingdom toward religious tolerance and understanding of Muslim science, military strategies, and agriculture, all of which increased the region's prosperity and power. The multiethnic kingdom appropriately produced a great work of international geography: royal edicts in Latin, Greek, Arabic, and Hebrew, and the Assizes of Ariano, which not only established European feudal law within a central government, but also freedom of worship and independent judicial procedures for Muslims, Jews, and Christians.

Above all, there were works of architecture resplendent with the techniques and treasures of this cultural crossroads, as Normans preserved and learned from Byzantine and Arab mosques, churches, palaces, and courtyards. Chief among these is the Cappella Palatina of Palermo, built by Roger II and consecrated in 1140, which embodies in all elements of its architecture a peaceful and harmonious intermingling of the Christian and Muslim faiths. Craftsmen of three different religious cultures created its Saracen arches and arabesques; its Greek columns with Gothic floral capitals and gargoyles; its glittering Byzantine dome and mosaics; and its texts written in Greek, Arabic, and Latin, all suffused in a golden glow. It's a UNESCO world heritage site, along with the cathedral of Cefalú and other structures such as the Royal Palace of Palermo, which bear Muslim features like cupolas and their own Byzantine legacy.

It's particularly amazing to think that the kings of Roger's line would have their final resting places beneath a timbered roof and ceiling that's considered one of the few surviving examples of Egyptian Fatimid art, possibly built by carpenters and painters from Cairo. Arabic arches and scripts decorate the roof, and eight-pointed three-dimensional polygonal stars, so typical of Muslim design, form a Christian cross. The Muslim designs literally enfold the largely Byzantine mosaics, which may have religious significance but are probably secular in origin and symbolize Roger's court. *Muqarnas*, ornamental honeycomb vaulting, decorate the band beneath the ceiling. Meanwhile every element is covered with vegetal and geometric decorations; paintings of animals, dancing girls and musicians; and inscriptions in Kufic script containing blessings. It's hard to think of a Western religious edifice so shaped by Islamic art—in fact it's hard to think that very thought in the early 21st century . . . but that cultural synthesis looms in all its glory on a square in Palermo.

Sicily's not that large an island but boasts (as does Italy) a quantity of UNESCO World Heritage Sites way out of proportion to its size. Much of that constitutes a remarkable celebration of a Norman-Arab culture that brought peace, architectural splendor, multicultural sophistication, and interfaith unity to Italy, but which had sadly vanished by the mid-thirteenth-century. Still, elements of its flourishing, especially under its peak influence during the reign of Frederic II, would travel north, where a little city named Florence was waiting for its world-historical lesson. (see "Wonder of the World" and "Flowering in Fiorenza")

♦ NEPOTISM'S LEGACY

The acorn doesn't fall far from the tree is an extraordinarily apt adage when it comes to the house of della Rovere (literally "of the Oak Tree," its coat-of-arms bearing that image and the emblem of an acorn). The della Rovere family were of modest beginnings and rose to prominence through acts of nepotism and ambitious arranged marriages by two della Rovere popes, Francesco della Rovere, Pope Sixtus IV (1471–1484) and his nephew Giuliano, Pope Julius II (1503–1513). But in this they were no different from any other family with a papal branch, because the whole concept of nepotism arises from the Papacy itself.

164

The term comes from the Italian word *nepotismo* with its Latin root *nepos* meaning nephew (no, it's not the popular "the son also rises"). During the Middle Ages until the late 17th century it was common for popes and bishops who had taken vows of celibacy, and therefore would bear no legitimate offspring, to award their nephews and other relatives positions of preference. Numerous popes took advantage of this and many cardinals got to be cardinals through this back door system of appointments meant to expand the family's power and control and continue the familial or papal dynasty.

No popes were more conscious of that power than uncle and nephew Pope Sixtus IV and Pope Julius II, who were not exactly gentle shepherds leading the flock and who took seriously their family motto "Fortune favors the bold." Both ruled more as monarchs seeking the aggrandizement of the Papal States while subordinating their duty as the Holy Church's spiritual head. Julius took his name from Julius Caesar and is remembered as the "Warrior Pope" for his Machiavellian tactics. Both Popes sought to have the grandeur of Rome eclipse all other Italian cities, were great patrons of the arts, amassed large personal art collections, and viewed art and architecture as a means to express power, prestige, and authority.

During "Uncle" Sixtus IV's pontificate, Rome was transformed from a medieval to a Renaissance city. He restored numerous public buildings and churches, and did it through heavy taxation and a kind of commercial expansion of nepotism: simony, or the selling of appointments and positions of power. But he knew how to use the original version; along with his nephew Guilano, he appointed numerous family and friends as bishops and cardinals. Although the Sistine Chapel's original building existed for centuries, the chapel as we know it today was restored by Pope Sixtus IV and named for him. Its dimensions and layout are based on the Old Testament descriptions of the Temple of Solomon; clearly the virtue of humility was also somewhat lacking in this Pope. But his finest legacy was that chapel. While the Sistine has become synonymous with Michelangelo's ceiling and Last Judgment, both later commissioned by Julius, Sixtus had a brigade of great artists fresco the walls: Sandro Botticelli, Domenico Ghirlandaio, Pietro Perugino, Cosimo Roselli, and Luca Signorelli.

The darker side of his legacy was the authorization of the Spanish Inquisition through a Papal Bull in 1478. It was a quest for religious purity that somewhat foundered with the accession of the next pope, Rodrigo Borgia, the infamous Pope Alexander VI, who was himself a *nepoti*, the nephew of Pope Callixitus III (*see* "Sympathy for the Borgia"). There was great animosity between the cunning and powerful Borgias and the della Roveres. Once Rodrigo Borgia was elected pope he plotted Guiliano's assassination; the cardinal fled to France where he lived for ten years. He returned to Rome after Alexander's death, and with the help of a little simony, was elected pope himself in 1503.

After Giuliano, as Julius II, ascended to the Papacy, he sanctimoniously banned the practice of simony in all future papal elections. His urge to consolidate power was expressed in his hiring of the young Michelangelo, on the basis of his *Pietà* and *David*, to sculpt the monumental tomb he boldly planned to immortalize his greatness. The original design of the tomb was to include forty-seven freestanding statues reflecting Pope Julius' larger than life personality and reputation; ironically such a tomb was never built due to the need to spend the papal budget on a more temporal use of power, Julius' early military adventures seeking to restore and expand the Papal States.

Those campaigns earned Julius II the title the "Warrior Pope," but he was also appropriately known as the "Renaissance Pope." After the death of Lorenzo de Medici the curtain may have fallen on the "Camelot" that had been Florence of the Quattrocentro, but under Guilano's ambitious vision and patronage, the masterworks that have come to epitomize the High Renaissance were created in Rome: Michelangelo's Sistine Chapel frescoes, Raphael's *School of Athens*, and the foundation for St. Peter's Cathedral, for which Julius laid the first stone on April 18, 1506.

During his rule of ten years, he was referred to as *Terribile*, which means fearsome but also suggests awesome, sublime, and superhuman (the same word used for his intense, angry, and supernaturally gifted artist Michelangelo). His ultimate tomb, sculpted by Michelangelo and his assistants—a two-tiered architectural assemblage with six statues in his family church San Pietro en Vicoli—was greatly reduced from Julius' original conception, but still radiates his power. Michelangelo, upon completing the bearded and horned Moses, eight feet of seated muscularity, pulsing with energy and fury at his people's worship of the golden calf, reputedly struck the sculpture's knee and cried "Now speak!", so alive did he feel this work was with (one suspects) the power of Pope Julius.

It was a power that gave the world a papacy tilted toward repression and war, and which relied on a dubious practice that thankfully, while it persists in spirit everywhere, at least is no longer standard operating procedure for Italy and the papacy. Instead Renaissance nepotism's ultimate legacy is a body of art and architecture that suggest a far better dimension of humanity.

◆ NERO'S GOLDEN HOUSE

We all know how Nero fiddled while Rome burned (well, no, that's just a legend, since there were no violins back then). What we are sure about is that Nero's rule gave us our modern definition of the word "grotesque"— not, surprisingly, because his reign was such a bad thing, but also because one of his creations turned out to be a very good thing. And to understand that mystery, we need to dig a little deeper (literally) into the story of his Domus Aurea, or Golden House.

There's a general consensus that Nero was perhaps the worst Roman emperor, and that's saying something, given that two emperors before him was the debauched and cruel Caligula who once made his horse consul. Beginning as a fairly generous and smart ruler, he slowly went mad (perhaps because of lead poisoning), suspected his mother Agrippina of plotting against him, had her killed, and gradually descended into criminal insanity. In fact, there are theories that he deliberately set the 64 CE Great Fire of Rome in part so he could build a new Rome in his image and in part so he could blame Christians for it and relentlessly persecute them.

He did take advantage of a tract of burned-out land to build a huge 80-hectare (197 acres) brick palace, with stuccoed ceilings inlaid with ivory and semiprecious stones, and gold leaf applied throughout its series of villas and pavilions, which gave the residence its name. With its artificial forests and vineyards, its altar in a sacred grove, it was *rus in urbe*, "countryside in the city," and even had a manmade lake. A lyre-player who fancied himself a great musician, Nero made sure that dominating his Golden House was a statue of himself over one hundred feet tall as Apollo the god of art. Perhaps the House's master touch was the first dome ever used for a nonreligious structure, with mosaics in the vaulted ceilings, a design that would become paramount in Christian art. And the greatest artist of the day, Fabullus, covered the walls with elegantly beautiful frescoes.

Complete with a revolving and (supposedly) perfume-scented banquet hall, it was perhaps the greatest party mansion ever. But most of Rome wasn't invited. Nero's combination of the Domus Aurea's showmanship and his predatory taxation and land confiscation to support the place, along with his decadence and cruelty, all fueled hatred by the people, the army, and conservative Roman senators.

And so the Domus Aurea was something his successors wanted to expunge from Roman history. The palace was stripped of its bejeweled ornamentation and built over by Vespasian and his heir Titus. From 72 to 80 CE they kept the Colossus Neronis, drained the lake (though it would later be reflooded for staged naval battles), and built the Flavian amphitheater the world would come to know as the Colisseum.

Colossus Neronis/Colisseum—it was not that easy to eliminate Nero's memory or, fortunately, his Domus Aurea. Forty years after Nero's reign the building was totally underground, beneath the Baths of Trajan and Temples of Venus and Rome . . . and that was what so effectively preserved not just the basic structure but Fabullus's frescoes.

And so in the 15th century, when all Italy was ablaze with discoveries and rediscoveries of classic art, the Domus Aurea was discovered by painters like Raphael and Pinturicchio who spelunked into its depths as if they were caves or grottoes, climbing down rickety ladders to admire Fabullus's art. They and later art visitors like Ghirlandaio and Filippo Lippi, not to mention Casanova and the Marquis de Sade, left graffiti signatures to let the world know they'd been there. The exuberant and imaginative style of the frescoes, their friezes of figures and landscape, their elaborate use of foliage and other motifs—including mythical beasts—in ornamental patterns, all influenced the loggias of the Raphael Rooms of the Vatican and other great works of Renaissance art, where the style became known as "*grottesco*," of a cave, or ultimately "grotesque."

Now the Domus Aurea is open to all of Rome at last. From the Octagonal Room domed salon and its spectacular frescoes, to terraces and fountains that remain from Nero's "countryside in the city" grounds, to spooky underground chambers, the world can see the fruit of Nero's madness that became the spice to Raphael's and other artists' greatness.

When, after a series of conspiracies and revolts and the collapse of his rule, Nero finally had his confederate help him commit suicide, he was said to cry "What an artist dies with me!" Posterity has emphatically disagreed. And yet . . . the world of the Golden House, which he commissioned and (according to Pliny the Elder and Tacitus) personally supervised, inspired the greatest Renaissance artists and the Neoclassical artists who came after them, making Fabullus, Nero's chosen fresco-painter, one of the most influential artists in the history of painting.

Only later did Fabullus's and then Raphael's "grotesque" style get a connotation that went beyond ornamental to extravagantly excessive, dark, and monstrous—and at that point, in a further irony, it described an art appropriate to the original emperor's personality. How strange, and yet, in many ways how Italian, that such a symbol of decadence and madness from a vicious chapter in imperial history left us an enduring aesthetic legacy.

- VIVA OLIVA!

- OVID'S TRANSFORMATIONS

- GLI OCCHIALI DA SOLE

- OCULUS, GATEWAY TO HEAVEN

- ORPHANS OF THE OSPEDALE

O

◆ VIVA OLIVA!

There is something deeply evocative of ancient, mystical times about an olive grove. The gnarled branches with delicate green-gray foliage that shimmer in the light are distinctively hardy and graceful; they conjure imaginings of old gray-haired Italian men and seem to symbolize fortitude and endurance.

And in this case the tough, weathered look does not deceive. The olive tree is an evergreen and the average life expectancy is five hundred years; the oldest living olive tree today is believed to reside on the island of Crete, over two thousand years old and still bearing fruit. Able to thrive in the poorest, rockiest of soils and ferocious Mediterranean sunshine—in fact *simpatico* with the climate due to its low water needs and great need for a long hot growing season— olive trees, like those old men, have truly won the battle of survival. They have come to epitomize the Mediterranean landscape, and olives and olive oil are key to the cuisines of the Mediterranean region, nowhere more so than in Italy, where approximately 3,150,000 tons of olives and olive oil are produced annually.

The olive is technically a fruit of many colors: green (ripening to black), purple, dark brown, even pink, from the largest (called a "donkey") to the smallest (a "bullet"), which gives an idea of the size range. Since olives are fruit, the olive oil produced is a fruit juice. Olives are pressed to release their juices in similar fashion to oranges and lemons, with about sixteen olives yielding one serving. That oil can be remixed with crushed olives and capers to make deliciously spreadable Italian tapenades.

Certainly a useful food, olives and olive oil have become much more than that: not only cosmetic and medicinal, but also ritualistic, achieving spiritual status and even standing in for the sacred.

Like figs, olives are biblical. The first vegetation brought back to Noah after the flood by the dove was the branch of an olive tree. The Egyptians and Minoans (who may have begun its mass cultivation) made olive crowns and extracted olive oil. The fruit also holds its place in Greek mythology, when Athena and Poseidon competed for possession of Athens. Athena beat Poseidon's trident blow and gusher of sea water simply by planting an olive tree beside the well; the court of the Gods ruled in favor of her more peaceful and fruitful gift. Homer, author of the *Odyssey* and the *Iliad*, called olive oil "liquid gold," and Hippocrates, Greek physician and "father of medicine," called it "the great therapeutic," as it found uses for everything from sun protection to eye shadow.

The Roman poet Virgil (70–19 BCE) associated olive with the goddess Pax (the Roman Eirene), and he used the olive branch as a symbol of peace in his *Aeneid*, which it has remained (on the flag now of seven nations, four American states, and the UN). It also became a commercial calling card; the historian Pliny, turning pitchman, maintained Italy had "excellent olive oil at reasonable prices . . . the best in the Mediterranean." And when, after Constantine, the Roman Empire became infused with the Christian religion, olive oil was used in virtually every part of the Catholic ritual. Saints and martyrs seem to have been anointed with olive oil at death as traces of it were found soaked into their bones. Olive oil was also used as the oil for the Oil of Catechumens, Oil of the Sick, the Rites of Baptism, the Sacrament of Confirmation, and the Ordination of priests and bishops.

Why? Why the spiritual aura around the olive and not the fig? Maybe it just goes back to nature. The olive tree survives and thrives in the most inhospitable, rocky terrain. With just the minimum of water it provides delicious fruit and healing oil, and as an evergreen it keeps its leaves throughout the winter while all others lose theirs. These facts alone might have mystified early civilizations enough for them to associate the olive with eternal values.

Little wonder that olives and olive oil have been treasured and even re-vered. Versatile and exceptional multi-taskers, they emblemize peace, live lightly on the planet, and offer virtuous pleasures to us all.

◆ OVID'S TRANSFORMATIONS

He was a *bon vivant* who once proclaimed himself Venus's "engineer of love." As a poet, he had no serious intentions similar to Virgil's desire to craft an epic of the founding of Rome for the betterment of Romans. He was a man whose given last name, Naso, became kind of a joke, suggesting he had a "nose" for trouble since the most significant response he ever got from the Roman cultural and political establishment was not honor but exile.

And yet Publius Ovidius Naso's major work of poetry, the *Metamorphoses,* is one of the founding works of the entire Western canon, fitting company with the Old Testament and Shakespeare. In fact, when it comes to the Bard of the English language, much of his work is unimaginable without Ovid.

Ovid was a poet who never exactly suffered for his art, at least not early in his life. A scion of a wealthy landowning family, he went to Rome to learn oratory so that he could establish a career in law and public office, but found verse more congenial to his talents. (Seneca thought his oratory was "loose poetry.") He sought out other poets, like Propertius and Horace. He took the "grand tour" of the time to Athens, Sicily, and Troy, got married and divorced, tried minor public office, then joined a pleasure-seeking circle led by Augustus's daughter Julia and wrote the *Ars Amatoria* (his Venusian engineering work), which caused (so far as we know) the puritanical Emperor Augustus to view him with disfavor. He then settled down with his second wife and wrote *Metamorphoses*, and went from high society in Rome to the highest ranks of literature.

This witty gentleman was something of a modern Italian in Roman times: a politically aware epicure alive to sensory stimulation of all kinds, with great curiosity about the natural and historical world around him and a tremendous knowledge of legends and stories. His fifteen books of *Metamorphoses* are a fairly complete encyclopedia of Greek myths, some of which would have been lost without him.

The Metamorphoses is nothing less than Ovid's record of cosmic history, from primeval chaos to an orderly world as Julius Caesar becomes a star in the heavens. It's an epic of human civilization involving humanity's creation and interaction with the gods, including the Trojan War and the founding of Rome; it even borrows from the *Odyssey*. It all flows together thanks to the poet's art, and it all shares one common theme: transformation, the passing from one form to another, often with devastating violence, and, in the case of women, involving rape by gods or man, even if the setting and psychology are sometimes quite beautiful, and the result is that sometimes the suffering victim rises to a higher or at least more beautiful form (a bear in the heavens, a laurel tree).

It's a fair poetic transfiguration of what life in a sometimes idyllic, sexually sophisticated, sometimes utterly brutal society must have been like, but done almost with an Italian shrug and appreciation of how an evolving universe and fate are beautiful and terrible things. It's most certainly an invitation to just take pleasure in marvelous stories. Underlying it all is the theme of *amor*, love, though in Ovid's hands it can be ridiculous as well as sublime.

Scholars and critics have long debated if there's a further meaning to Ovid's epic. It may be that we are all just constantly changing visions of one great soul energy through time, that "naught may endure but mutability," as Shelley wrote. But the moral neutrality of the storytelling resists any interpretation. Ovid desacralizes the mythology, shrewdly suggesting at various points they may all be tall tales. He believed in art for pleasure's sake and had no moral agenda. His great work was perhaps the first example of style over substance, art over meaning. It was for others to draw on his work as a poetic resource.

"Others"—as in much of subsequent Western literature. Ovid's *Metamorphoses* influenced the emerging national literatures of the Middle Ages, even though his tales were totally pagan, often having to do with sexual appetites and relations (divine, human, or in between) that could in no way be Christianized. The French troubadours took many of their lays (so to speak) from him. Dante put him in his "*bella scuola*" of the greatest poets and embellished his *Divina Commedia* with some of Ovid's stories. Shakespeare borrowed many of his tales and classical allusions from him, drawing on him directly for his narrative poems, *Venus and Adonis* and *The*

Rape of Lucrece, and using elements of his stories in *Titus Andronicus, Midsummer Night's Dream, A Winter's Tale,* and *Romeo and Juliet.* In the twentieth century James Joyce used one of Ovid's lines as an epigraph for *Portrait of the Artist as a Young Man,* "And he turned his mind to unknown arts," referring to his protagonist, Stephen Daedalus, an Ovidian young artist with an Ovidian name.

The *Metamorphoses* has been more widely illustrated than any other book except the Bible, and great artists have drawn, painted, and sculpted its stories. Raphael learned history and the attributes of his *Galatea* from verses by Ovid. Titian turned to his tales for his great cycle of mythological paintings.

Above all there's Gian Bernini's lifesize, gorgeous, and heartbreaking sculpture *Apollo and Daphne* created between 1622 and 1625 and housed in the Galleria Borghese. In Ovid's tale, the avowedly chaste nymph Daphne, pursued by Apollo, pleads with her father Peneus to make her no longer beautiful or available to the god, and so Peneus transforms her into a laurel tree. Bernini captures the exact moment of the metamorphosis: Apollo, so close he can breathe on her hair, sees her fingers turning into leafy twigs even before she figures out what is happening to her, and you can sense him start to recoil. Daphne's mouth seems to be shrieking. The delicacy of her finely sculpted fingers splaying into twigs and her toes into roots is incredible, sculpted so thinly it's almost translucent. Rendered in one long beautifully curving line, the statue is a freeze-frame, utterly dynamic and emotional, of divine transformation.

Ovid would not be spared his own ugly change of circumstances at the end of his life. Just when his epic was nearly complete, in 8 CE the emperor Augustus banished him to Tomis (Tomi, near modern Constanța, Romania) on the Black Sea. Ovid believed the reasons were possibly his *Ars amatoria* and an offense which he doesn't specify, which might have been his nod and wink toward the adultery of Augustus's daughter, Julia, or his politi-

175

cal support of Germanicus as Augustus's successor and not the ultimate emperor Tiberius.

Whatever the reason, Ovid was never in any danger, but his new life at a half-barbarian port was very much a punishment for this refined man. He kept up a stream of pleas for pardon in his "Letters from the Black Sea," and even burned his copy of the *Metamorphoses* in despair, although fortunately other copies survived. But he never would be allowed back to Rome before his death.

He took some comfort in the fact that while humans and their civilizations are transformed and destroyed, just as Apollo made the laurel that Daphne became into his emblem, there is an eternity, as the *Metamorphoses'* epilog states, to works of art. And he correctly predicted his own final transformation: *parte tamen meliore mei super alta perennis astra ferar, nomenque erit indelebile nostrum.* "Yet in my better part I shall be borne immortal, far above the stars on high, and mine shall be a name indelible."

✦ GLI OCCHIALE DA SOLE

Who hasn't watched Italian films or seen Italian fashion magazines over the years and said, at some point or other, "I want those sunglasses?"

For most people glasses are worn to correct vision or protect it from UV rays, but for Italians eyewear has long been a fashion statement and *gli occhiali* and *gli occhiali da sole* are most especially an essential element of the Italian wardrobe from little tots on. Designers change frames with each seasonal collection and customers spend lots of money for these highly visible status symbols; one wears sunglasses inside and out, as an elegant substitute for a hair band or a chic accessory tucked into the neckline of a designer tee.

Perhaps that's because of the long, *long* history of glasses and magnifying lenses in Italy. The Roman tragedian Seneca (4 BCE–65 CE) read "all the books of Rome" with the help of a glass globe of water for magnification. Emperor Nero watched gladiator fights through polished gems, an example—on so many levels—of how *not* to wear glasses.

176

$$ \bullet \; O \; \bullet $$

Most historians believe that the first form of eyeglasses was produced in Italy by monks or craftsmen in Pisa (or perhaps Venice) around 1285–1289. The first spectacles were shaped like two small magnifying glasses to assist reading and crudely set into bone, metal, or leather mountings that could be balanced on the bridge of the nose. The first known artistic representation of the use of eyeglasses was by Tommaso da Modena's in 1352. His painting depicts monks reading and writing manuscripts, one wearing that early form of glasses.

Fortunately, over the years, and especially in recent centuries, regular *occhiali* and *occhiali da sole* have become considerably more stylish. On or off the beach, Italians feel naked without them.

♦ OCULUS, GATEWAY TO HEAVEN

When Michelangelo first saw the Pantheon in Rome in the early 1500's, perhaps the best preserved building of antiquity, he said it was of "angelic not human design." Brunelleschi took it as his inspiration for Florence's Duomo. By then the Pantheon was already more than 1350 years old, but even with the passage of five more centuries it remains one of the most influential buildings ever created. Its simple exterior masks an absolutely astonishing interior of perfectly harmonious proportions, and one of its most commanding features is the oculus, sometimes known as a "gateway to heaven:" five rows of carved coffers lead one's gaze perspectively to this eyelike hole in the center of its dome.

In Rome it would have been thought of as a link to the sun that put one properly in mind of worship of the gods. For a long time, the gods did not return the favor. There may have been an ancient Pantheon built to consecrate Romulus's death in the eighth century BCE; if so, no trace of it remains. But in all probability Emperor Marcus Vipsanius Agrippa built the first Pantheon in 27 BCE, a regular rectangle of a building with masonry walls and a timber roof. It burned in the great fire of 80 CE and was built again by Emperor Domitian only to be struck by lightning and burn again in 110 CE.

Ten years later, Emperor Hadrian planned a far more ambitious structure with a circular domed rotunda or vault, which would create a perfect sphere, its height at the oculus matching its diameter, and the oculus and its shaft of light being the only light source. In that way Hadrian meant to "reproduce the likeness of the terrestrial globe and of the stellar sphere..."

with himself on his throne directly beneath the oculus, a demigod around which the very heavens revolved.

This Pantheon not only lasted, it became a model building for the ages, and after the 5th century it ceased to be a shrine to Roman gods when Pope Boniface IV renamed it Santa Maria ad Martyres. Many believe centuries of divinities looking down through its oculus have protected it; very strong *pozzolana* concrete and a brilliantly solid foundation is a more likely explanation.

So it served its purpose of conferring on Hadrian the mark of some kind of divinity, both in his time and for generations to come. But it may have served another purpose as well: that of a sundial. The shaft of light coming through the oculus might have marked the passage of time by working its way around the dome to mark the noon hour and, on the equinoxes and April 21, the traditional anniversary of Rome's founding, striking Hadrian's doorway with a beam of light to celebrate the emperor's divinity. It was the emperor's job to manage the calendar after all; why not dramatize that in the Pantheon and grab some extra glory in the process?

The Pantheon may have marked the time and held many statues of  the gods in Roman days. But in its modern incarnation—beloved by the greatest builders and thinkers from Michelangelo to Palladio to Christopher Wren to Thomas Jefferson (and reflected in his University of Virgina library) it simply inspires us with its somber, perfect beauty, crowned with a beam of light.

✦ ORPHANS OF THE OSPEDALE

By the 17th and 18th centuries, the Republic of Venice had long since slipped into a steady state of commercial and political decline. Especially during the ever-expanding *Carnevale* season, its principal commodity seemed to be that of decadence, as its grandees siphoned off the residual wealth from more productive times. Nearly coincident with (and hardly coincidental *to*) the general decline of the Republic, and signs of its creeping societal dysfunction, was the emergence and growth of a remarkably *functional* institution, the Ospedale della Pietà.

Along with three other *ospedali* operating in Venice at that time, the Ospedale della Pietà had come into being centuries before as a hotel for Crusaders. But as the Crusades receded into the past and the Republic's fortunes also began to ebb, the Pietà and other *ospedale* evolved in their charter to address more local needs: most notably those of orphaned children and foundlings, quite a few of the latter being the products of Venice's increasingly "indiscreet bourgeoisie." (Infants could be left inside a tiny window at the Ospedale della Pietà, not unlike the night depository in a 20th century bank.)

The *ospedali* were extraordinarily progressive institutions in a number of respects. First of all, they represented a rare public/private charitable partnership: the Republic provided some baseline funding but they could not have survived without private donations. Secondly, the *ospedali* were microcosms of resourcefulness and productivity within an otherwise ever more indolent Venetian culture. Young boys were prepared for apprenticeship in trades, and the girls—the great majority of the *ospedali's* residents—were engaged in a variety of revenue-generating pursuits such as making lace, dyeing silk, and mending sails (not to mention producing ethereal music, discussed shortly) to help meet operational expenses as well as to build their own savings and dowries. In fact, an individual bank account was set up for each girl who produced some income. Thirdly, the *ospedali* were remarkable centers of female empowerment, in many cases affording girls opportunities to learn, earn, save, and advance on the equivalent of "career tracks" either to possible leadership positions within the institution or to advantageous marriages or employment beyond it; indeed, many young women who started life orphaned or abandoned in the *ospedali* ultimately fared better than their female counterparts on the outside in a society with far more circumscribed roles for women.

But the *ospedali*, and the Pietà in particular, were most renowned in their own time for the transcendent performances of their female musicians and singers, the latter called *figlie di coro* or "daughters of the choir." Although all the female residents experienced at least some basic education in the musical arts, the most promising girls were nurtured with the utmost attention and discipline, a natural outgrowth of the institution's religious organization. (Although none of the *ospedali* were officially affiliated with the Church, their internal activities were structured around those of a convent or monastery.) In time the concerts and other performances by these young women attracted widespread attention, and the consequent revenues came to represent a substantial portion of each institution's funding. Some of the most accomplished young performers were showered with gifts, invited to vacation in villas on the mainland, offered marriage proposals by well-heeled admirers, or blessed with professional opportunities beyond the institution.

But why did the Ospedale della Pietà achieve preeminence in the Venetian musical landscape? Largely on account of a single figure: the composer, conductor, and violin virtuoso, Antonio Vivaldi. He spent nearly thirty of his last forty years in positions from violin master to overall music master at the institution. Dubbed *Il Prete Rosso* (The Red Priest) for his shock of bright red curly hair, Vivaldi was excused from his ecclesiastical duties for respiratory or cardiac health reasons, but he proved hearty enough during his tenure at the Pietà to compose, conduct, and often perform in hundreds of his own concerti and other works. He also created and managed productions for the Teatro San Angelo, a Venetian opera house, and for opera companies elsewhere on the Italian peninsula. Never modest, Vivaldi once boasted to a patron that he could compose faster than a copyist could write out his scores.

Besides being prone to exaggeration, *Il Prete Rosso* was notoriously thin-skinned, preemptively parrying the anticipated slights of critics in the introduction to his first published set of scores. Yet for all his personal eccentricities, there is no detracting from Vivaldi's formidable talents and influence. An original and leading light in the expressive yet controlled style known as the Baroque, Vivaldi served as perhaps the greatest source of inspiration to none other than Johann Sebastian Bach. For all that, mere decades after his death at age 63 in 1741, Vivaldi's reputation fell into obscurity for nearly a century and a half until the early 20th century, when Bach scholars began to revive it. Perhaps, ultimately, the reinstatement of Vivaldi's reputation as a seminal figure in the Baroque is Bach's greatest "resurrection."

◆ PRIMAVERA SPRINGS ETERNAL

Primavera—can there be a more delightfully pictorial or euphonious Italian word? The derivation of this Italian word for "spring"is from two Latin roots: *primo* meaning "first" and *ver* meaning "spring" (as a verb "spring" means to well up, leap forth, and to come into existence, and the verb has become a noun that describes the cycle of nature it characterizes). And it sounds as lovely as its season.

No wonder Italians seem to want to use it in all sorts of categories: from the culinary to the musical to the visual arts.

~ Culinary: The whole world knows and enjoys Pasta Primavera, a light dish made with crisp vegetables such as broccoli, carrots, peas, spring onions, bell peppers, and tomatoes, typically featuring aromatic herbs, bright colors and a sauce of garlic and olive oil finished with Parmesan cheese. But surprisingly this dish is NOT traditional at all and, in fact, under this name, it was an American creation ascribed to Italian-American Sirio Maccioni, owner of New York City's Le Cirque in the early 1970s.

~ Musical: As previously noted, Antonio Vivaldi (1678–1741), Italian composer, priest, and virtuoso violinist born in Venice, is regarded today as one of the greatest Baroque composers and renowned for his instrumental concertos for the violin. His best known work is a series of violin concertos known as *The Four Seasons*, considered one of the boldest examples of program music (music created with a certain narrative or central purpose) of that time. This work both tells a story and paints a picture with Vivaldi capturing the essence of each season, especially the carefree, revivifying nature of spring. By one estimate, the first concerto, "Primavera," is the most well-recognized and loved piece of classical music in the world (with the first bars of "Spring" rivaling the opening of Beethoven's Fifth Symphony).

~ Visual Arts: *Allegory of Spring,* also known as *Primavera*, was painted in 1482 by Sandro Botticelli and has, like his *Birth of Venus*, become a beloved icon of Western art. The work depicts a group of mythological figures in a garden and is an allegory for the fecundity of spring, so much so that the elaborate scenery has been shown to contain over 500 identified plant species and about 190 different flowers.

In the allegorical framework of the painting (reading right to left), the biting March wind Zephyrus, depicted as a bluish male creature with the aggressively puffed cheeks, kidnaps nymph Chloris, the maiden with flowers springing from her mouth. He then "marries" her and transforms her into the deity Primavera, the goddess and personification of Spring. Primavera then becames both the face of Venus and Flora and bearer of eternally reviving life, and is represented by the flower-crowned figure in a floral-patterned dress scattering roses on the ground. Clustered on the left, the Three Graces dance in diaphanous white watched over by Mercury, who guards the garden, providing a spiritual balance to nature's fecundity on the right. Somewhat set apart from the others, but very much in the center of all the springtime action, and harmonizing it all, is Venus, goddess of love and grace, who serenely presides over the garden and invites us to join in the celebration of *la primavera.*

♦ PAPARAZZI

It's become one of the most famous and infamous of Italian terms, denoting the ever-present horde of publicity photographers; Lady Gaga has sung about them and famous celebrities have slugged some of them.

The word "paparazzi" is an eponym (meaning the name of a real or fictitious person given to a particular place, era, discovery, or other item) that originated in the 1960 film *La Dolce Vita*, directed by Federico Fellini. A character in the film is a news photographer whose surname was Paparazzo, hence the connection to the usage of the word today.

The origin of the name Paparazzo is disputed, but its similarity to the Sicilian word for a large mosquito, *papataceo,* connects with Fellini's statement: "'Paparazzo suggests to me a buzzing insect, hovering, darting, stinging." That's expressed in the staging and filming of the scenes of the paparazzi chasing the main characters in *La Dolce Vita* and swarming them at every opportunity. Fellini also drew one of his famous caricatures of the character—a humanoid figure lacking any bone structure that looked like a vampirish insect—suggesting that paparazzi, like mosquitoes, are also parasites … or at the very least shutterbugs.

♦ PATRON SAINT OF CHEFS … AND COMEDIANS?

A patron saint in Roman Catholicism is regarded as a heavenly advocate. Every day of the year; every aspect of life; every nation, city, occupation or craft, activity, class, clan, family, or person has its own protector. For example, if you lose something you invoke Saint Anthony, if you have what seems to be a lost cause, Saint Jude. And the "patroni" are not randomly attributed; rather there is an associated link to the saint's life story and miraculous works.

Saint Lawrence is the patron saint of chefs, comedians, and firefighters. These connections seem wildly incongruous until you know the story of his martyrdom. Lawrence was a deacon in Rome in the early third century CE when Christians were being aggressively persecuted. He was responsible for his church's treasury. The Prefect of Rome demanded that Lawrence relinquish the riches of his church to the Empire; in defiance Lawrence gave away everything to the poor and then presented his indigent, crippled, and suffering congregants and said they were the true treasures of the church. One account records him declaring to the Prefect, "The Church is truly rich, far richer than your emperor." He was sentenced to death on the gridiron. He is always depicted in art with his grill (known as his "attribute"). While being roasted over hot coals (now you understand chef and firefighter connection) he was reputed to have cheerfully cracked a joke (the comedian connection) quipping "I am well done, turn me over."

If you find this too gruesome for words, don't be upset; most historians believe the roasting to be apocryphal. He was certainly martyred, but most likely by beheading, which was the standard fate of recalcitrant Christians. The "roasting" is thought to have been a mistranslation caused by the omission of the letter *p* in a crucial text: *assusest* means he roasted, while *passusest* means he suffered, which would be more typical (perhaps one should appeal to the patron saint of proofreaders).

What does the creation of a saint based, essentially, on what might be called black humor say about the whole assignment of *patroni*? You could call it religious absurdity or a compassionate exercise of the imagination. There's something about the practice that's guileless, loving, gentle and rooted in the people's hopes and dreams in a way that transcends papal politics. The *patroni* serve as a down-to-earth tool to help maintain spiritual grace. In that sense, as Lawrence might have said: well done.

♦ THIS LITTLE PIGGY CAME FROM PARMA

Prosciutto, pancetta, bacon, coppa, capicola, speck . . . What's the difference?

They all have a similar look and they all have a similar taste and they can often be substituted for each other. And when glimpsed on a menu by a non-Italian-speaker they are inevitably bewildering. Here's how these tasty morsels are different.

Pancetta versus Bacon: Pancetta (from the diminutive of the Latin *pancia* for "belly") and bacon are both from pork belly and both are cured for a period of time, considered raw, and need to be cooked before eating. How they are cured is how they are different. Pancetta is salt-cured but with a little creativity it can be flavored with a whole variety of spices. Bacon is also cured but it is cold-smoked afterwards; the taste we all love can be further enhanced with a variety of woods infused with flavors such

186

as apple or maple. Pancetta and bacon are interchangeable, but for a smokier flavor choose bacon.

Prosciutto and Speck: These are two related salumi with no similarity to pancetta, even if prosciutto also begins with a "p"—not to mention that "speck" sounds slightly frightening and maybe not even like a food term. The term prosciutto is derived—surprise—from Latin, as in *pro* for "before" and *exsuctus* (to suck moisture away from); both prosciutto and speck are made from the hind leg of a pig. The quality of the prosciutto depends on how it's cured, and on what kind of mix of salt and spices the piggy is rubbed with. That spicy massage is meant to, as prosciutto's name implies, extract the moisture while the ham air-dries (and that can take up to several years). Once cured, prosciutto is usually thinly sliced and eaten as is—technically raw, it's hardly ham sushi when it's been cured as long as primo dry-aged beef. Prosciutto di Parma is considered the gold standard of Italian prosciutto, and it has been for centuries, enjoying the coveted Protected Denomination of Origin (PDO) status.

Speck, on the other hand, is typical of the northern regions of Alto Adige and Südtirol, where the cool dry climate is perfect for curing meats. Speck goes through a two-part curing process: first it's rubbed with a blend of spices (supposedly a well-kept secret but it's usually juniper, bay or laurel, pepper and garlic) and salt-cured; then it's cold-smoked in the central European tradition, which gives it its characteristic smokiness. It can be eaten like prosciutto and also holds up well in cooking, giving dishes a flavor similar to bacon but without a lot of extra fat. You can substitute it for bacon, pancetta, or prosciutto in most recipes. It also makes a most excellent midnight snack.

Capicola and Coppa were virtually the same. In Piedmonte the *salumi* is called Coppa, and in parts south like Calabria it is Capicola. Made from the neck or shoulder of the pig, its name derived from *capo* ("head") and *collo* ("neck"). It is distinct from prosciutto because, in the curing process, it is coated in either black pepper or hot red pepper which defines the taste as either being sweet when cured with black pepper, or hot when red pepper is used. The neck and shoulder of the pig is particularly tender because of the higher fat content, and the marbled fat is very important to the final flavor as it helps to balance the sharpness the spices impart. Capicola is also known as "gaba'goul," made famous by *The Sopranos*, so when you're having it, you're in good bad company.

♦ PECORINO, CHEESE AND WINE

Sheep rule in Sardinia. There are more than twice as many sheep as people (4 million vs 1.6 million) so not surprisingly the Sardinians are famous for their "sheep cheese," or Pecorino Sardo. "Pecorino" comes from the word *pecora*, meaning "sheep."

Pecorino Sardo is a hard un-cooked cheese but quite distinct from its more famous cousin Pecorino Romano, with a richer, less salty, and less biting flavor. Of the two main varieties, Pecorino Sardo Dolce and Pecorino Sardo Maturo, the Dolce variety is young and soft and matures between three weeks to two months; as the name suggests, it's sweeter than the older version and labeled with a green emblem to distinguish it from the Maturo. Maturo is aged for about four to twelve months, is tangy and a little crumbly, and is labeled in blue.

What might surprise you is that, more and more, Pecorino also turns up on wine lists! For pecorino is also a unique Italian white grape varietal native to the Marche and Tuscany regions that got its name because the shepherds, while tending their flocks, also tended the vines and named the grape based on its pretty pale blush color which reminded them of the color of a sheep's sheared skin. Pecorino is a deliciously different dry white wine with a nice minerality and that lovely straw-yellow blush hue, and it has a sophisticated floral bouquet of acacia and jasmine, sometimes tinged with a faint hint of licorice.

This excellent grape almost went extinct. While steadily cultivated in the Marche for hundreds of years, it had been a lower-yielding grape, and in the last century the vines had been steadily replaced by more prolific grape varieties like Trebbiano until, by the 1950s, Pecorino was thought to have vanished. Thankfully, in the 1980s, a local producer investigated a rumor that proved to be true: that there were still some forgotten vines in an overgrown vineyard. With characteristic Italian ingenious industriousness not to mention a nose for profits as well as wine, cuttings were taken and propagated, and eventually they grew to make a very good wine by the 1990s. Since then, the variety's plantings have increased tremendously, and Pecorino is now cultivated in Marche, Abruzzo, Umbria, and Tuscany.

Coincidentally a perfecto pairing for Pecorino is … Pecorino!

◆ PEGGY'S PALAZZO

Her great passions were art, men, and her little dogs too.

She was known as the Mistress of Modernism, and she titled her memoirs *Confessions of an Art Addict*. Peggy Guggenheim's life, beginning in America but culminating in the most artistic realm of Italy, was as passionate and colorful as her stunning art collection that sits rather unobtrusively on the banks of the Grand Canal in Venice. She and her artistic tastes played an important role in the modern art movement in the United States, and it is thanks largely to her influence that Venice became a mecca for contemporary art and the Dorsoduro an arty bohemian neighborhood.

Born in 1898 to wealth and some sadness—her beloved father died on the Titanic when she was thirteen—she moved at a young age to the immortally bohemian Paris of the early '20s and became part of Hemingway's "Moveable Feast" for the next twenty years. Her lifetime passion for art began with Renaissance painting, and she wrote after her arrival in Paris "I soon knew where every painting in Europe could be found." Although not artistic herself, she immersed herself in art circles and loved being surrounded by boundary-busting creative activity. She was close to those iconoclasts who created it, the avant-garde—life's underdogs. That was the exact opposite of her life, and this greatly appealed to her, both in mind and body. She had countless lovers in Paris (as she did her entire life) and two marriages that ended in divorce.

In 1938 she hit upon the idea of starting a modern art gallery in London, utilizing the great eye she had for those artists she'd met in Paris who would be the prime movers of 21st century art. At her new Guggenheim Jeune, she gave Kandinsky his first London exhibition, followed by a show of contemporary sculpture featuring Henry Moore, Jean Arp, Constantin

Brancusi, and Alexander Calder. Her gallery succeeded brilliantly and she moved on to the next step: a modern art museum. The one slight problem was that Europe was on the brink of war, but instead of hightailing home she got out her checkbook and fearlessly went on a buying spree (assisted by Marcel Duchamp) famously resolving to "buy a picture a day."

Artists and dealers fleeing Europe with no idea of what the future might hold were happy to sell to her what the Germans considered "degenerate art" at grossly knocked-down prices. She had no idea of that future either, but bought surrealist works by Dali, Braque, Picasso, Mondrian, and Leger in the winter of 1939, and in the spring of 1940 acquired Miros, Picassos, paintings by Max Ernst and sculptures by Brancusi. As the German army advanced on Paris, she finally fled France in July of 1941 (with Max Ernst, her then husband) and headed for New York, having spent only $40,000 to amass her original collection.

In 1942 she opened a gallery in Manhattan to exhibit her acquisitions. Although she was wealthy by any standard, and could've lived merely as a professional heiress with a hedonistic social life, she instead gutsily persisted in an art world then dominated by men, raising New York's art profile to international levels. As European artists' work flowed through her New York gallery she began supporting unknown Americans whose own visions were energized by those works and who would ultimately show in the gallery themselves, like Robert Motherwell, Mark Rothko, and the gallery's star attraction, Jackson Pollock.

After the war she cast her own spell on the city of magical illusions and reflections when she was asked to exhibit her collection at the 1948 Venice Biennale. Her collection of European artists, her Pollacks, Rothkos, and Gorkys shown for the first time in Europe was a hit and was thought to epitomize modern western art. The next year she bought the Palazzo Venier Dei Leoni which, after her collection toured major cities in Europe, would become its permanent home. Art suffused every room, including an Alexander Calder silver headboard adorned her bed, and American sculptor Claire Falkenstein was commissioned to create the main gates of the compound featuring welded iron rods around large colored pieces of Venetian glass.

Peggy's is the smallest of the Guggenheim collections, yet it continues to capture the imagination of art lovers the world over and is one of the most visited modern art museums in the world. And she herself was a jazzy work of art very much at home in Venice and truly enlivening the city, an audacious American woman fond of flamboyant earrings (which she displayed on her bedroom walls), gowns by Fortuny, and above all her signature butterfly-winged glasses designed by artist Edward Melcarth. She commissioned galas and parties until the end of her days and owned 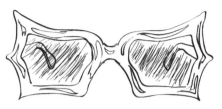 one of the last private gondolas in Venice. Fun, fabulous, eccentric images of her are still famous today, showing her cruising the canals in her signature sunglasses (perhaps their "wings" were really meant to be the wings of the Lion of Venice), draped in jewelry, with red lipstick, pouffed hair, and one of her faithful and equally pouffed little Lhasa Apsos.

In 1951 Peggy began opening the Palazzo to the public during the summer months and continued adding to her collection over the next thirty years, ultimately bequeathing it all to the Solomon Guggenheim Foundation. After her death in December 1979, she still kept two of her passions close to her; her ashes were buried in a corner of her sculpture garden, near the final resting places of her fourteen beloved little Lhasas.

♦ PONTE VECCHIO'S SURPRISE SAVIOR

Ponte Vecchio means simply "old bridge," and, true to its name, it's the oldest bridge in Florence. It crosses the Arno at its narrowest point and is believed to be a successor to a Roman bridge erected on the same spot. The current bridge was rebuilt in 1345 and has been the home of the city's goldsmiths, whose shops form an utterly unique cubist assemblage on its flank for nearly 500 years.

The Ponte Vecchio was the only bridge in Florence to have survived World War II. Its fortuitous survival was not due to divine intervention (quite the opposite) and its fate was directly linked to the Vasari Corridor: a kilometer-long covered passageway supported by arches that passes over the Ponte Vecchio and all the bustling activity of the goldsmith trade.

Named for its architect, Giorgio Vasari, the elevated and well-camouflaged passageway was commissioned in 1565 by Cosimo I, the great-great grandson of Cosimo de Medici and grandson of Lorenzo, on the occasion of the wedding between his son, Francesco. and Joanna of Austria. The corridor would assure that the Medici could move freely, safely, and privately between the government headquarters at Uffizi and their home at Palazzo Pitti. There were small windows through which they could survey the streets and the river. At this time the Ponte Vecchio was populated with butcher shops since it was convenient to toss their waste into the river. The sight was not so pretty, nor was the smell coming through the windows, and so in 1593 the Medici Grand Dukes ordered the butcher shops off the bridge and had them replaced with the goldsmith shops which to this day characterize the Ponte Vecchio.

For the first two hundred years the corridor was used only as a passage back and forth between the government offices and residence and, although it was just a kilometer long, the trip was usually done by a small carriage suitable for two passengers. According to the final will of the last Medici, Anna Maria Luisa d' Medici, the Uffizi and the Vasari Corridor became public property and the Vasari Corridor lost its function as a private passageway.

Today the Vasari Corridor is closed to the general public but it can be visited on a guided tour with a reservation through the Uffizi. You enter a silent space and experience an inaccessible place that seems a world apart from the crowded museum. The collection of artwork displayed along the corridor comprises works by 15th and 16th century artists and a unique collection of artist self-portraits from Andrea del Sarto to Marc Chagall. After you have crossed the Arno over the Ponte Vecchio there is a view into the small church of Santa Felicita, where the Medici worshiped. There is a large window (now fenced) onto a balcony that looks directly into the church; from here the Medici were able to attend mass from a privileged vantage. Artwork aside, what is most exceptional about being in the Corridor is the elevated perspective. This was of great importance to the Medici—the ability to see everything going on while no one knows you are looking. You can feel a little bit like Florentine royalty as you pass through and observe the city completely unnoticed by the people on the streets below.

The central part of the Corridor that passes over the Arno is the most beautiful, with an incredibly panoramic view point exactly halfway over the Ponte Vecchio. Mussolini loved this particular spot and its view to Santa Trinità. In anticipation of Hitler's official visit to Florence in 1939 he ordered that the small windows be enlarged. The story goes that Hitler was so moved by the magnificent panorama that when the Germans were in retreat he ordered all bridges in Florence be destroyed except for the Ponte Vecchio. Though it seems utterly inconceivable that Hitler could show any mercy to anything connected to humanity, even to something inanimate, the Ponte Vecchio and Vasari Corridor still stand today.

♦ PLAGUE DOCTOR

It's a Bird … It's a Beast …It's *Medico della Peste*—the popular, highly distinctive plague doctor mask, or perhaps more aptly put, "the birdman of the black plague."

In the Venice of today, with its overabundance of visual stimulation—bridges, canals, watery reflections, dazzlingly colored glass, and curiosities of all descriptions, not to mention all sorts of outlandish costumes and masks worn fairly frequently throughout the year—it seems reasonable not to give something even that macabre a second thought. But think of this: why not just a mask of a bizarre avian beast, or simply one with a larger-than-life schnozzola from the country that gave us Pinocchio? Why this particular, and particularly bizarre, head-to-toe design?

The answer is that this costume is a fairly accurate rendition of a 17th-century "biohazard" suit doctors wore when treating plague victims. Here is a description of the suit written by Charles de Lorme, the personal physician to Louis XIII of France who is credited with inventing it:

> *The nose (is) half a foot long, shaped like a beak, filled with perfume with only two holes, one on each side near the nostrils, but that can suffice to breathe and carry along with the air one breathes the impression of the (herbs) enclosed further along in the beak. Under the coat we wear boots made of Moroccan leather (goat leather) from the front of the breeches in smooth skin that are attached to said boots, and a short sleeved blouse in smooth skin, the bottom of which is tucked into the breech-*

es. The hat and gloves are also made of the same skin...with spectacles over the eyes.

The bird-beaked mask probably predates the full ensemble by a few centuries; it served as a sort of gas mask filled with perfume and herbs. Doctors based the design on the incorrect assumption that the plague was transmitted by a cloud of poisonous vapor in the air known as miasma, created by decay and identifiable by a bad smell. Following the logic that bad-smelling air carried the disease, it made perfect sense that you could "cure" the air by making it smell good. Hence the perfume and the long nose designed to be stuffed with pleasantly aromatic material.

Versions of the mask survive today bearing black circles around the eyeholes connected by a curved black line: these represent actual spec-

tacles the plague doctors had on their masks to further block the pernicious miasma from the doctors' faces. The mask was tucked into the long black coat. Including gloves and boots, the leather ensemble was a covering designed to protect the doctors' skin from contact with the disease. And everything was waxed so the suit was impermeable. The final touch to the plague protection was a wooden stick that allowed the doctors to poke and prod while making as little physical contact with the infected patient as possible.

Despite the total erroneousness of the whole bad air concept, the costume was a fairly effective way to protect the doctor against disease. However, one has to wonder what possible good a doctor looking like the angel of death (and prodding the sufferer with a wooden stick) could do for the overall mental and emotional resilience of the patient.

The epidemics took thousands of lives throughout Europe. Venice, a major port city and crossroads to the Orient for ships in the lucrative spice trade, was especially susceptible to what turned out to be bubonic plague bacteria carried by shipborne rats and fleas that hitched rides along with their precious cargoes. Fortunately the only legacy of those terrible years that remains in Venice are three major plague churches (Saint Rocco, Il Rendentore, and Santa Maria Della Salute) and two annual festivals celebrated in gratitude for the end of two very deadly epidemics.

As well, of course, as those present-day versions of the plague doctor mask and costume which, in fine Italian fashion, have transmuted a terrible passage in European history into a note of sardonic life-enhancing humor in Venetian revelry. They're associated with the *commedia dell'arte* character Il Medico della Peste, and the Carnevale decorative rendition of the plague doctor mask is now a familiar sight. And the mask hasn't escaped the notice of filmmakers, especially one of the most perceptive of them all; it makes the orgy scene in Stanley Kubrick's *Eyes Wide Shut* just a little bit spookier.

◆ PLINY THE ELDER, STORYTELLER OF THE WORLD

Second only to Aristotle, Gaius Plinius Secundus, known as Pliny the Elder, was probably the most influential scholar of Antiquity. Former cavalry officer, advisor to Emperors, holder of numerous official positions, and author of at least seventy-five books (plus 160 volumes of unpublished notebooks) Pliny, clearly an over-the-top workaholic, is remembered for just one of those books (the only one to survive): the thirty-seven volume *Historia Naturalis* (Natural History). A man with a  voracious hunger for knowledge of all kinds, his stated ambition for *Historia Naturalis* was "to set forth in detail all the contents of the entire world." As a Roman citizen, he had reason to believe that the world was encompassed by the Empire to which he belonged. Thus Rome, through Pliny, gave us the world's collection of "encyclic culture," or *enkyklios paedia*: the first encyclopedia, and a fascinating window into life in ancient Rome and the worldview of his fellow Romans.

Volume 1 alone, with the Table of Contents and a preface dedicated to Emperor Titus, was seventy pages when translated to English. Volumes 2–6 covered cosmology, astronomy, and geography; Volume 7, Man (as a general topic); Volumes 8–11, zoology; Volumes 12–19, botany; Volumes 20–27, the medicinal use of plants; Volume 28–32, medicines derived from animals; and Volumes 33–37, rocks, metals, and precious stones and their use in art. The importance of his work lay in how he carefully observed, identified, and organized previously random facts, patterns, and important details missed by others—especially in fields like botany and agriculture. He once, for example, described an ox-driven grain harvester in Gaul that was considered fantasy until a 1958 discovery of a 2nd-century relief depicting its use. His volumes on plants and the medicinal use of plants shaped scientific and medical theory up through the Middle Ages, and contain much of the beginnings of today's herbal medicine.

Given the limited historiographic and fact-checking resources of the time (such as the difficulty of going to Africa—and as for libraries on the natural history of the continent his book was the first and only one anyway), accuracy wasn't always his work's strong suit. Some of the *Historia Naturalis* stretched nature quite a bit, based on secondhand accounts of faraway lands that were, to say the least, fanciful. Plus he was ecumenical and eclectic, to put it mildly, in his philosophy of what facts he wanted to report: he stated "*Aliena memoria salutamus, aliena vivimus opera, alienis oculis agnostimus* ("We welcome unfamiliar memories, we preserve unfamiliar work, we observe with unfamiliar eyes").

And so he wrote of the real and fantastic: dog-headed people who bark, snakes that propel themselves skyward to catch birds, evil-eyed Illyrians, bear cubs born as shapeless lumps that had to be licked into shape by their mother, monsters from places like India and Ethiopia. He described the origin of cinnabar as the blending of elephant and dragon blood resulting from a vicious battle between the two. Magic and superstition were all over the Natural History, and would influence much subsequent pseudoscientific thinking. Modern science historian Brian Cummings has described Pliny as "endearingly batty." However, he must have possessed a modicum of skepticism—he qualified much information with "some say" or "so the story goes," which certainly made him a lot less "batty" than many writers on the Internet today.

His history of his own culture is far more accurate and useful. Much of what we know of day-to-day Roman life and specific events comes from Pliny, including cities that have long since ceased to exist. We owe to him the first recording of the location of notable sites and detailed descriptions of ancient Roman works of art, and his writings became incredibly helpful during the Renaissance as a combination map and interpretive guide for Renaissance scholars and artists who revered ancient Rome and wanted to cull as much information about the city as possible.

Pliny is, of course, no longer the authority he was up to the sixteenth century, when his errors became increasingly, even comically obvious. But he's remembered as first of all a relentless reporter of a world both real and imaginary, always accompanied on his walks by someone taking his dictation. He was also the Ben Franklin of his day, as many quotes from his work attest:

> *In wine there is truth (In vino veritas).*
>
> *In all matters, the only certainly is that nothing is certain.*
>
> *Home is where the heart is.*
>
> *The happier the moment, the shorter.*
>
> *From the end springs new beginnings.*
>
> *Lead by example; example is the softest and least invidious way of commanding.*
>
> *An object in possession seldom retains the same charm that it had in pursuit.*
>
> *It is generally more shameful to lose a good reputation than to never have acquired it.*
>
> *There is always something new out of Africa.*
>
> *The most valuable discoveries have found their origin in the most trivial accidents.*
>
> *Nature is to be found in her entirety nowhere more than in her smallest creatures.*

But he also, as a Roman and Italian, exemplified the combination of ornery courage and curiosity that would fuel so much intellectual discovery on the peninsula and in the Western world in later centuries. That natural curiosity compelled him, while commanding a fleet in the Bay of Naples, to seek to get close to Vesuvius while it was exploding in August of 79 CE. He went out into the Bay of Naples in a boat to examine and document the volcano's smoke cloud and died of asphyxiation; his body was later found on the beach, a martyr to the natural science he helped to create.

◆THE QUEEN
WHO REFINED THE FRENCH

◆ ◆ ◆

◆RENAISSANCE MAN

◆ROCK STAR OF THE RENAISSANCE

◆ROCKS OF CAPO TESTA

◆RELICS, REST IN PIECES

◆ROCCO, PATRON SAINT OF DOGS
AND MORE

◆RUNNING OF THE SAINTS

◆ROME'S DECORATOR

◆RIDOTTO "ROYALE"

✦ THE QUEEN WHO REFINED THE FRENCH

It took an Italian orphan to trigger a revolution of culture and cuisine in France.

Caterina, great-granddaughter of Lorenzo the Magnificent, lost both her parents within three weeks of her birth. She was a bright child who managed to obtain an excellent education from demanding nuns overseen by two Medici popes. At the age of only fourteen, wearing elevated shoes—the first high heels—she was married to Henry of Orleans (also only fourteen), the son of King Frances I of France, by her uncle Pope Clement VII, who had taken a keen interest in the strategic alliance represented by their union.

She arrived in France with her dowry, which included her Florentine chefs and samples of her favorite vegetables and legumes, some of which had never been seen in France, including broccoli, peas, savory cabbage, and the exotic artichoke. Although her teenage husband neglected her for the charms of Diane de Poitiers, a beautiful woman twenty years his senior, her father-in-law greatly enjoyed Caterina's company and found her to have a sharp mind and quick wit, and to be better educated than the ladies at court, as well as being especially skilled in equestrian arts. Caterina, incidentally, is credited with inventing the sidesaddle; in fact, a bit of a cult has developed around her regarding a variety of cultural contributions. On a good day she can also be credited with the creation of britches.

The culinary realm was the truly productive aspect of her reign. Over the next several decades, Caterina's chefs helped cultivate an appreciation in the French court for veal, sweetbreads, aspics, onion soup, duck a l'orange, and other well-sauced delights. Caternia was especially fond of spinach and a dish including it that was called "*alla Fiorentina*" in her honor. She had quite a sweet tooth too, and brought to her court the charms of sorbets and ice cream, fruits in syrup, pastries, zabaglione, custards, and frangipani. She also popularized gracious table settings, luxurious silverware, and even the humble fork, which had come to Italy from the Byzantine Empire and Constantinople via Venice and was used in Italy at a time the rest of Europe looked upon it as pretentious.

From elegant Venetian glass goblets to perfumes, fine lingerie, and the ballet, she fostered the cultivation of many refinements. She also brought woman into the dining room. Before her reign Frenchwomen ate separately from the men because chewing was thought to distort their faces; perhaps this odd perception was based on the fact that table manners, if they could be called that, were abominable at the time. She was also a bit of an impresario and was known for orchestrating elaborate garden festivals including ballet and dramatic performances, and contributed to the design of the Tuileries and the lyrically harmonious architecture (featuring beautiful arches) of the Chateau de Chenonceau.

So the French can be thankful for the period when her husband was King and left her with so much idle time on her hands. As it turns out, not that much idle time—she ultimately bore the king ten children—but she remained in the shadow of Diane until Henry's death in a fluke accident during a jousting tournament in 1559.

As a more politically involved widowed queen and regent she lived another thirty years, and here her record is definitely mixed; her obsession with the destiny of her children and her lack of understanding of the Huguenot crisis would mean that political history would be less than kind to her and

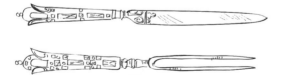 characterize her as dictatorial and unscrupulous. She lived in turbulent times and was something of an outsider in her adopted country.

But it's worth remembering that, true to the Medici legacy, she was a real Renaissance woman, and that the *haute cuisine* of France owes a great deal to a highborn Italian.

R

• RENAISSANCE MAN

If Cosimo de Medici was the founder of Renaissance Florence, his grandson Lorenzo the Magnificent (known as Il Magnifico) was its finest personification. After the brief and unfortunate reign of his father Piero, he succeeded to the position of de facto leader and chief statesman of the Florentine Republic during the height of the Renaissance and became the most remarkable public figure of his time. Not only a wily diplomat and politician, he also headed what we would now call a "salon" of scholars, artists, and poets. And while not the most attractive of his contemporaries, as busts of him with his squashed nose and nearsighted appearance show, he became the idol of a cadre of charismatic young men, for he was accomplished in the manly arts of jousting, hawking, hunting, and racehorse breeding. Devoted to his city, his family, the church, and the pursuit of art and learning, and an accomplished poet himself, was also known to dabble in alchemy and Kabbalah and loved pranks and bawdy humor. *L'uomo universale*, to be sure.

About as much a fortunate son as one could be in Florence (he's even depicted as Caspar the youngest Magi in the Gozzoli masterwork in his grandfather's Magi chapel) he was thrust toward his responsibilities early. He was fifteen when Cosimo died and his father Piero (not hugely respected; he was dubbed "the Gouty") took over Cosimo's duties. By the time Lorenzo was twenty his father's reign had ended and control had passed to his hands—where it was almost snatched from them by members of the Pazzi family conspiracy, who killed his beloved brother and wounded him in a vicious attack (their name became one of the words in Italian for "insane"—as in trying to stop the Florentine Renaissance).

Lorenzo had the conspirators ruthlessly punished, sparing few in their family, and as a result of their assault ruled more despotically than his ancestors with an army of bodyguards and spies. Still he was described as a "pleasant tyrant" by Florentine historian Francesco Guicciardini, in part because he wasn't interested in power for its own sake. Lorenzo once wrote, "In Florence, it's difficult to stay wealthy without controlling the state," and later, in his poem *The Triumph of Bacchus and Ariadne*, "And what's the good of being wealthy/If it doesn't make you happy."

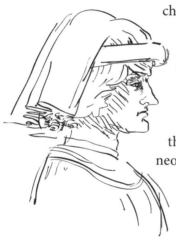

He continued the wise foreign policy of his grandfather, weaving alliances, especially with Naples, to keep Venice in check and to guard against the growing threat of invasion by France. He continued the Platonic academy and created his own salon, which included older artists like Botticelli and the young, impressionable, and brilliant Michelangelo, whom he even housed for awhile. Botticelli, influenced by the thoughts of that salon and the academy's neo-Platonic doctrine of a mystic love that approached Christianity, would paint his two most lushly beautiful and poetic works during Lorenzo's reign: the *Primavera* and *Birth of Venus*.

Lorenzo kept his own personal balance by taking great pleasure in scholarship and the company of learned men, enjoying the company of a circle that included not only artists but Marsilio Ficino and Pico della Mirandola. Perhaps Lorenzo's greatest contribution was to the evolution of the Italian language. He continued his grandfather's efforts to disseminate the knowledge of antiquity. But as a patron of poets and scholars like Politian and della Mirandola, he opposed the new classicists' preference for Latin texts and championed the vernacular of Dante and Boccaccio. Under his patronage, della Mirandola wrote his *Oration on the Dignity of Man* concerning the great chain of being from animals to angels that man can travel, and challenging Church doctrine, especially by accepting elements into his thought of other religions. Meanwhile Lorenzo's friend, Politian, and Lorenzo himself became the outstanding poets of their world. Lorenzo composed in the vernacular, often in sonnet form, poetry of love and nature and *canti carnascialeschi*, songs for Florence's lavish and exuberant carnivals.

To the sustained admiration of his fellow-citizens (now virtually his subjects) of Florence, Lorenzo displayed personal genius, charisma, passion for life, and generous support of art, poetry, philosophy, and music. He loved and collected fine furniture, ceramics, and gems. He managed, in a truly Italian balance, to blend Catholicism and humanism, gaiety and an awareness of life's tragedies. And somehow he managed to combine sagacity as a ruler with a love of satiric verse, pranks and course humor, games, and ruinously overspending the family's fortune. Machiavelli commented on what seemed his impossible combination of the serious ruler and the inveterate gamesman and joker.

With his death in 1492 and the end of his benign and cultured rule, discord would soon come to Italy, signaled by the ruin of the Medici bank. Machiavelli called his death a disaster. A future loomed of Borgia misrule, Savonarola's bonfires of the vanities, and the invasion from France that Lorenzo had worked so hard to prevent. While his grandson Cosimo I would come to power, build the Uffizi, renovate the parish church of San Lorenzo (which houses the Medici tombs) and create the Laurentian Library, the days of Florentine preeminence would soon die away, and Pope Julius II (*see* "Nepotism's Legacy") would move the center of the Renaissance to Rome.

A poem lamenting the loss of beauty and youth by Lorenzo, the first stanza of *The Triumph of Bacchus and Ariadne*, could also stand for the passing of the Camelot-like glories of the Florentine Renaissance after his death:

> *How lovely is our youthful time,*
> *Which flees and brings on endless sorrows!*
> *Let all who will, enjoy their prime—*
> *Not place their trust in vague tomorrows.*

✦ ROCK STAR OF THE RENAISSANCE

Raphael is the painter who was said to have achieved the most graceful grace: *graziosissima grazia*. He was great-looking, charismatic, and charming (he acquired his most excellent manners while in the employement of the elegant court of Urbino), the perfect painter of numerous commissions and the perfect guest; at only twenty-five Raffaello Sanzio was the toast of the town in Florence and then Rome, and everyone invited him to dinner, and often for after dinner besides. Michelangelo, always moody and introspective, was resentful of all the attention the young man received and was said to comment "all that Raphael knows of art he got from me." While it seems ludicrous to think of Michelangelo playing Salieri to Raphael's Amadeus, the dour titan of the arts was after all responding not so much to Raphael the artist as Raphael the rock star of his world.

That reputation was sealed when Raphael made his way to Rome under the patronage of Pope Julius II, who gave him the commission for the incredibly ambitious Stanza della Segnatura (the Signature Room), the Pope's private apartments in the Vatican, used by the Pope as a library.

One wonders if there was an encounter then between him and his angry artistic rival: Michelangelo was painting the Sistine Chapel at the same time Raphael was painting the Stanza. Raphael was friends with Donato Bramante, then architect of the Vatican, who had the keys to the Sistine and let Raphael in for a nocturnal visit. Allegedly Michelangelo was there.

Did (to paraphrase W.B. Yeats) Raphael acquire Michelangelo's knowledge or his power by viewing his masterpieces, as Michelangelo alleged? However much of a libertine Raphael was, he was deadly serious about learning his art, so much so that he risked bodily harm to climb down ladders into the grottoes that at the time concealed Nero's *Domus Aurea* to study the ancient frescoes and learn from them (see "Nero's Golden House").

Raphael utlilized all his learning and skill and rose to the occasion of the Pope's commission with his mural the *School of Athens,* the theme of which was the synthesis of classical Greek and Christian thinking. The Signature Room contains two other of Raphael's best known works: the *Parnassus,* and the *Disputation of the Holy Sacrament.* Theology, Poetry, Philosophy, and Justice, corresponding to the main fields of scientific knowledge of the time, are thus all represented.

The *School of Athens* memorializes the philosophers and men of learning above all, with Plato at the center (with the features of Leonardo da Vinci) pointing skyward, while Aristotle next to him points to the earth. Among the other figures is a Heraclitus with the features of Michelangelo done in what seems to be Michelangelo's style, suggesting Raphael was indeed stunned by the Sistine Chapel. He in turn stuns with this work. Beneath a towering arched basilica decorated with statues of Apollo and Minerva that recedes to an almost impossible distance, numerous wise figures of classical Greece and the Renaissance debate or silently meditate in a widescreen and densely populated but beautifully harmonized tableau, both in terms of the grouping of ideas and human figures. Beautifully chosen colors guide one's eye through the assembly, and the architectural vaulting conveys an unparalleled depth and loftiness of perspective. The mural is considered one of the great masterpieces of *disegno* (the basic drawing that underlies ideally proportioned work).

The School of Athens was an immediate success and would become one of the signature works of the Cinquecento, along with the Sistine Chapel and Leonardo's *Mona Lisa*. Raphael would complete three other Papal apartment rooms in the Vatican (known as the Raphael Rooms), along with numerous altarpieces and portraits, and was to remain in Rome serving successive popes until his sudden death in 1520.

The story of his death became as noteworthy as those of his paintings. Discovered in Raphael's studio at the time of his death was the painting known as *La Fornarina* (*The Bakeress*) and the woman in the painting is thought to be Raphael's Roman mistress, Margherita Luti, the daughter of a baker from Siena. A marriage to a mere peasant girl, the daughter of a baker, might have seriously damaged Raphael's reputation with the Roman and Florentine aristocracy, possibly ending his career. (At the time he was engaged to Maria Bibbiena, his friend Cardinal Medici Bibbiena's niece, for over six years, though evidencing a certain lack of enthusiasm.)

But Margherita is thought to have been the woman Raphael secretly loved until the day he died; according to Giorgio Vasari, in his *Life of Raphael*, Raphael was so in love with his mistress that he could not paint without her by his side. She even had to be smuggled in to live with him in secret so that he could complete his frescoes at the Villa Farnesina, the pleasure palace of his wealthy friend, the Sienese banker Agostino Chigi. In some versions of these stories Raphael's mistress is also smuggled into the Vatican so that he could finish his frescoes for Pope Leo X.

And thus the urban legend of Raphael the sex maniac was born. For the story went around that the ever-carnal and amorous painter died of too much sex with Margherita. After a particularly lusty evening, he came down with a high fever, was bled according to the treatments of the time, and he grew weaker and died on Good Friday. He was thought to be the same age as Jesus at the time of the Crucifixion, or so many in Rome whispered as they universally mourned his passing—except the curmudgeonly genius Michelangelo, who was reputed to have commented, "My thief is dead."

But whatever the circumstances of his death and their life together, there was an artistic marriage and true harmony between Raphael and the baker's daughter in the many portraits for which she doubtless served as a model, with the special liveliness and radiance that characterize so many of Raphael's subjects. In *La Velata* or *La Donna Velata* (*The Veiled Woman*) the model wears a pearl bauble in her hair in both portraits; the name Margherita means "pearl" in Italian. She is thought to have modeled for several Madonnas including the *Madonna della Seggiola* (known as *Madonna of the Chair*), painted around the same time. In the *La Fornarina* portrait she wears a wedding ring and an armband on which is written the name Raphael of Urbino, framed by myrtle branches, symbolic of love and marriage—and these details were only discovered recently when a restoration of the portrait revealed that these symbols had been painted over, apparently by Raphael's discreet assistants after his death.

And so it's right that Raphael is not only in the pantheon of great artists but buried in the Pantheon (along with the fiancée he never wed).

◆ ROCK FORMATIONS OF CAPO TESTA

Sardinia is second largest island in the Mediterranean and one of the most ancient land masses in Europe; it is aligned geologically with Corsica along a mountain chain that arises from the sea floor, and unlike Sicily and mainland Italy, it is not earthquake prone. That beautifully sheltered quality is one of many reasons the Smeralda (Emerald) Coast on Sardinia's northeastern shore has become the playground of billionaires, famed for its giant yachts hosting oligarchs and celebrities like Julia Roberts and Donatello Versace, and for Porto Cervo, a faux-Mediterranean village lined with the most fashionable of emporiums. But beyond this emblem of opulent Italy is an example of immemorial Italian countryside where, even if you can't party like the super-rich, your imagination can play forever with the towering granite bluffs that line the coast, called by natives the realm of the thousand shapes. Hues of peach, pink, and gray predominate, depending on the natural state of the rocks and the light. Stark dramatic forms are carved by the Mediterranean mistral, reminding onlookers of human faces, Roman columns, or clouds. Descending to the headland Capo Testa region near Santa Teresa di Gallura, by car or perhaps (much more Italian) Ducati motorbike, your eyes feast on translucent blue waters; you inhale the juniper,

myrtle, rosemary, and oregano scents of silver-green macchia on the hillsides; perhaps you pause for a swim or a snorkel. But above all your eyes linger on the mighty stones, sculpted by nature in ways that suggest the wildest possible artistry, while losing yourself in a calm Mediterranean beauty that no plutocrat's villa can match.

◆ RELICS, REST IN PIECES

If Italy is a land bountifully blessed with natural and cultural treasures, it's even more so a portal to Heaven, judging from its seemingly endless supply of the one commodity that eclipses all earthbound riches: those myriad artifacts known as religious relics.

When you venture to even the smallest of Italian towns you should not be surprised to find in the local church some form of relic: say, a sacred piece of fabric; or a finger bone enshrined in a gem-encrusted rock crystal reliquary;

or even an entire saint clad in ecclesiastical finery and visible through a glass sarcophagus set into the altar. Such relics—from the Latin *reliquus*, meaning "left behind"—serve as objects of veneration, sources of healing, and even objects of civic pride, power, and prestige. Venice was not the only city in the Middle Ages to "steal" the remains of a saint (see "Leone"), and did so several times; so too did Bari, Siena, and Conques, among others.

Although the veneration of relics is not unique to the Christian faith, the Roman Catholic Church has made their classification into something of a science. A 1st Class Relic would include any part of a saint (say, a bone or tuft of hair) or one of the instruments of Christ's passion. A 2nd Class Relic might include something owned by a saint, or an instrument of torture used against a martyr; 3rd Class Relics—a boon to less privileged parishes—include any object touched by a 1st or 2nd Class Relic.

In a 2010 feature article, *Time* magazine identified what it considered the "Top 10 Religious Relics." Although the list included Muhammad's Beard (preserved at Topkapi Palace in Istanbul, Turkey) and Buddha's Tooth (found in Sri Lanka), fully half of the relics were claimed by Italy: the Shroud of Turin; the Blood of San Gennaro (Naples); Mary's Holy Belt (Proto); John the Baptist's head (Rome, although Muslims claim it's actually in Damascus, Syria); and the Chains of St. Peter (Rome).

Regular celebrations attend some of the more famous relics. Each year on the September 19th anniversary of the martyrdom of St. Gennaro, the people of Naples gather to see the miraculous liquefaction of their patron saint's blood, always regarded as an auspicious sign for the city's well-being. The mysterious and inexplicable annual liquefaction has been occurring for hundreds of years with the first written reference to it dated 1389. On at least two occasions when the saint's blood failed to liquefy, the city endured the calamity of a plague (1527) and an earthquake (1980). When the blood liquefies, the "miracle" is announced accompanied by a 21-cannon salute and the people of Naples cheer as if they had just scored a World Cup goal.

The Feast of San Gennaro has also been celebrated in New York's Little Italy since 1926, a then enclave of newly arrived Neapolitan immigrants. Today it is a much anticipated annual street fair featuring colored lights, sausages, zeppole, and games of chance which culminate in a moving candlelit procession in which a statue of San Gennaro is carried from its home in the Most Precious Blood Church through the streets of Little Italy.

Another curious Italian relic is St. Anthony's tongue. St. Anthony died of natural causes in 1231, was canonized shortly thereafter, but then exhumed in 1263. The saint's body had completely decomposed except for his tongue which remained wet, as in life, and "incorrupt." This miraculous finding was quite naturally associated with Anthony's legendary powers of persuasion as an itinerant preacher throughout Italy and France. Today the saint's "silver" tongue lies in state within a gold reliquary in his namesake basilica in Padua. There parishioners and pilgrims alike venerate "the patron saint of lost things."

The tongue of St. Anthony (as any other sacred relic) still speaks to legions of the faithful.

♦ ROCCO, PATRON SAINT OF DOGS AND MORE

The enterprising, crafty, superstitious, and hot-for-the-ducat Venetians understood the future value of obtaining the bodily remains of the son of a noble governor from France well in advance—about one hundred years—of his eventual canonization. It was not the first time the Venetians had gone to great lengths to secure holy or potentially holy relics for the Republic. St Roch, Rocco in Italian, was eventually designated patron saint of dogs which, granted, is fairly important, since the dog is man's best friend, but that prospect alone would not have merited such a clandestine smuggling mission.

Saint Rocco's story is crowded with more legend than most lives of the saints. He was born of a noble family at the end of the 13th century with a miraculous birthmark on his chest in the shape of a red cross that grew as he grew. Some say he may have studied medicine. Like his mother, he was very pious; when his father, governor of Montpellier, died when his son was twenty, instead of assuming the governorship by his birthright, Rocco stepped aside in favor of his uncle, chose to distribute his substantial fortune among the local poor, and then set out for Italy disguised as a mendicant pilgrim.

En route he fearlessly ministered to those suffering from plague. He affected many cures by his touch or by making the sign of the cross. He soon contracted the plague himself and went into the forest to die, where he was found by a hunting dog who brought him bread and licked his wounds, which began to heal (hence the connection to dogs). One day the dog's owner followed his dog, discovered Rocco, and became his first acolyte.

After Rocco recovered his health he returned home to Montpellier where he was accused of being a spy and imprisoned by his uncle, who failed to recognize him. It was only after he died in prison five years later in 1327, accepting his suffering without complaint, that he was recognized by the red cross-shaped birthmark on his chest. After his public funeral numerous miraculous healings were attested to and he was, in effect, given sainthood by the people, although he was not officially added to the Roman Martyrology of saints until 1590.

And so, in 1414, when a plague broke out in the nearby city of Constance, the town council ordered public prayers in honor of, as they dubbed him, Saint Roch; shortly afterwards the plague abated. After this, intercessions to Saint Roch and his miracle cures built to a cult following. Enter the Venetians who were especially prone to plague as the residents of a port city and who had lost a third of the city population to various epidemics. They built the Church of San Rocco and consecrated it in 1489 four years after they had exhumed and "acquired" Saint Rocco's remains for the Republic. Aside from the protection such prized relics were believed to offer the people and city of Venice, they had the practical effect of enhancing the prestige of the city. And in a common phenomenon in the Italy of those times (and not entirely forgotten today), the remains attracted many pilgrims seeking the Saint's protection. So there was a kind of religious *arrangiarsi* at work.

It still works. St Rocco's feast day remains August 16th and features a popular procession. In addition to being invoked against plague, he is also invoked for cholera, skin diseases, and knee problems; and beyond being "Patrone" of doggies he also specializes in the protection of bachelors, the falsely accused, invalids, and ironically, gravediggers! A saint for the modern age, Rocco has proved to be a multitasker—and portable as well.

• RUNNING OF THE SAINTS

In a beautiful spot that almost seems caught in a pre-Renaissance time warp, in the fortress town of Gubbio (in the region of Umbria just south of Tuscany), the Festa dei Ceri takes place every year on May 15. It celebrates the anniversary of the death of the town's patron saint, St. Ubaldo, in 1160, and is an authentic medieval festival that's an almost hallucinatory fusion of gaiety and religious devotion.

The *ceri* (as in "cherry"), or "candlesticks," are three gigantic wooden structures, beautifully built out of octagonal sections so that they look almost like chess pieces. They are over twenty feet high, 400 kilos in weight (up to 900 pounds), and each are crowned with carvings of the saints Ubaldo, Giorgio, and Antonio (who, respectively, protect masons, merchants, and farmers).

The start of the festival could be a ceremony from a Peter Jackson fantasy movie: amid horn and drum fanfare and a colorfully costumed horde of spectators—a dedicated color for each of the saints (yellow for Ubaldo, blue for Giorgio, and black for Antonio) —three youths leaning on the bases of the giant *ceri* pedestals spreadeagle themselves horizontally toward the crowd to help tilt the platforms to their vertical position. With a roar from the multitude, the *ceri* are caught and hoisted up by the teams of other local young men, the *ceraioli*, who will haul the giant pedestals along the Corsa dei Ceri, at running speed, to their destinations.

But there are no special effects here, though you might think so seeing videos of the rocking *ceri* towering over and moving through the crowd. The shouts of the multitude accompany the *ceraioli* every step of the way, from their circling of the central Piazza Grande to their downhill, then uphill journey (often switching out porters) on a very difficult, tiring, even dangerous 2.5-mile path to the Basilica of St. Ubaldo at the top of Mt. Ingino. Though it takes the ritual form of a race, it's not one you want to bet on, given that it's preordained that St. Ubaldo wins every time, so as to herald a year of good fortune for the town.

The authenticity and abiding continuity of the festival is such that the *ceri* are exact replicas of the originals, are over one-hundred-twenty-five years old, and were restored just three years ago. For the men who become their porters, it's a rite of passage; they train for it throughout their lives.

The festival inspires such passion among people of the region and their descendants that homesick Italian soldiers enacted it within the bloody landscape of World War II. And in the United States, Jessup, Pennsylvania, just outside of Scranton, performs a nearly identical "Race of the Saints" to celebrate St. Ubaldo's day on the Saturday of Memorial Day weekend.

What accounts for the enduring appeal of the festival? The springtime date, the almost Bacchic level of group celebration and the distinctive shape of the proud "candlesticks" (which observers have frequently likened to phallic symbols) give it the spirit of a more ancient fertility ritual. The dates curiously coincide with an older pagan festival. Perhaps the five hour lunch break (this is Italy after all) and the increasingly exuberant parties during that lunch and after the race's conclusion are both feasts of nature's renewal and invocations for abundance to come. It wouldn't be the first time in world history—and especially in Italy's—that elements of Christianity have fused with earlier pagan rites. It just happens to be one of the happiest and most colorful.

◆ ROME'S DECORATOR

Among the many artistic treasures displayed in Rome's not-to-be-missed Borghese Gallery is *The Rape of Persephone*, a marble sculpture that depicts the mythical kidnapping of the daughter of Zeus and Demeter by Hades, god of the underworld. Nearly airborne in her abductor's arms, Persephone tries mightily to twist away, the pivotal moment frozen in stone for posterity. As powerful as the overall drama of these struggling figures may be, many observers find one detail especially compelling: where Hades' right hand grabs Persephone's thigh we can see his fingers indent her soft flesh, the hard marble miraculously incarnate.

Less than an hour's walk west, just across the Tiber, we can stand within the monumental square of St. Peter's Basilica and find ourselves in a more welcoming and spiritual embrace—in the massive curved arms of its twin colonnades—as have millions of pilgrims before us.

One remarkable man was the stage master of these two quintessentially Roman experiences plus a great many more: Gian Lorenzo Bernini (1598–1680), the Baroque genius of gestures grand and small. It is difficult to recall another artist whose lifetime achievements made a greater difference in the look and the life of a major city.

214

Those achievements were the product of unusually auspicious circumstances, a singularly prodigious talent, a cyborg's capacity for grueling physical labor, and the bonus of a long life.

Bernini was fortunate to be born to a sculptor father, Pietro, who moved from Naples to Rome to work for Cardinal Scipione Borghese and the cardinal's uncle, Pope Paul V, when he was just seven. Young Gian Lorenzo studied classical works of the Renaissance masters Michelangelo and Raphael in the Vatican Museum, and apprenticed with his father. When the skills and talents of his young boy seemed destined to eclipse his own, the elder Bernini reputedly said, "It doesn't bother me, for as you know in that case the loser wins." Around age eleven the younger Bernini sculpted a bust of Giovanni Battista Santori that caught the eye of Pope Paul V who reportedly declared, "We hope that this youth will become the Michelangelo of his century."

The pope's nephew, Cardinal Borghese, offered young Bernini his first major commissions, including *The Rape of Persephone* (completed at age 23); an intently focused David, about to hurl the rock that would topple the Biblical Goliath; and *Apollo and Daphne*, the spectacular piece of mythical stagecraft and technical virtuosity that would seal Bernini's reputation as Rome's leading sculptor.

Cardinal Maffeo Barberini, another patron, became Pope Urban VIII in 1623 and reportedly told the prodigy: "Your luck is great to see Cardinal Maffeo Barberini Pope, Cavaliere, but ours is much greater to have Cavalier Bernini alive in our pontificate." For the next twenty-one years the pontiff would make good on his implied promise, a promise which doubtless arose from both a political impulse as much as aesthetic one: to buttress the cause of the Catholic Counter-Reformation, church leaders recognized the need for a style of religious art that was more emotionally charged, vigorous, and realist: in short, engaging the masses though aesthetic "shock and awe" and demonstrating (especially to the Catholic monarchies of Europe) the vitality of the church and it's ecclesiastic primacy. Bernini's highly expressive and realistic style—the first compelling instance in sculpture of the "baroque" style pioneered in paint by Carracci and Caravaggio—perfectly fit the bill.

Almost at once Bernini set to work on the 64-foot high bronze Baldacchino (canopy) over the altar of St. Peter's and the tomb of the first Vicar of Christ in the Basilica. Part sculpture, part architecture, and part proscenium-in-the-round, this dynamic yet stately structure alone would have easily served as the crowning achievement of almost any other artist's career. Inspired in part by the namesake portable canopies used in religious processions, Bernini's Baldacchino has the lightweight appearance of a fabric covering, complete with simulated fringes and tassels, despite its use of more than 100,000 pounds of brass. Once again, the Baroque master transcended his medium: just as he had given marble the softness and suppleness of flesh, he bestowed on brass the airiness of cloth. His "interior design" for St. Peter's also included the Cathedra Petri—or throne of St. Peter—a dramatic assemblage of gilded bronze sculptures illuminated by a yellow stained-glass window in the apse.

Pope Urban VIII died in 1644 and incoming Pope Innocent X showed little inclination toward Bernini, instead favoring Francesco Borromini and others. Making matters worse, a bell tower that Bernini had created for the façade of St. Peter's proved structurally unsound, needing to be demolished in 1646. But just as Bernini's good fortune appeared to desert him, he created his own luck. He used this period to begin work on what many critics consider his greatest masterpiece: the Cornaro Chapel of S. Maria della Vittoria, a virtual stage set for his enthralling *Ecstasy of St. Theresa*. Around the same time, Pope Innocent X decided to commission a fountain for Piazza Navona. Although Bernini was not invited to compete for the project, he nonetheless created a model which ended up capturing the pope's attention. When advised that it was by Bernini the pontiff reputedly said, "The only way to resist executing his works is not to see them." Today Bernini's Fountain of the Four Rivers is among Rome's most handsome and beloved attractions.

Despite the bell tower debacle, Bernini has come to be regarded by many as the preeminent Baroque architect as well as sculptor. His Jesuit church of Sant'Andrea al Quirinale is an exquisite ovoid space sometimes called, "the Pearl of the Baroque."

While Bernini might rightfully be called "Rome's Decorator," he might also be thought of as the choreographer of Catholic pilgrims' final approach to St. Peter's. As they would cross the Tiber atop the Sant' Angelo Bridge they would pass between a gauntlet of Bernini-designed angels, each bearing an instrument of the crucifixion. Then making their way to the basilica, pilgrims would enter the awe-inspiring St. Peter's Square surrounded by its distinctively curved double colonnade of 284 travertine marble columns with 140 statues of popes, martyrs and evangelists installed on top, described by Bernini himself this way: "These are the motherly arms of the church, reaching out to embrace the faithful and to reunite heretics (protestants) with the church."

In his nearly eighty-two years, Bernini served eight popes. Longevity alone would not account for Bernini's remarkable life output of sculptures, fountains, and edifices, only several of which are mentioned here. While he employed a team of assistants during most of his career, Bernini was also celebrated for his own prodigious work ethic and stamina: he would work seven hours without interruption on a block of marble, and claimed that his lifetime's worth of dining and slumber would likely not have exceeded a full month. (His daily diet reportedly consisted of a small portion of meat and copious amounts of fruit.)

Throughout his career, from the early remark of Pope Paul V onwards, Bernini was cited as the artistic heir to the genius of Michelangelo. Whether he ultimately measured up to that lofty goal can be left for others to argue. But, beyond debate, we must give this to Bernini: the man who made marble emote remade Rome.

◆ RIDOTTO "ROYALE"

Around the year 1500, at the very height of its mercantile power, Venice was likely the richest city on the planet. In the centuries to follow, the Most

Serene Republic's supremacy as a trading center would erode with realignments toward the west, and the cost of its numerous naval engagements (both offensive and, more and more, defensive) would be increasingly felt. Nevertheless, the Republic's moneyed elites would remain prosperous for generations, and as elites tend to do they would allot a share of their wealth to "diversions."

One such diversion was gambling, both rampant in scale and clandestine in nature by the early seventeenth century. As a legally prohibited activity it became the province of secret gambling houses known as *ridotti*, from Medieval Latin *reductus* ("place of refuge, retreat"). But the civic and safety problems arising from this underground commerce—plus, no doubt, the revenue opportunity it represented—prompted the Venetian government in 1638 to authorize and create the first legal gaming house in the Western world. Appropriating the name Ridotto, it occupied a lavish four-story wing of the Palazzo San Moise.

The splendid Ridotto featured a large entrance hall, dining rooms and some of the finest artwork around including, ironically, Gerolamo Colonna's *The Triumph of Virtue over Ignorance*. All the well-heeled visitors had to wear a three-cornered hat, mask, and cape before they were allowed to play. This form of anonymity allowed them to more freely indulge in spirited mischief and still retain their public reputations for probity while also shielding wins or losses from their fellow Venetians. (There's the story of a 17th-century masked gambler who incurred the wrath and punishment of the civic authorities by trying to pass himself as a member of the noble gentry while cheating; one might infer that the former was considered the greater infraction!) Famous guests included Casanova, the philosopher Jean-Jacques Rousseau, and Lorenzo da Ponte, opera librettist for Mozart.

One could almost imagine that the "stately pleasure-dome" of Kubla Kahn had levitated from the river Alph of Coleridge's poem to the Grand Canal.

218

The Ridotto had a good run but was closed in 1774 by a morality-minded majority of the same governing council that established it 136 years before. Gambling activity went back underground, and the Republic itself would last only another twenty-three years when the beleagered city surrendered without a fight to Napoleon.

◆SYMPATHY FOR THE BORGIA

◆STRANGLED PRIEST

◆SINS OF THE FATHER

◆SHAKESPEARE IN AMORE

◆LA SERENISSIMA

◆THE SALUTE

◆SNOW IN AUGUST

◆THE FIRST SNOWBALL FIGHT

◆SCENT OF A TRUFFLE

◆ SYMPATHY FOR THE BORGIA

From the great novel *The Romance of Leonardo da Vinci* by Dmitry Merezhkovsky to a world-famous television series, the verdict seems to be in that the Borgia family was the nadir of Renaissance cruelty and excess. But measured against the libertinism, corruption, and violence of the era, the story gets a little more complicated.

For example, by current standards, a pope who fornicated with at least two women we know of and probably bribed his way into the papacy seems . . . pretty bad. But Rodrigo de Borja, who became Alexander VI, the second Borja pope after Alfons de Borja, Pope Callixtus III, reigned in an age when the Holy See had secular power and wealth rivaling other Italian city-states. Using devious tactics to gain the papacy was not unheard of; nor was charging money for forgiveness of sins, known as simony; nor was it unusual for the Pope to consolidate or expand his power through nepotism and warfare using papal armies; or to have a mistress, as Alexander VI undoubtedly did in the person of Vannozza dei Cattanei.

Caesare Borgia may have been the most infamous of the Renaissance's warring princes: while Alexander was pope, he undertook a northern Italian campaign to create his own kingdom out of the holdings of the petty tyrants of the State of the Church, and left a trail of assassinations in his wake. But again, it wasn't unusual for relatives of popes to embark on such murderous campaigns to add to their land holdings, especially if they came originally from a landless cash-strapped parvenu Spanish family like the Borjas turned Borgias.

And was Caesare's sister, the infamous Lucrezia, an incestuous whore, poisoner, murderer, and witch? Some sources say otherwise, depicting her as a woman respected by the nobility and intelligentsia of her day. Was the Borgias' "Banquet of the Chestnuts," long considered one of the Renaissance's ultimate orgies, for real? We have only the accounts of Johann Burchard, an anti-Borgia papal official.

The point may be that the victors get to write history—and blacken the losers' names. The Borgias originated in Valencia, Spain, and thus were loathed by many 15th-century Italians. Pope Alexander in particular, through flagrant practices like living publicly with his mistress and their children, drew such condemnation that he gave traction to the fanatical anti-papal Savonarola in Florence and his bonfires of the vanities—not to mention the beginnings of the Protestant Reformation.

Caesare Borgia's conquests ended after Julius II, the "warrior pope" from the more successful and long-established della Rovere family, came to power. The Borgias didn't even leave much art behind, though Alexander had the master Pinturicchio paint lush frescoes in his Borgia Apartments downstairs from the Vatican's Raphael Rooms, which include (they were completed in 1494) perhaps the first picture of a Native American in European history.

These apartments were closed off in black crepe by Pope Julius II, who spurned his predecessor, and not reopened until 1889, which symbolizes the job history did on the Borgias. All in all, it's not as if the Borgias didn't earn their bad reputation—but by the standards of the Italian Renaissance, they were overpaid.

✦ STRANGLED PRIEST

Strozzapreti literally translates to "priest choker" and is a pasta similar to penne but with a distinctive twist. Also known as "strangled priest," it originally hailed from Emilia-Romangna, notorious as a land of sin and sinners as well as for curious and tasty culinary delicacies.

As legend has it, back in the day when the region was part of the Papal States the people were resentful of the onerous taxation by the church and the custom of priests expecting to eat for free in parishioners' homes. Wives would prepare the meal while their more anticlerical husbands would joke that they hoped the priest would choke on the pasta before the more expensive secondi piatti, usually a meat dish, was served. Another less political interpretation of the evocative name's origin was given by Signor Pozzetto in *La Cucina Romagnola*, Franco Muzzio Editore, 1995, relating it to the sharp and firm movement the Romagna housewives would have used to shape the pasta by "choking" the strips of dough.

◆ SINS OF THE FATHER

The term "sins of the father (or fathers)" goes back at least as far as the Bible and the Books of Exodus, Numbers, and Deuteronomy and refers to the sins of one generation passing on to the next. Of course the underlying notion of nasty deeds and their bad consequences afflicting an entire lineage goes back even further: to Greek mythology and the benighted House of Atreus. The root concept of intergenerational sin and guilt runs deep in Western culture.

Such was the legacy of Reginaldo Scrovegni, a wealthy moneylender so infamous for his usurious greed and heartlessness that he was banished to the seventh circle of Dante's *Inferno*. Placed on burning sand and showered with fiery rain, Reginaldo was weighed down for all of eternity with a moneybag tied around his neck and bearing the Scrovegni coat of arms. Reginaldo's reported last words in life were "Give me the keys to my strong box so that no one may get my money."

So what was Reginaldo's son Enrico to do? In a brilliant act of karmic *arrangiarsi*, the younger Scrovegni made a grand and lasting gesture to expiate the sins of his father (while also, presumably, retaining some of his ill-gotten bequest): he commissioned a cycle of murals by the then-renowned Giotto di Bondone to adorn the interior of an otherwise nondescript brick chapel in Padua in northern Italy.

The rest, as they say, is art history. The Scrovegni Chapel's forty panels represent a masterful orchestration of images which dramatically depict key scenes from the lives of Christ and his mother, the Virgin, all culminating in a "universal judgment" fresco covering the entire wall beyond a triumphal arch. There Enrico is depicted as himself on the side of the blessed, those whom Christ has chosen to go to Heaven, kneeling and presenting the chapel to the Virgin Mary who is flanked by two angels. Created at the apex of Giotto's career, the Scrovegni frescoes far surpassed contemporaneous paintings in their convincing use of spatial effects like volume and depth and in their compelling figuration. Giotto's crowning work both prefigured and preordained the art of the Renaissance. (see "Giotto, Master of Emotion")

Astonishingly, the Scrovegni Chapel is not listed on the long roster of Italy's UNESCO World Heritage Sites— it's only on the waiting list! Perhaps Reginaldo Scrovegni's redemption (or at least his son's) will only be complete once the UNESCO grandees have made their own last judgment.

♦ SHAKESPEARE IN AMORE

Like so many Brits, the Bard too had a great love affair with Italy. Of the thirty-eight of his plays that survive, fourteen were at least partly set in the sunnier climes of La Bella Italia: *Julius Caesar* (Rome, Greece), *Romeo and Juliet* (Verona), *Two Gentleman from Verona* (Milan, Mantua), *Much Ado about Nothing* (Messina), *Othello* (Cyprus, Venice), *The Merchant of Venice* (Venice, Belmonte), *The Taming of the Shrew* (Verona, Padua, England), *Coriolanus* (Ancient Rome), *All's Well that Ends Well* (Florence, Paris, Marseilles), *Titus Andronicus* (Ancient Rome), *Winter's Tale* (Sicily, Bohemia), *The Tempest* (Mediterranean Sea), *Cymbeline* (Rome, Wales), and a scene in Rome from *Anthony and Cleopatra*.

Running one's eyes over this census of genius, one can see some common features of his Italian plays: blood running even hotter than in his most dramatic British work, often with tragic consequences; the moral ambiguities and the commercial chicanery of Venice; fiery romance; light and airy and sometimes wild comedy. He seems to have grasped the essence of Italian culture so well that it's been theorized he traveled to Italy. Only someone who was there for a time, like the Earl of Oxford, could have "gotten it" that way.

But Shakespeare might have never left home and still have been tremendously aware of the Italian culture and literature of his day, widely disseminated throughout Elizabethan England. Many motifs and themes of the Italian Renaissance were circulating throughout his lifetime in the sixteenth and seventeenth centuries, in written and unwritten mediums, and they found their way into the imagery and poetry of his plays. His compatriots and his acting company in all probably visited the country. And perhaps the greatest adapter of other stories as source material who ever wrote in English, he knew how to absorb the home truths of other cultures into his work.

Finally, it's reputed that one of the fountainheads of Italian literature, the Roman poet Ovid, was Shakespeare's favorite author. One can certainly see Ovid's influence in Shakespeare's sonnets and classical references; a play like *A Midsummer's Night Dream* borrows its structure from Ovid's great epic collection of tales *The Metamorphoses*, where often one story surrounds another with all sorts of shenanigans within. And that whole play is a kind of antic ode to the freedom of shape-shifting and discovering other selves, both as (one can imagine) a writer and as a human being. As in *The Metamorphoses*, such transformations can be terrifying, but at least in this phantasmagoric comedy they can be balanced with joy. If Bottom is transformed into a donkey, thanks to Titania's transformed perceptions, at least there's plenty of consolation for Bottom when this beauteous queen of the fairies falls in love with him.

In fact, Shakespeare cheerfully pillaged Ovid not just for imagery and themes, but for stories like "Pyramus and Thisbe," which is given an uproariously funny bad performance by the Players in *Dream,* and which in Shakespeare's far more capable hands was adapted into *Romeo and Juliet.* From Ovid's transformations to Pico della Mirandola's chain of being to stories of elegant and murderous courts freely derived from Renaissance events, Shakespeare dug deep into Italian literature, philosophy, and history. And *The Tempest* has magical illusions and creations, images of "sea change," character metamorphoses, a lovely romance, and an underlying story of courtly intrigues avenged within realms of nature and fantasy, all finally resolved in a tableau of rebirth and Christian forgiveness. In this final masterpiece, in which "we are such stuff as dreams are made of," Shakespeare wrote in a way that evokes Italian art and literature from Ovid to Dante to Botticelli to Fellini. He may have been the pride of England, but he earned honorary dual citizenship in Italy.

✦ LA SERENISSIMA

The Republic of Venice is traditionally known as *La Serenissima*, "The Serene Republic," and has long been a captivating city of color, light, and hauntingly beautiful reflections that has inspired generations of artists, writers and musicians the world over. And as Goethe said, "Venice can only be compared to itself"…

dawn's light seen
through a lavender lantern
darkly

a polychrome map
of worn stucco and brickwork
where Polo set out

Piazza S. Marco
pigeons transfigure
to pixels

in silent mist
the Bridge of Sighs
goes missing

moonlit lagoon
a mask shop merchant dons
his galoshes

stitching the darkness
the glint
from a gondola's prow

◆ THE SALUTE

Gazing across the Grand Canal from St. Mark's Square in Venice, especially in the quiet of the morning, it is difficult not to be moved by the ethereal beauty of a great dome taking shape out of the mist from the opposite bank. That iconic edifice is the church of Santa Maria della Salute—or, more colloquially, just The Salute—built beginning in 1631 as a gesture of civic gratitude. The plague had taken the lives of a third of the Venetian population in the prior year, and the Senate pledged to erect a grand church to honor the Virgin Mary if their republic was delivered from further harm. And so when the pestilence miraculously subsided, Santa Maria della Salute ("the church of the Virgin Mary in good health") arose, just as three older churches in Venice had been erected under similar circumstances. Much of the architectural beauty of Venice came in response to deliverance from this terrible disease.

The church is an unusual and compact "Marian" structure (a church dedicated to the Virgin Mary) featuring architectural symbolism associated with the Virgin Mother. True to their word, the Venetian authorities gave the Virgin a prime parcel of real estate at the tip of Dorsoduro, where the Grand Canal merges with St. Mark's Basin directly across from Piazza San Marco.

The architectural commission for the Basilica was awarded to a twenty-six-year-old unknown named Baldassare Longhena, who won the design competition with a highly original plan that would take over fifty years to complete. The church's round shape represents Mary's womb, the dome her crown, and the octagonal interior her eight-sided star. There are thirty-two roses on the polychrome marble floors symbolizing the beads of her rosary.

The Baroque exterior is highly decorative with exuberant scrolls and more than 125 statues. The sensory assault falls away as you enter the serene, light-suffused, cavernous, yet perfectly proportioned "womb." There are altarpieces by Luca Giordano, the *Marriage at Cana* by Tintoretto, and ceiling paintings and portraits by Titian, the great Venetian artist who most dominates the interior.

The church was consecrated during the Feast of the Presentation of the Virgin (November 21) with a magnificent procession of the city's officials from San Marco to La Salute crossing the Grand Canal on a specially constructed pontoon bridge. The Festa della Madonna della Salute has since become an annual event celebrated by the locals. Gondoliers bring their oars to be blessed by a priest who recites his incantations from the church steps. The huge main doors of the basilica are opened, and Venetians walk across the canal to pay their respects to the Virgin Mary—or at the very least to Venice's tradition and a symbol of the city that has inspired artists from Canaletto to Sargent and Turner, towering above the Grand Canal of Venice as a glowing symbol of thanksgiving.

♦ SNOW IN AUGUST

Not to be outdone by Florence's annual Easter "Explosion of the Cart" or Venice's "Wedding to the Sea" each Ascension Day, Rome has a strange and wonderful ecclesiastical tradition all its own.

If you happen to be walking past the Basilica di Santa Maria Maggiore at a certain nighttime hour on any August 5th, you can be forgiven for thinking that you've stepped into the Dolomites in January: it will appear to be *snowing!* Though you and your fellow witnesses may be clad in shorts and sandals, you'll be engulfed in a veritable blizzard—of snow-like soap bubbles.

This faux-meteorological rite traces to a dream that reputedly occurred over a millennium and a half ago. In the fourth century a wealthy Roman named Giovanni dreamed that the Virgin Mary appeared to him in a snowstorm at that very spot, instructing him to build a basilica there in her honor. When Giovanni confided in Pope Liberio about his dream the Pontiff of Rome said that he too experienced the very same nocturnal visitation, and so the deal was sealed. (Another version of the story has it that actual snow fell on that spot over an otherwise hot August night.) The basilica was completed in 440, and the rest is alternative climate history.

• THE FIRST SNOWBALL FIGHT

When we think of the art of the Middle Ages one principal association will usually come to mind: Christianity and the Christian life of devotion. The imagery is plainly religious and the tone unequivocally solemn. Focus was on the spiritual realm and little attention was paid to natural world and scenery let alone climatic conditions. It never never rains in heaven.

But even a Medieval has gotta have fun—at least those in the upper echelons of Middle Age society! Thus we find, as the late Middle Ages were drawing to a close, the first known representation in the history of art of . . . a snowball fight! In the Eagle Tower of Trento's Castello del Buonconsiglio (formerly the bishop's residence) is an early 15th-century fresco cycle of the months. The month is January and the Bishop and his noble companions are enjoying a snowball fight on the sunny day. The Castle and Bishops are featured as well as several companions (including ladies) all garbed in medieval finery. One enterprising woman combatant is thoughtfully fully-armed with a lap full of snowy orbs and is shown taking aim like a seasoned pitcher.

• SCENT OF A TRUFFLE

If you're a late night stroller in the Piedmont region during certain times of year and you spot an alertly suspicious man with his dog, chances are he's not taking the dog for a *passegiata* (walk). But nor is he up to anything dicey. He's merely using the best tool at hand to locate rare white truffles for which wealthy gourmands will pay a fortune.

To clear up a point of confusion, Italian truffle hunters do not use pigs; they use dogs. It's the French who occasionally hunt truffles with pigs. No self-respecting Italian man would ever consider it. Granted, pigs have a keen sense of smell; no one disputes that. But that's also the problem. Truffles give off an aroma that, to be blunt, turns a pig on. So at that point you've found the truffle only to lose it to the jaws of your three-hundred pound sexually-charged sow. Dogs on the other hand are easily distracted with happy words and a mere doggie treat.

While the masters get the riches, it's the dogs (in Italian *cani* pronounced "KA-nee") who are the real hunters. In Piedmont, there used to be a college degree granted for that . . . for the dog! The Universita dei Cani da Tartufo (University of the Truffle Hunting Dogs) wasn't exactly Oxford, located in the garage and two-story home of Giovanni Monchiero near the village of Roddi outside of Torino. However, it did have an august history of successful alumni going back to its founding by his great-grandfather in 1880. Now there is a small "museum" where the school used to be. You can learn the history of its distinguished *cani* and even go out with a dog and hunter on a "hunt," really a demo.

There are many truffle varieties, but the Piedmont region is the *only* area in the world where the White Alba Truffle (known as King Truffle or White Gold) can be found under the roots of trees. Found only for a few weeks in November, this delicacy is so coveted that it sells for about $350 an ounce—that's over $4,000 per pound!

Thanks to these prices there are an estimated 7,000 to 8,000 licensed truffle-hunters in Piedmont. They take their dogs out in the middle of the night for easier scent detection in the moist evening air, but also secrecy and even protection. Top truffle-hunting dogs are very valuable creatures and, appalling as it may sound, the business is so brutally competitive that some super-sniffers have been kidnapped or even poisoned by rival truffle hunters.

The end result is a prize for both hunter and diner. The scent of fresh truffles fills a room almost instantly. White truffles are generally served uncooked and shaved over steaming buttered pasta or salads, transforming these familiar dishes into a foodie fantasy. The flavor of black truffles is far less pungent than that of white truffles and reminiscent of fresh earth. Truffle oil is often used as a lower-cost substitute for truffles to provide flavoring or to enhance the flavor and aroma of truffles in cooking. However, most truffle oil is a synthetic product containing no actual truffles. (Chocolate truffles are a whole other treat, invented by French chocolatiers and named for the famous funghi because of their similar size.)

So, does your dog have what it takes to be a champion truffle hound? Monchiero used to find out by introducing a dog to truffles and observing how it reacted to the scent; it would, after all, have to smell its quarry three feet underground. If a dog has what it takes, it will still require four years of nightly hunting before it can really become truly proficient. But with that four-year investment in his or her "education" your best friend might just become your benefactor too.

◆TRULLI, HOBBIT HOUSES OF PUGLIA

◆TREVI

◆TIBERIUS'S SWIMMING POOL

◆TERRACE OF INFINITY

◆TEARS OF CHRIST

◆TEMPEST IN A TIRAMISU CUP

◆TORRI SARACENE

◆TUSCAN TAROT FANTASY

❖ TRULLI, HOBBIT HOUSES OF PUGLIA

While touring Puglia, you could be forgiven for pausing in front of one of the region's unique *trullo* homes and expecting to find a hobbit, maybe an old "Bilbetto" at the window smoking a pipe. These tiny homes, with their rounded stone walls and conical rooves, have an elfin Tolkienesque charm that's irresistible and so unique that the town of Alberobello, which contains over 750 *trulli*, has been declared a World Heritage Site.

But looking at their history, it's amazing how practical they are, thanks both to beautifully efficient architecture and—this being Italy, the land of countering greedy governments with a touch of *arrangiarsi*—a great way to dodge taxes.

In the 16th and 17th century, the peasant families of Puglia lived in and built these *trulli* out of solid limestone rocks from the area (a fortunate source of material, since Puglia was primarily deforested for cultivation of olive oil and grapes, except of course for olive trees). The building technique had been known for a very long time; Puglia had been colonized by the Greeks in the 8th century BCE, and the "dry" mortarless masonry technique was also used in the Tholoi, or domed tombs, of Mycenae.

The circular shape was extremely efficient, the thick stone walls were great insulation against both heat and cold, and the peaked rooves were perfect for channeling rainwater away, often to underground water tanks. *Trulli* were so economical to build that families would build adjacent ones for their horses or livestock, or dual connected *trulli* as their families grew.

They were also fairly easy to dismantle—which is where the tax dodge comes in. The nobility and the King of Naples steeply taxed permanent roofed dwellings. Because all the roof stones were built around a keystone that prevented the roof from collapse, a *trullo*-dweller, learning the tax collector was en route, could in effect demolish his *trullo* simply by extracting the stone. It may be a legend, but it's certainly not the most outrageous tax dodge ever devised.

Further "protection" against tax collectors and the evils of the outside world came in the form of a "Pinaccolo" or pinnacle on the roof, either in a ball shape, which some claim is the symbol of the sun, or a cross; and some *trulli* are painted with hex charms or astrological symbols, adding to their bewitching fairy-tale appeal to modern visitors. No wonder many wealthy foreigners and locals are now buying or renting *trulli*; some have even become boutique hotels. Their mystique and charm is undeniable—and rather than tax dodging, why not have a lovely little Italian *trullo* for about half the price of a pied-à-terre in Paris or New York?

♦ TREVI

As you approach, you hardly hear the sound of rushing water. Curiously tucked between three narrow streets, the theatrical Fontana di Trevi greets you as you round the corner. At 85 feet high and 65 feet across, it is Italy's largest and most famous fountain of the Baroque era and a timescape of Italian history.

Roman engineers had an illustrious relationship with water and Rome has always been a city of fountains, with over 1,200 back in the days of the Empire. Today's Trevi is located at the site of the city's oldest water source (dating to 19 BCE) when it was the terminus of the Acqua Vergine Aqueduct. The fountain's name is derived from the Latin word *trivium* for the crossing of three roads and now marks the junction of Via Dei Crocicchi, Via Poli, and Via Delle Muratte.

Bernini is associated with this monumental structure, but though he did sketch renovations for Pope Urban VIII in 1629, he would not be its creator.

The project was abandoned with Urban's death and only revived a century later by Pope Clement VII who held a competition (contests were very much in vogue at the time) to redesign the fountain. Many important architects joined the fray and by some accounts it has been suggested that Alessandro Galilei (a relative of the famous Galileo) was originally awarded the commission but was deprived of his win due to a public outcry. Why? Galilei hailed from Florence while Nicolas Salvi, who ultimately redesigned the fountain, was a Roman. Civic pride runs deep in the Italian consciousness.

The fountain took thirty years to complete and Salvi died before he could behold his extravagantly imaginative masterwork. On a sunny day in Rome there is no more dazzling sight than the Trevi, an architectural harmonization of stone outcrops, five fountains spouting 2,824,800 cubic feet of water daily, and triumphant statues of a god and mermen sculpted out of travertine marble. The central figure of the fountain is Oceanus, believed by the Romans to be the incarnation of the world-encircling sea, who stands stripped to the waist aside a chariot shaped like a shell and flanked by sea horses who burst out of the water barely controlled by the Tritons of legend.

Over the centuries the Trevi has been celebrated in literature (Nathaniel Hawthorne's *The Marble Faun*) and film (the delightful '50s romantic comedies *Roman Holiday* and *Three Coins In A Fountain*, which also yielded a hit song of the same name). The tossing of coins in the fountain over one's shoulder to express a wish to return to Rome or simply find one's own Roman holiday is not without its religious history either; it dates back to a pagan tradition of an offering to the goddess of the waters to ensure the safe return of a loved one from an ocean voyage. And nowadays it has a Christian purpose: the 3000 euro worth of coins that cover the basin at the end of the day are donated to Caritas, a Catholic charity that provides for the indigent families of Rome.

The Trevi found perhaps its most iconic image in Frederico Fellini's *La Dolce Vita* when blonde bombshell Anita Ekberg waded into its basin, sweeping her black dress along as it clung ever more tightly to her figure and calling in ever more festive and inviting tones to her companion, the gossip columnist Marcello, played by the great Marcello Mastroianni. As already noted, so much did this cinematic symbol of the seductive sweetness of Italian life (as well as Mastrioanni's performance) engrave itself on the imagination of Rome that when Mastrioanni passed away, the Trevi was draped in black in his memory.

Now that the fountain has emerged from its restoration shell of scaffolds, it once again shines in all its glory in front of the Poli Palace, thanks to funding by Fendi. It also was given new lighting, making a visit to its dappled waters after nightfall a must. Just resist the temptation to wade in.

♦ TIBERIUS'S SWIMMING POOL

It's a sight that made the author Hans Christian Andersen feel as if he'd stepped into a landscape from one of his own fairy tales; every year it amazes thousands of tourists.

Capri's Grotta Azzurra (Blue Grotto) is literally the greatest draw in Capri—as in the tide pauses and, while visitors duck low, their oarsman pulls his craft and they are sucked into an opening in the cliff face and taken into the grotto. Once there, in an arched cavern about one hundred and sixty feet long, one hundred and twenty feet wide, and seventy feet high, they take in the unearthly deep blue glow—created by refracted sunlight through one visible and one submerged opening—of waters of seemingly infinite depth.

There's no lighting better in any indoor pool on earth, which is why the Emperor Tiberius chose the Grotto as his personal natatorium when he moved the administrative capitol of the Roman Empire to Capri in 26 CE and ruled remotely for the remaining eleven years of his reign. It was a highly unorthodox move; some have speculated that he chose to live out his life and reign in relative seclusion so he could indulge in vices he had struggled to conceal throughout his life. Others suggest he had "had it" with the political machinations of Rome and preferred a more contemplative seaside existence. Another intriguing theory is that Tiberius wanted to get away from his domineering mother, Livia (see "Livia's Painted Garden") who expected to co-rule with her son as she had as wife, confidant, and silent advisor to the powerful Augustus Caesar during his forty-year rule. Whatever the reason, Tiberius loved Capri and his Grotto and so built a residence at the top of Mount Jovis a thousand feet over the Mediterranean; being a capable multitasker, he also made it serve as a launch pad from which to throw dissenters of his rule to their deaths.

The grotto was long known to residents, who called it Gradola and avoided its supposed monsters and evil spirits. But it was rediscovered for the rest of the world by German poet August Kopisch in 1926 and became part of the European Grand Tour. Mark Twain celebrated it with uncharacteristically lavish prose in *Innocents Abroad*. Beyond the grotto and its 150-meter deep waters, the cave actually branches out further, to a Sala dei Nomi, "Room of Names," where visitors have scrawled messages over the centuries, and then to passageways yet to be explored. Three statues of the sea gods Neptune and Triton were found there in 1964, remnants of Tiberius's original ornamentation of the Grotto, and are now on display at a museum in Anacapri.

Whether as a source of legend, archaeological treasure, or illicit excitement (as in intrepid athletes sneaking into the grotto to defy the "no swimming" rule), there is no natural wonder in Italy more famous or more gorgeous. And if the project being undertaken by the environmentalist association Marevivo and the archaeological superintendency of Pompeii comes off, which will reconstruct the original Roman statuary and bring the Grotto back to the way it looked in Tiberius's time, the Grotto will be more dazzling still.

❖ TERRACE OF INFINITY

The Amalfi coast is by no means undiscovered and even the small town of Ravello, perched up in the cliffs stretching out along a promontory 1,200 feet above the sea, has attracted Grand Tour travelers since the 18th century. There is a very special place though, accessible only by foot, that still remains relatively unknown.

Just outside of town you'll find a meandering path more suitable to donkeys than cars, or, thankfully, tour buses, which leads to Villa Cimbrone with its sumptuous eclectic architecture and gardens and the spellbinding panaroma that has become known as the Terrazzo dell'Infinito—the Terrace of Infinity.

An 11th century villa that would become part of the monastery of Santa Chiara—Cardinal Della Rovere, later Pope Julius II who commissioned Michelangelo to paint the ceiling of the Sistine Chapel, would place the papal coat of arms on the wooden gateway himself—Villa Cimbrone would afterwards languish for centuries until rediscovered by the Englishman Ernest William Beckett, Lord Grimthorpe, while traveling on the Amalfi Coast in the late 19th century. He found solace here after his beloved wife died in childbirth and not only restored the gardens but, a true Italy-besotted Brit, he made those gardens and the villa itself into a fantasia of classical and mainly Italian salvaged architectural styles: a temple with a statue of Ceres, a cloister reflecting Arab and Sicilian motifs, a grotto dedicated to Eve, and even a Gothic crypt.

Lord Beckett's names for his garden pathways are as evocative as their views. As you enter, your eye is drawn down the long Avenue of Immensity best seen in the summer when its pergola is abloom with white and blue wisteria. But he outdid himself with the Terrace of Infinity, turning the ancient cliffside belvedere into a promenade lined with imposing 18th-century marble statues of no particular provenance, mainly trusting the view itself to inspire absolute awe. The mountainous coastline of the Bay of Salerno plunges to the Mediterranean, and on a sunlit day the blue sea and sky seem to merge into an endless sphere of light. Gore Vidal, who bought a home in Ravello, was so enthralled by the Terrace of Infinity that he considered it the most beautiful view in the world.

Over the years the Villa Cimbrone and its world-famous Terazzo became a favorite of guests like E.M. Forster, Virginia Woolf, D.H. Lawrence, Tennessee Williams, Greta Garbo, and Winston Churchill, and it still hosts the rich and famous today. As for Lord Beckett, he never left; he died in

1917 and his body was buried at the foot of the Temple of Bacchus in the gardens, his epitaph borrowing lines from Catullus celebrating the return of the traveler to rest from all cares in his longed-for home.

❖ TEARS OF CHRIST

The richly fertile lower slopes of Mount Vesuvius, with their volcanic soils, are covered with vineyards and have been producing a variety of grapes and wines since the time of Magna Graecia and Imperial Rome. The winemakers of this area seem to have had an equally rich (and very much Italian) talent for naming the wines with the kind of imagery and story-telling that's far more ingenious than the teasing non sequiturs or fanciful labels with cute animals of American wines. Even before there was a need to break though marketing clutter, Italians named their wines in an unfor-gettable way (as in remembered over centuries, and mentioned by Dumas in *The Count of Monte Cristo* and Voltaire in *Candide*) especially when it comes to a beauty among Neapolitan wines, Lacryma Christi del Vesuvio.

The variations on the basic story of how the wines got their name are even more intriguing and evocative than the name itself. In the simpler "tears of joy" version, when Jesus was on his way to up to heaven, he glanced back down to earth and beheld the Bay of Naples and wept with joy to witness its beauty. His tears fell on Mount Vesuvius's scarred lava soil and a new breed of vine flourished.

Then there's a "tears of sadness" version, slightly darker and more complicated: when Lucifer and his band of fallen angels were cast out from heaven, they clutched a corner of heaven as they were cast out. As they fell, pieces of paradise scattered from their grip and landed on Mt. Vesuvius. When Jesus, up in heaven, saw the calamitous fall, he wept from pity, and again, when the sacred tears fell like rain, vines miraculously sprouted on the volcano's slopes and from those vines Lacryma Christi is made.

Finally, there's yet another similar story which alledgely predates Chris-tianity. In the earliest version, it was the Roman God Bacchus who, upon seeing such beauty, wept and created the vines. However the tears were shed, and without casting aspersions on the beautiful legends, the story behind the wine is literally one of the great branding strategies of all time.

And the poetry of the wine doesn't stop at the bottle. Lacryma Christi del Vesuvio wine is slightly higher in alcohol content and produced in several styles: red, white, rose, and sparkling. The red, a rich garnet color, juicy and well-balanced, is made from a blend of grapes called Piedirosso, or "red feet," referring to the reddish stems, and Aglianico, which may be a dialect version of *vitis hellenica*, or "Greek vine." Piedirosso is also known as Palombina or Per'e Palummo, "little dove" and "dove's foot," because of the three stems of the vines that resemble the feet of a native dove. The crisp dry white wine is made from a blend of Coda di Volpe, meaning "fox's tail" (due to the way the grapes grow in a long bunch), and Falanghina, from the Latin word for "vineyard stakes" that support the grapes, or Greco di Tufo, named after a southern Italian town. It's a veritable vintner's tour of Italian myth, images, and history.

♦ TEMPEST IN A TIRAMISU CUP

A global phenomenon, tiramisu is the fifth most recognized Italian word among non-Italian speakers, behind pizza, spaghetti, espresso, and mozzarella. Its distinctive combination of marsala-soaked sponge cake, espresso, and yummy mascarpone custard dusted with bitter cocoa make it one of the world's best-loved desserts, but a not-so-sweet debate has erupted in Italy over the provenance of this beloved confection.

For starters, most assume it to be a "classic" Italian dessert with a long illustrious history. This is not the case. Caterina D'Medici had nothing to do with it nor are there old family recipes passed from generation to generation; tiramisu is an entirely modern culinary invention.

For years the town of Treviso in the Veneto region has proudly claimed itself Tiramisu's birthplace. In *The Timeless Art of Italian Cuisine—Centuries of Scrumptious Dining*, author Anna Maria Volpi states the following: "... the oldest recipe I could find was in the book by Giovanni Capnist, *I Dolci del Veneto* ('The Desserts of Veneto')." The first edition was published in 1983 and has a classic recipe for tiramisu. Recent recipes with infinite variations from the town of Treviso, says Capnist, reflect its discovery by other restaurants rather than family tradition.

According to Volpi the final word on the origin of tiramisu is found in *Gastronomica* by Fernando e Tina Raris La Marca, published in 1998, a book entirely dedicated to the cuisine of Treviso. The authors recount an article by Giuseppe Maffioli in 1981 stating that tiramisu was born ten years prior at the Alle Beccherie restaurant, owned by Alba and Ado Campeol, where the dessert and its name became instantly popular, and where it was immediately copied by countless restaurants, first in Treviso and then throughout Italy.

The Alle Beccherie narrative has been corroborated by another culinary researcher, Pietro Mascioni, who further identified the restaurant's pastry chef as Loli Linguanotto and noted he had spoken directly with the Campeols. The matriarch, Alba, recounted the circumstances that led to the dessert's creation. After the birth of one of her sons she had been exhausted and weak; to perk her up, her mother-in-law made her a special zabaglione spiked with coffee. That was both the inspirational spark for several defining ingredients and tiramisu's uplifting name, which literally translates to "pick (*tiru*) me (*mi*) up (*su*)."

Recently however, Italian food writers Clara and Gigi Padovani claim to have found documentary evidence that a concoction of sponge fingers, cream, coffee, and mascarpone was first conceived in Friuli-Venezia Giulia in the 1950s, at least twenty years before Alba Campeol's "eureka" moment. The newly discovered recipe refers to a dessert called "tirime su" produced by a chef named Mario Cosolo from a town near the border of Slovenia; additionally, they also discovered a recipe for "tirimu su" served in 1959 in a restaurant in the town of Tolmezzo, near the Austrian border.

The Padovanis' findings are in their new book *Tiramisu—History, Curiosities, and Interpretations of Italy's Best-loved Dessert*. Not surprisingly their thesis has ignited indignation in Veneto, with the governor, Luca Zaia, aggressively supporting his region: "Don't question its origins in Treviso. No one can swindle us out of tiramisu—it was invented by the Alle Beccherie restaurant in Treviso. That is set in stone. They can claim that it was invented in Bulgaria, if they like. . ."

Mr. Zaia previously had led a campaign to have Treviso recognized by the European Union as the home of tiramisu, as Naples has been recognized as the home of pizza. "If others have copied it, that's because it's the best and most genuine dessert in the world. In every sector, the best things are always copied, from Ferrari to great wines to great fashion brands. This is not the first time someone has tried to hijack tiramisu," Mr Zaia said.

In response, the Padovanis commented: "We Italians are like this—we engage in a futile argument over who created tiramisu while it conquers national boundaries and becomes part of the heritage of the whole world."

While Veneto and Friuli-Venezia Giulia wage their battle, other food writers have proffered a far more salacious theory—tiramisu was born in a brothel in the 1950s as an energy-boosting pick-me-up for ladies of the night. When it comes to Italian food, feuds, and prostitutes, all you can say is the beat goes on.

✦ TORRI SARACENE

They loom over seashores like broad squat obelisks with windows, turrets without castles, lighthouses without lights. They're the proud, stony, if gloomy remains of an era when, at the height of the Ottoman Empire,

residents of the Sorrentine and Amalfi coast had a lot more on their minds than making Limoncello.

The very word "Saracen!" was enough to set the population trembling. "Barbary pirates" and Corsairs, typically Turks and North Africans collectively known as Saracens, repeatedly attacked ships and raided coastal towns from southern Italy, France, Spain, and Portugal to as far north as the British Isles, although the Italian coast bore the brunt of their hellish assaults. It is estimated that from the sixteenth to the nineteenth centuries the pirates captured 800,000 to 1.25 million people, who were then sold in slave markets, put into harems, or worse. The most infamous of these Saracen Pirates was Pasha Hayreddin, known as Barbarosso, which means Red Beard. He was one of four brothers who were the most feared pirates of their time.

Defensive watchtowers have always been a part of the coastal landscape from early Greco-Roman times. They were the sole "early warning system" to alert townspeople to the pirates' approach. Many of these towers still stand today as they did hundreds of years ago. Others are partial remains or just piles of rocks; still others have been restored as private residences or restaurants, nightclubs, and boutique hotels. These towers have become known as the Saracen Towers or Torre Saracena. From Gaeta to Amalfi alone, there are more than 350 of them.

Saracen Torre a Mare in Praiano, midway between Amalfi and Positano, may have been erected as early as 1278. Today it has been cleverly repurposed as an artist's atelier. Paolo Sandulli is a painter and a ceramist; you can meet him along with his dog and his goats, and he will gladly offer you a glass of wine and show you his paintings and his terracotta artworks. His work reflects the world he sees around him as well as his sense of humor and whimsy; most remarkable are his terracotta busts of women with sea sponge hairdos. Many a head (having a bad hair day?) has gone home with a foreign visitor; thankfully these days it's not the other way around.

♦ TUSCAN TAROT FANTASY

If life is a game of cards, we are born without knowing the rules,
yet we must play our hand throughout the ages ... philosophers,
alchemists, artists have devoted themselves to discovering their meaning
—Niki de Saint Phalle, 1995.

The quote describes the famed deck of Tarot cards, used for centuries to attempt to interpret and predict humanity's fate according to a universal series of archetypes depicted in their imagery (like the Empress, Hanged Man, and Sun and Moon). These words are etched into a cement path in the Tarot Garden, or Giardino dei Tarocchi, on the coastline of the Maremma region of southern Tuscany near Capalbio (about 75 miles north of Rome). Surrounded by views of the classically Italian Tuscan landscape is the utterly unexpected sight of twenty-two vividly multicolored, playfully bizarre sculptures—some huge, even big enough to walk into—which depict the Major Arcana of the mystical and mythical Tarot cards.

The garden is the public art masterwork of Niki de Saint Phalle, a self-taught French-American artist who blended elements of pop, folk, outsider art, and surrealism into her paintings, lithographs, sculptures, jewelry, and other aspects of her world-class oeuvre. Her art and life were unpredictable. Beautiful as any French actress of her day, she became a sensation in the early '60s with "shooting paintings," where she fired rifles into sacs of paint on plaster surfaces to create works of art. She then painted a series of eccentrically voluptuous, colorfully abstract "nanas" (rough translation: broads). They had the proportions of earth goddesses and the whimsicality of adult cartoons, a spirit that soon found its way into de Saint Phalle's exuberant, mischievously grotesque sculptures. But when she experienced surrealist architect Antonio Gaudi's Parc Guell in Barcelona, she was inspired to move in a whole new direction and create her own outdoor world of dream and fantasy.

A lover of Italy with wealthy Italian friends, she was granted the land on which to create her gardens. Beginning in 1978, and financing the work in part by sales of a perfume she created, Niki de Saint Phalle worked on the project for over seventeen years.

The result is a 20th century version of Italian fantasy gardens of the 15th, 16th, and 17th centuries like the Villa D'Este in Tivoli and Parci dei Monstri in Bomarzo: a visitor leaves traditional Tuscany behind to enter a world of massive tarot card symbols that have a French playfulness and wit, but are also hauntingly otherworldly and beautiful. From the Empress to the Hierophant, Niki de Saint Phalle, with the help of her partner Jean Tinguely, built the sculptures out of steel and concrete, giving each dazzling shell inside and out of mosaicized colored glass and ceramics. The Empress, or *Imperatrice,* is so huge she has a viewing terrace and a walk-in mirrored cavern with her own palatial bedroom and bathroom.

In Giardino dei Tarocchi, one is of course supposed to admire the art, but also climb the Tower and play with the Wheel of Fortune and the Star. Niki de Saint Phalle meant for her spot of Eden to be touched and enjoyed by adults and children with all their senses, a evocation of—but also a brief respite from—the lifelong game of chance that is the story of the Tarot.

- UGLY BUT GOOD
- UCCELLO'S BATTLE
- UNESCO BONANZA
- UNSWEPT AWAY

✦ UGLY BUT GOOD

Brutti ma buoni means "ugly but good," an endearingly comical name for an amazing cookie that isn't exactly the prom queen of the cookie tin. These are funny-looking, misshappen beige meringue blobs (not so much ugly as nonconforming) laced with crushed nuts—usually hazelnuts, but not necessarily so—and often chocolate flavored. They have a crisp exterior and a soft and chewy interior, and as a bonus are even gluten free. *Brutti ma Buoni* originated in Northern Italy where hazelnuts are plentiful. . . at least until they find their way to these very tasty morsels and become the amazing disappearing cookies.

✦ UCCELLO'S BATTLE

Paolo di Dono, known as Uccello (his nickname, meaning "bird," for his love of drawing birds) was an early Renaissance painter in Florence as well as a mathematician. Uccello was a bit of an artistic outlier, an idiosyncratic transition artist who incorporated elements of the medieval Gothic—pageantry, pattern, and decorative effects—within the Renaissance's new science of rendering space through linear perspective. He was so fascinated by the principles of perspective he was said to have spent days and nights drawing objects in foreshortening; and according to Vasari's *Lives*, he was so obsessed by it that even when his wife called him to come to the bedchamber he would say "What a lovely thing this perspective is."

His most famous work, *The Battle of San Romano*, is considered to be one of the greatest Renaissance paintings of the *quattrocento,* and it introduced an entirely new subject into 15th-century art: the battle. Yes, this is the first battle scene on a High Renaissance canvas, and it's no surprise that the Medicis loved the painting, a large-scale tour de force executed as a three-panel triptych (each panel being approximately six feet high by ten feet wide) depicting a critical battle fought between Florence and neighboring Siena in 1432.

The painting is remarkable for its grasp and depiction of the geography 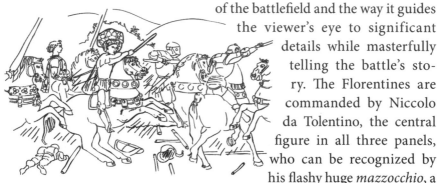 of the battlefield and the way it guides the viewer's eye to significant details while masterfully telling the battle's story. The Florentines are commanded by Niccolo da Tolentino, the central figure in all three panels, who can be recognized by his flashy huge *mazzocchio*, a kind of Florentine turban. The battle took place over eight hours and each panel shows its course throughout the day: dawn, when Tolentino and his men, who were greatly outnumbered, were ambushed by the Sienese; midday, when the Sienese leader was struck by a lance and knocked off his horse; and finally dusk, when reinforcements arrived and the Florentines counterattacked and ultimately prevailed.

The atmosphere is otherworldly—a colorfully crowded but bloodless battle, with knights attired in elaborate armor clashing on steeds with decorative harnesses, shown through a series of superimposed, intersecting, and action-packed perspective planes. The design offers scientific clarity applied to the fog of war; the broken lances and battle debris recede like a chessboard to a fixed vanishing point, creating a mathematical illusion of space. Many areas of the paintings were covered with gold and silver leaf; the gold leaf, found on the decorations of the bridles, has remained bright while the silver leaf, found particularly on the armor of the soldiers, has oxidized to a dull blackish-gray. The original impression of the gold leaf and burnished silver and strong colors must have been dazzling.

There has been debate as to who commissioned the paintings; it seems they originally were commissioned by another wealthy Florentine (Leonardo Bartolini Salimbeni) and were greatly admired, not the least by Lorenzo de Medici. Lorenzo so coveted the work that it is alleged he purchased one panel and had the remaining two panels forcibly removed to the Medici palace and installed in the large hall known as Lorenzo's room—at least according to the National Gallery in London, which, along with the Louvre and the Uffizi, now shares the three panels.

It has been hundreds of years since the panels have been displayed together; it would be a true victory for the forces both inside and outside modern Europe's first painted clash of men at arms if they could once again be assembled into a triptych, as Uccello meant it to be shown.

◆ UNESCO BONANZA

"Heritage is our legacy from the past, what we live with today, and what we pass on to future generations. Our cultural and natural heritage are both irreplaceable sources of life and inspiration." So states the United Nations Educational, Scientific, and Cultural Organization (UNESCO) on its website. If you're looking for inspiration at a UNESCO World Heritage Site, Italy is the best place in the world to find it, hands down.

With fifty-three such sites of cultural or natural significance, Italy tops the list of all 195 participating nations. Although Italy represents less than one-tenth of one percent of the planet's land-mass, it accounts for nearly five percent of the current total of 1,073 World Heritage Sites: fifty times the statistical average.

So, relatively speaking, it's hard to turn around in Italy without bumping into a World Heritage Site! (China is next on the list with one fewer sites spread over thirty-two times Italy's geographic area.)

Italy's World Heritage Sites cover the gamut from prehistory (La Valle Delle Incisioni—the Valley of Engravings—Europe's largest assemblage of petroglyphs); to antiquity (most famously, Pompeii and Herculaneum and classical Rome); to pivotal places of the last two millennia (dozens of others); plus a handful of natural wonders including Monte San Giorgio ("possibly the best fossil record of marine life from the Triassic Period") and the magnificent Dolomites.

At least one more notable Italian candidate for World Heritage Site status has been waiting in the wings for a decade now: the Scrovegni Chapel (*see*

"Sins of the Father"), the "Sistine Chapel of Padua." Perhaps someday soon the site of Giotto's best surviving work will take its rightful place on a list that includes the site of one of Leonardo da Vinci's most famous creations: Santa Maria dell Grazie, home of *The Last Supper*.

✦ UNSWEPT AWAY

This curiously fascinating floor mosaic is in the Vatican Museum. The objects are utterly realistic, with three-dimensional solidity and shadows cast in a way that prefigures *trompe l'oeil* and chiaroscuro. Rather than a heroic mythological subject, impressive geometric patterns, or exotic plants and animals, we see food scraps seemingly cast on the floor. The debris, which one would ordinarily expect to be swept into the garbage, includes fish bones, snails, fruit rinds, chicken bones, a lobster claw, and, as a final touch, a marauding mouse gnawing at a walnut shell.

This design motif was popular in ancient Rome and cropped up in dining rooms in posh private homes in Pompeii, Tunisia, Hadrian's villa, and in this case, from a villa on Aventine Hill. According to Pliny (see Pliny the Elder, Storyteller of the World) it was called the "Unswept Floor" and was inspired by the original mosaic floor created for the royal palace of Pergamum by the Greek artist Sosus of Pergamon in the second century BCE.

So. . .what does it speak to? What does it mean? We know the Romans were great adapters, so it's no surprise that they sought to emulate the Greeks. But what was its original intent? Was it a sign of hospitality, or a badge of conspicuous consumption marking the residence as a place of opulent banquets? Was Sosus showboating and showcasing his craft or did he

just have a quirky patron with a wry, sophisticated sense of humor? We may never know, but we can marvel at this surprising and enigmatic mosaic and what it may or may not tell us about one of our founding civilizations.

- VENUS'S NAVEL

- VENICE'S VENUS

- "LITTLE VENICE" AND VESPUCCI

- THE VESPA

- VESUVIUS

- VITRUVIUS, THE MAN

- VIN SANTO E BISCOTTI

- VOLARE

♦ VENUS'S NAVEL

The "creation myth" of tortellini involves Venus, the mythical goddess of love. It's a little suspicious: it's not set way back in the day, and it actually sounds a bit like a Sophia Loren-Marcello Mastroianni movie. But suspend your disbelief for this fun little folly, as it does lead to actual fun in the real world.

Tortellini are rolled and filled dough in the shape of tiny dumplings, a beloved member of the pasta family that hails from Emilia-Romagna. Once upon a time, in the small town of Castlefranco Emilia between the gastronomic giants of Bologna and Modena, Venus (or in some versions, simply a beauty from out of town) happened to be traveling alone and decided to take shelter among mortals. She was recognized by the keenly observant (actually voyeuristic) innkeeper, who could not resist checking out his immortal guest by peeping thought the tiny keyhole to watch her undress. He glimpsed only a small part of her beauty. But inspired by what he saw, he rushed to his kitchen and, to the best of his ability, using egg pasta to better approximate her luscious skin tone, he created a pasta to immortalize her... divine navel!

For the residents of Castelfranco, this story is more than just a flight of fancy. Each year, on the second week of September to be exact, the nameless inventor of the sensually shaped pasta is celebrated with ceremonial pomp, Renaissance costumes, and a staged reenactment of the Eureka moment

253

. . . the MC shouts: "Inspired by the sight of the divine navel, our innkeeper invents the prestigious tortellini!"

Actually, the pasta was in all probability created in the late 1500s. In the Emilia-Romagna region, the tortellini, not exactly *cucina povera* (fillings like prosciutto or parmesan cheese can make it expensive), has always had a special place, reserved for big occasions like Christmas, Easter, and weddings . . . or if Venus happens to be disrobing in your guest room.

♦ VENICE'S VENUS

Thomas Mann referred to Venice as "the most improbable of cities." Like Venus, goddess of love and beauty, Venice too arose from the misty lagoons to become the pleasure capital of Europe. Her unworldly allure and physical separation from the mainland gave permission for visitors (and residents) to conduct themselves outside of the restrictive moral boundaries of the times. So inevitably Venice became the dominion of the most beautiful and skilled courtesans of their time.

The word courtesan is derived from Italian *cortigiana* (sharing, not improbably, the root of both "court" and "cohort") and these women made up about ten percent of Venice's population in the 16th century. Class distinctions reigned even in the realm of prostitution and there were two strata: the first fit the standard notion of a prostitute today while the second, known as *cortigiana onesta* (so-called "honest courtesans," for which Venice was particularly renowned), were like brainy high-priced call girls. Not only beautiful, they were well-educated and cultured, knowledgeable in art and literature, occasionally skilled musicians, and certainly able to engage in intellectual discourse with the rich and powerful. With a better education and a broader knowledge base than most married women, even those of noble birth, the most refined "honest courtesans" were sometimes more highly valued for their opinions than were the wives of the powerful, and they not only maintained a subtle political influence but sometimes even engaged in political espionage! For a beautiful woman of substance, becoming an honest courtesan was an avenue to a more independent life and to personal wealth—provided she could hold her own against the most beautiful, clever, and shrewd women of Venice.

Venice being Venice, Popes always seemed to be excommunicating the fiercely independent Republic (to little effect), but paradoxically the Church took a laissez-faire approach to the courtesans and prostitution. There are documents still in existence that show that prostitution and courtesans were believed to curtail the spread of sin rather than being a sin in their own right. The Church seems to have believed that prostitution had positive influences in serving to reduce homosexuality and sodomy, which, beyond being mortal sins, were punishable by torture or death.

One Venetian courtesan stood above the rest, a supreme curtailer of sin, and it was not simply because of her chopines. Veronica Franco (1546–1591) was immortalized by the likes of Tinteretto and Titian, and the movie *Dangerous Beauty* was based on her life. She was the daughter of a famous courtesan who made sure she had an excellent education, learned Latin and Greek from her brothers' tutors, and became a talented lute player. Seeking a different life for Veronica, her mother arranged for Veronica to marry a wealthy physician. But Veronica chose to leave her husband very shortly after their marriage and the birth of a son and began her life as a *cortigiana* to support herself financially.

Wealthy men helped her throughout her life, including Domenico Veniere who included Veronica in his literary salon, which was the most influential in Venice at the time. She was not only well educated but a gifted writer and poetess, addressing themes of love and the rights of women in writings that are still highly regarded today. Her most famous client was King Henry III of France, son of Catherine De Medici. While the story may be apocryphal, she apparently presented the King with the portrait of herself and also included two sonnets dedicated to him in her publication called "familiar letters to various people." Despite having powerful supporters, Veronica was unable to catalyze a political change she sought in city life; in 1577 she proposed the establishment of a home for poor women for which she would become administrator but was turned down by the Venetian Council.

She eventually gave up her life as courtesan and sought to dedicate herself to her literary pursuits, including two important volumes of poetry. It was in these later writings that she ultimately regretted her life and advised a friend against allowing her daughter to become a courtesan, saying it was giving "your body in slavery."

Her fortunes began to decline following one of Venice's plague epidemics, which forced her to flee the city. When she returned she was charged with witchcraft; although she was eventually freed, she descended into poverty and died at the age of forty-five. The woman who had risen in Venice to command its realm of pleasure realized toward the end of her life that it was not only improbable but, while remembered fondly, not to be trusted:

> *"We danced our youth in a dreamed of city,*
> *Venice, paradise, proud and pretty,*
> *We lived for love and lust and beauty,*
> *Pleasure then our only duty.*
> *Floating them twixt heaven and Earth*
> *And drank on plenties blessed mirth*
> *We thought ourselves eternal then,*
> *Our glory sealed by God's own pen.*
> *But paradise, we found is always frail,*
> *Against man's fear will always fail."*
> ~ Veronica Franco ~

♦ "LITTLE VENICE" AND VESPUCCI

The great Age of Exploration was in part an age of confusion. Christopher Columbus set out to reach India sailing west, landed in the Caribbean, called the islands the "Indies," and stuck native Americans with the term "Indians." Later he would be called the discoverer of America although he never reached either of the land masses that bear that name.

To Amerigo Vespucci went that honor (even though he never landed in "America" America either). He did however discover South America, which he called the New World; both his given name and his names for the continent then traveled north.

There was one place that one of these men landed in and named accurately. In 1499, Vespucci's expedition across the Atlantic landed on what we now know as the Venezuelan coast. The stilt houses in the area of Lake Maracaibo reminded him of the city of Venice—*Venezia*—so he named the region "*Venezuela*," meaning "little Venice" in Italian. The word has the same meaning in Spanish, where the suffix *-zuela* is used as a diminutive; thus, the term's original sense of "little Venice" carried over to the territory's ultimate possessors.

What all this reminds us of, other than that the most mind-bending and revolutionary discoveries naturally involve some mistakes at first,

is that while the empire-builders
of the New World would be the
Spanish, Portuguese, French,
and English, the navigators
and explorers who first made
it all possible were Italians. And
they knew each other: Vespucci,
a Florentine, having worked with

merchants who supplied the Genoan Cristoforo Colombo, met with him
in Seville in 1496 after Colombo returned from one of his later voyages.
Inspired by the other's tales, and with his own business floundering, Vespucci, knowing that King Ferdinand and Queen Isabella of Spain were still
funding voyages of discovery, followed in his countryman's footsteps (or,
more accurately, wakes) and joined him in Italian and global immortality.

◆ THE VESPA

Introduced over seventy years ago, the Vespa, both sexy and practical,
has become synonymous with stylish spontaneity, freedom, and *la dolce
vita*. And it can be parked almost anywhere—in the narrow cobblestone
alleyways of little hill towns or in the triple-park traffic nightmare in Rome.

Following World War II an inexpensive alternative to the automobile
suitable for maneuvering around the bomb-damaged cities was needed, and
only in Italy could a homely mini-military vehicle inspire the invention of
a cultural icon.

Industrialist Enrico Piaggio was determined to get his factories working again, and began building prototype scooters resembling the U.S.'s
olive-colored Cushman Airborn motorcycles that had been parachuted into
the northern industrial regions of Italy and used by the troops against the
Germans. The early prototype was a funny shaped ugly duckling nicknamed
"Paperino" (after Donald Duck). Piaggo didn't like it and assigned aero-
nautics engineer Corradino D'Ascanio to redesign it. D'Ascanio preferred
aircraft to motorcycles, seeing the latter as cumbersome and dirty. With
a mind for the practical and an eye for the sleek, he created the prototype
which stands as a marvel of modern design engineering.

Blending aircraft features with those of a motorized scooter, D'Ascanio
abided by the ethos of "form follows function." For easy access, the

gearshift was moved onto the handlebar and, thinking aerodynamically, he altered the shape of the scooter's body and designed it to protect the driver from rain, mud, and road dirt. Another game-changer was a seat which made the vehicle both safer and more comfortable to ride, with the greasy inner working of the motor concealed behind the seat panels to keep a rider's clothes in *la bella figura* condition. And the practical step-through frame meant it was also perfectly suited for skirt-wearing *signoras* and *signorinas* to zip around in. The story goes (and one only hopes it's true, because truth here is indeed beauty) that when Piaggio saw the prototype, because of its narrow chassis and buzzing sound, he instantly named it la Vespa, meaning "the wasp."

Vespa sales skyrocketed in 1953 when Gregory Peck took Audrey Hepburn for a spin around the eternal city in the film classic *Roman Holiday*, and its popularity has never waned. Today over 16,000,000 Vespas buzz through Italian streets, and it's the vehicle of choice of businessmen, nuns, teenagers, and grandmothers.

♦ VESUVIUS

Refuting the old axiom "ignorance is bliss," residents of the resort towns of Pompeii and Herculaneum never saw it coming. They might have felt it coming if only they had understood the link between seismic and volcanic activity and if they had actually known Mount Vesuvius, fertile and abundant with wine and olive groves, was a volcano. Vesuvius had been dormant for over eight hundred years. And though a deadly earthquake had occurred seventeen years earlier and tremors were considered common, Pliny the Younger had written that the rumblings "were not particularly alarming because they are frequent in Campania."

The course of the unforeseen cataclysm that would destroy these Roman cities has been reconstructed based upon letters written by Pliny who, with his father Pliny the Elder, did not survive, but observed and recorded the eruption first hand, along with the accounts of the Roman historian Tacitus and archaeological discoveries.

On the afternoon of August 24, 79 CE, Vesuvius began spewing volcanic ash and rocks thousands of feet skyward in a cone of fiery smoke that eventually flattened out, prompting Pliny to describe the appearance of the gray cloud as a stone pine tree. The prevailing winds were blowing toward the southeast, causing eight to ten feet of volcanic material to fall primarily on the city of Pompeii and the surrounding areas. Most roofs and buildings collapsed, destroying much of the city on the first day while neighboring Herculaneum was only mildly affected, receiving a mere dusting of a few inches of ash and giving many (though not all) of its residents ample time to flee.

During the night came the first deadly pyroclastic surge of superheated gases and rock, followed by a succession of six flows and surges afterwards. Recent research has lead to the conclusion that exposure to this heat of at least 250° C was the main cause of death for those who did not escape, rather than the suffocation which had been previously assumed. It has been estimated the Vesuvius eruption released one hundred thousand times the thermal energy of the Hiroshima bombing.

Then the rains came and mixed with the ash, forming a sort of concrete which froze everything and everyone in time, preserving what was left of the cities. The mostly evacuated town of Herculaneum was then buried but with little damage, miraculously preserving structures, frescoes, objects, and victims almost intact. And so these cities' terrible losses became history and archaeology's gains.

There are exceptional frescos from the ruins of Herculaneum that give a glimpse of residents' daily life. Female slaves were common and performed a wide range of duties, depending on the needs of the household, from cooking and cleaning to being nannies and wet nurses and serving as personal attendants of their wealthy matrons, caring for their hair among other responsibilites.

In the neighboring and more bacchanalian Pompeii, there are murals that show a range of far more illicit activities, but also artistic ones, such as the near perfect mosaic of Street Musicians, signed

by Dioskourides of Samos and found in the so-called Villa of Cicero, one of the finest surviving works from the ancient Roman world. Figures are playing musical instruments typically connected with the cult of Cybele: the tambourine, small cymbals, and the double flute. Cybele had a powerful reputation connected with agricultural abundance and military victories.

Far more unique to this disaster than these frescoes, the ruins of buildings, or even the wealth of objects unearthed from the volcanic debris (like carbonized furniture and even figs) are, in effect, mummifications of the residents of Pompeii: the volcanic ash that formed a hard shell over them later could serve as the foundation of body casts that would further define them. Preserved in their final solitary moments, or as they embraced and kissed each other goodbye, they remain a reminder of the need to live as well as possible in the present, and a warning of how much that present can be at risk from a lack of knowledge (or willful denial) of the laws of nature.

✦ VITRUVIUS, THE MAN

Perhaps no quote more sums up the way the Renaissance dispelled the darkness of the Middle Ages than that of the ancient Greek philosopher Protagoras: "Man is the measure of all things." And no image more incarnates that thought than Leonardo da Vinci's immortal drawing of the Vitruvian man.

Vitruvius was an actual architect and aesthetic philosopher who lived in ancient Rome in the first century BCE and who wrote a book on Roman buildings (and many other matters), *De Architectura*, which became a guidebook for Renaissance architects—especially Leon Battista Alberti, who wrote his own *De Re Aedificatoria* based on Vitruvius. Renaissance passion for the architectural embodiments of classical geometry and architecture (the simple forms of the circle and the square) found an ideal guide, via Alberti and other writers, in Vitruvius's work.

And nested in Vitruvius's book was a description, using those universal forms, of how man might exemplify the ideal measure of the universe. In his Book III, Vitruvius frames a vision of man linked to ideal proportion in terms of a circle and a square. In the circle, the center is man's navel, the arms and feet extending to the circumference. Meanwhile, in a square, man's head-to-toe line and extended arms also travel to the lines of the square. There was only one problem: the two didn't match up. How do you square the circle?

Enter Leonardo da Vinci one of the great minds of the age (or any age), not just a sublime artist but also a keen observer of nature and thinker about science and mathematics. He saw "Vitruvian man" as a puzzle to be solved, and he solved it—by a slight cheat: as drawn by Leonardo, the man occupies a circle and square that are slightly unequal in area. Later mathematicians would see Leonardo's elegant solution as reflecting the fact that the indefinite number *pi* itself makes any equality of areas of circle and square impossible.

Even with that little imbalance, with one foot in the Classical past and the other resting in observation of nature, Vitruvian Man, drawn by Leonardo, expresses the Renaissance notion that man himself is the most harmonious expression of Creation, and that to understand him is to understand the harmony of the universe at large.

The drawing is in the Gabinetto dei Disegni e Stampe of the Gallerie Dell' Accademia in Venice and is only very occasionally on public display. But the image drawn by Leonardo—its beauty, its hopeful poetic depiction of how we might be able to unite the physical and intellectual sides of humanity—is everywhere, including the obverse (national) side of the Italian one-euro coin. Carlo Azeglio Ciampi, former prime minister of Italy, observed that this represents the "coin to the service of Man," instead of Man in the service of money.

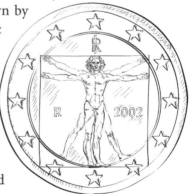

Long may the beauty of Vitruvian Man grace our currencies, T-shirts, mouse pads, and coffee cups. We need to be reminded of him now more than ever.

• VIN SANTO E BISCOTTI

When in Italy, instead of the good old comfort of cookies and milk, dip your postprandial biscotti in some Vin Santo.

Biscotti trace their origin to Roman times. Biscotto derives from *bis*, Latin for "twice," and *coxit* or "baked." Originally made to be durable for travel and carried off to war by the Roman legions (their version of hard-tack), biscotti helped fuel the expansion of the Roman Empire as far east as Iraq and west to Great Britian. It is that second trip to the oven which draws off all the moisture, resulting in their hard dry texture and extremely long shelf life. Roman scholar Pliny the Elder boasted they would be edible for centuries!

Hopefully that meant that some biscotti made it through the Middle Ages. At least the recipe did, for when cuisine, like so much else, came back to life in the Renaissance, biscotti reemerged in Tuscany and ingredients like almonds were added to the previously pallid and uninspired pastry. Today creative bakers in every region have developed their own style. The twice-baking still results in a dry crunchy texture, and this makes the biscotti (also known as *cantucci*) ideal for soaking up the traditional sweet local wine—Vin Santo.

Vin Santo is a style of sweet wine typical of Tuscany, usually made from white grapes and produced by drying the grapes on straw mats in warm and well-ventilated areas or by hanging them on indoor racks. There are a few theories on how Vin Santo or "holy wine" got its name. The most plausible was the wine's historic use at Mass where sweet wine was preferred. Another popular theory has to do with how the wine is actually "aged"—with fermentation around All Saints Day followed by the bottling of the wine during Easter week. Fortunately, this holy wine is available for any and all secular occasions.

• VOLARE

What can you say about a romantic ballad that begins with the kind of spoken word musical *recitatif* you might find in an opera, and is as much about beautiful Old Master art as young love? Number one, it's probably Italian. Number two, it probably won't travel well.

In the case of the world-famous song "Volare," you'd be right about the first conclusion, and totally wrong about the second one. Written by Franco Migliacci and Domenico Modugno and sung by Mr. Modugno, its original title was "Nel blu dipinto di blu" ("In the blue-painted blue") and was inspired by the paintings of Marc Chagall. The story has it that Mr. Migliacci woke up from vivid dreams inspired by a little too much wine and stared at a Chagall reproduction where a man, his face half blue, soared through magical landscapes. That became the inspiration for what he called his "sogno in blu," and once he began writing it with Mondugno, the idea of painting oneself and flying was combined with the idea of soaring with one's lover in romantic ecstasy.

The song, now titled "Volare," was chosen as the Italian entry to the Eurovision Song Contest in 1958 (the granddaddy of all shows like *The Voice*) where it won third place. But once out in the world, its popularity far exceeded that of many long-forgotten first-prize-winners. It would sell 22 million copies worldwide. Mondugno's version, propelled by a charming appearance on the *Ed Sullivan Show*, would become Grammy winner for Song of the Year in 1958 and was also Billboard's Number One single for that year. No non Anglo-American group would snag that double prize again until 1994's "The Sign" by Swedish group Ace of Base.

Mondugno's sensational success changed the global reach and style of Italian popular vocal music, but most people in the United States heard the song as rendered by, among others, Dean Martin, Bobby Rydell, Louis Armstrong, Ella Fitzgerald, and by David Bowie in the movie *Absolute Beginners*. In 2005, on the 50th anniversary of the Eurovision Song Contest, "Nel blu dipinto di blu" came in second on the list of all time Contest favorites, beaten only by ABBA's "Waterloo"—and Benny Andersson himself voted for it over his own tune. And in 2008, the song's 50th anniversary was celebrated with a stamp showing a man flying against a blue background, returning "Volare" to its original very Italian inspiration in great works of art.

Volare (to fly), oh oh
E cantare (and to sing), oh oh oh oh
No wonder my happy heart sings
Your love has given me wings

•WHERE THE WILD BOAR ROAM

•THE WOLF WHISPERER

•WORD-PLAYING WITH YOUR FOOD

•WINDMILLS OF SICILY

•THE WONDER OF THE WORLD

◆ WHERE THE WILD BOAR ROAM

It may not be Italy's equivalent of the American bald eagle, but the *cinghiale,* the wild boar, holds a valued place not only in Italy's culture but on its dinner tables.

The wild boar likely predates the Etruscans and might even represent Italy's oldest bloodline. They've been denizens of the deep dark woods and have roamed the mountains for thousands of years. It's said that the Greek sailors named the island of Capri Kapros—Greek for boar—because there were so many. Today there are no *cinghiale* on Capri, but they are everywhere else on the Boot.

They may be delectably beloved, but they're not loveable: a big, ferocious three feet tall at the shoulder beast weighing four hundred pounds. Though they have bad eyesight—which is why they hide in thickets to avoid predators—they can eat and fight almost anything they encounter; both the males and females have white tusks but only the males will charge and fight to the death.

Boar hunting is a popular Italian sport with a long tradition very much tied into the country's cultural identity. Going back to Roman times, it was initially pursued by the nobility, almost like British foxhunting, and so there are many depictions of the hunt in Italian art. Centuries ago, before rifles, wild boars were hunted with dogs wrapped in padding who would chase the boars and try to bite them and slow them down so that the hunters could finish them off with spears . . . not exactly a healthy gig for the dogs. Nowadays dogs go along only to flush the *cinghiale* out so the hunter can get a clear shot.

Currently there's a population boom of *cinghiale*, and a physical growth spurt as the wild boars have gotten even bigger crossbreeding with Eastern European wild boar who have been migrating west. So the hunt is now not just a tradition but a necessity to thin the population and keep them healthy.

And it's not just for sport; naturally the Italians have taken this un-prepossessing animal and turned it into great cuisine. Fall is the best time to hunt wild boar; even though at this stage they are at their most ferocious, they are also at their fattest and tastiest. Their meat takes many delicious forms—as *salsiccia* or a hard salami (you will see stuffed wild boar in village *salumeria* everywhere); eaten as ham, steak, or sausage; or as part of a rustic ragu. Tusks turn into jewelry, pendants, or knife handles, and their hair is used for hairbrushes.

As is typical of Italy, each region proudly boosts the virtues and superiority of their local *cinghiale*. Tuscans say theirs is best because of their diet of Tuscan chestnuts; the Sards say their boars are superior thanks to the acorns from their oaks; but the Umbrians seem to hold the bragging rights with a claim of Umbrian boars making regular snacks of the region's black truffles.

And of course the boar has made it into Italian art, most notably a Florentine 17th-century bronze sculpture in a fountain at Mercato Nuovo just off the Ponte Vecchio. Known affectionately as *il porcellino*—the piglet—it's a copy of a Hellenistic marble original that was found in Rome and removed to Florence by the Medici. If you place a coin in its mouth it's for good luck and if you rub its nose that assures your return to Florence. *Il porcellino*'s nose gleams.

♦ THE WOLF WHISPERER

Among the many roles played by St. Francis of Assisi in his brief but storied life, perhaps none was more startling than that of "wolf whisperer."

For a time in the early 13th century the neighboring Umbrian town of Gubbio was terrorized by the threat of a vicious and stealthy wolf. When Francis learned of this local crisis he immediately set out for Gubbio and then, ignoring pleas of the townsfolk, he ventured into the woods beyond. Sure enough, the wolf charged towards Francis, but he stood resolutely in place invoking a higher power. Rather than attack, the wolf then lay down at Francis's feet and listened to his terms of peace. Francis recognized that "Brother Wolf" was just another one of God's creatures who was only acting badly on account of his extreme hunger. So Francis proposed that the townsfolk would feed the wolf if, in turn, the wolf threatened no further harm. The deal was sealed hand in paw, and the wolf and townsfolk of Gubbio lived together amicably after that day.

When Brother Wolf died of natural causes a couple of years later, he was mourned and accorded burial in a chapel dedicated to Francis, one of the great peacemakers of his or any other time.

Is the wolf of Gubbio story apocryphal? What's indisputable is that in 1871 workmen found the skeleton of a wolf near Gubbio's church; it was subsequently buried inside.

One of the great Italian filmmakers, Roberto Rosselini, depicted nine episodes from St. Francis' life in *The Flowers of St. Francis*. The original Italian version of the movie used "chapter markers" to separate each of those episodes, reflecting the text upon which the film had been based. (The very same device was used forty-five years later in the international blockbuster *Babe*—produced and co-written by George Miller and directed by Chris Noonan—about a saintly, Francis-like pig who could also communicate with other animals, bringing love, hope, and peace to his rural realm). In a country that venerates a host of saints, St. Francis, with his doctrines of poverty, humility, and devotion; his generous and forgiving deeds; his caring for the poor; and his love of animals holds a very special place people's hearts, and naturally, *arte*.

٠ WORD-PLAYING WITH YOUR FOOD

Not only do Italians have a way with food but they have a way with words about food: many gastronomic terms are not simply descriptive but rather evocative, designed to tease and inspire the appetite and bring a sense of playful celebration to the dining experience.

There's no better example than *saltimbocca*, which doesn't have anything to do with pounded veal or the prosciutto and sage that so deliciously lines and tops the dish. "Salto" is the word for jump and "bocca" the word for mouth, suggesting how quickly one can and will want to eat these morsels.

Peppery *puttanesca* sauce is named for Italy's notorious ladies of the night. The name derives from the Italian word *puttana* which means whore and *puttana* in turn arises from the Latin word *putida* which means stinking. The story is that the ladies cooked up *pasta alla puttanesca* and placed pots of the spicy red sauce in or near the windows so the scent would draw in customers, because of course it's not stinking but salty and tangy (thanks to the olives, capers, garlic, hot pepper, and often anchovies) in a far more enticing manner (kind of like when Sophia Loren played a call girl).

Bagna Caudo, meaning "warm bath," is a traditional Piedmonte dish made of olive oil, butter, garlic, and anchovies; it's kept warm in its own specially designed terracotta tub atop a little heater for dipping raw or cooked vegetables in at the start of a meal. And *Osso Buco*—more descriptive and rather pedestrian by comparison—simply means "bone with a hole" (*osso* bone, *buco* hole), a reference to the marrow hole at the center of the cross-cut veal shank, although there is nothing pedestrian about this dish.

You'll frequently find *gelato affogato* offered in bars and gelateria throughout Italy. The word *affogato* literally means "to drown" and refers to what happens to gelato when you pour a shot of steaming espresso over it, adding a clever touch of theatricality.

An *affogato* is typically served with a gelato flavor such as pannacotta (*panna* for "cream" and *cotta* for "cooked") or *fior di latte* ("flower of milk," or sweet cream). When "drowned" by steaming espresso, the result is like and an ultra creamy latte. However with some improvisation and imagination, all sorts of other interesting "adult" combinations can be created:

~ Chocolate gelato "drowned" in Amaretto becomes *Casanova's Kiss*
~ Coconut gelato "drowned" in Limoncello becomes a *Coco-Motion*
~ Espresso gelato "drowned" in Frangelico becomes *The Naughty Friar*

It's hard to top gelato, but you can make it even more intoxicating.

◆ THE WINDMILLS OF SICILY

One of the most striking and unexpected panoramas in Sicily is the Via Del Sale (the salt road) on the west coast of the island between the harbor towns of Trapani and Marsala.

Marsala was named by its Arab traders "marsal Allah" (God's harbor), perhaps for its welcoming beauty. And that beauty has not changed too much over the centuries: a juxtaposition of white salt dunes, orange tile roofs rising to the blue sky, and the calm harmony of movement of the coast's peak-roofed, centuries-old windmills.

The *salinas*, enclosed salt marshes, add more subtle colorations to the scene, changing hues with the concentration of their brine: some clear and reflecting the azure Sicilian sky; others tinted with shades of pink, purple, dark blue; some white with pure salt.

Seen at sunset from the hill town of Erice, the view is an enchanting multicolored checkerboard like nothing else in the world.

The economic heft of the salt marshes has been a significant factor in Sicily's history. We think of salt as enhancing the taste of food, but in older times it was also a vital preservative and a primary source of iodine, a deficiency of which could be deadly. Salt has been cheap since the mining of rock salt in the nineteenth century but before then only deposits near the surface could be extracted and at great expense.

And so it was known as "white gold" for its value and, in many lands, its rarity. For centuries salt was part of the wages for soldiers; in fact the word salary is derived from "sale," and a skillful fighting man was said to be "worth his salt." The mineral was even thought to have magical properties in many cultures; Sicilians scatter salt on the ground to protect themselves from the evil eye and they believe salt given as a gift brings good luck.

So the Sicilians had very much a going concern in the Trapani-to-Marsala stretch of geography, with perfect conditions for salt harvesting—and there's still a salt works there extracting it the Old World way. It takes patience and luck to extract salt from the sea via evaporation, along with a flat coastline adjacent to very shallow sea, continuous sun, and here's where those beautiful windmills standing sentinel over the landscape come in—powered by the steady wind they pump sea water from pool to pool, causing faster and faster evaporation and leaving the wealth of salt behind.

How local are these windmills? The windmills are used to power Archimedes screws, screw-shaped surfaces inside pipes, which pump water upward from sea pool to sea pool as each successive pool undergoes more evaporation and makes the salt more concentrated. And the man who created this ingenious device which bears his name, while of course a Greek, was a "Sicilian" born in Siracusa. Talk about a local boy made good—as in immortal. The great Greek thinker's gift to his now-Italian people still powers a clean and valuable industry in the 21st century, not to mention fairytale windmills that are among the most delightful human-scale landmarks in Italy.

♦ THE WONDER OF THE WORLD

What can we say about a man who one of the greatest of all Italian literary figures, Dante, called a light of the ages but nonetheless consigned to the sixth circle of hell?

Other than that he was perhaps unfairly treated by literature (a tough business at best), we can certainly say he was complicated and that he had a powerful influence on his times. But actually Frederic II was known as *Stupor Mundi*, the Wonder of the World, and his expansion of his reign and its cultural achievements from the Kingdom of Sicily to most of the Western and much of the Muslim world is part of a virtual secret history of Europe, a history that leads directly to the cultural awakening of the Italian Renaissance.

No literary lion, not even a Dante or Shakespeare, could have invented the life of Frederic II, which began with a birth that, literally, had to be seen to be believed. His mother, Constance, Queen of Sicily, a Norman princess and daughter of Sicilian ruler Roger II (*see* "Norman Arab Sicily"), was on her way to meet her German husband Henry VI of Hohenstaufen who, as Holy Roman Emperor, was about to be crowned King of Sicily. The Holy Roman Empire was a vast swath of central Europe carved out of former Roman territories, often seemingly up for grabs among dynasties that would then add to their holdings by everything from papal dispensation to marriages to conquest. Along the route, since Constance was forty years of age and was concerned the population would never believe her child and heir to Henry's dynasty was legitimately hers, she gave birth in a tent in public, in the town of Jesi near Ancona, with clergy and other spectators to witness her royal son's arrival.

Though Italian by both birth and choice, Frederic was destined to rule over two dominions. His Court, begun by his grandfather Roger II, simultaneously Italian and multicultural, was a bright spot in the dark ages of medieval times. And he would continue its progress toward a modern centralized state while giving further impetus to Italian poetry and the other arts, religious tolerance, and the revival of Greco-Arabic learning in the west; like grandfather, like grandson.

But Frederic would be more prodigious than Roger II in both his achievements and excesses. Growing up with an Arab best friend, he quickly learned that language along with Greek, Latin, and many others. At the age of twenty-five, he vanquished his closest rival and in 1220 was crowned Holy Roman Emperor in St Peter's by Pope Honorius III. Before his mother's death she had appointed Pope Innocent III as his guardian and protector—but when he became the ruler of the lands north of Rome along with Sicily, geographically pincering the Vatican, that earned him their enmity.

He would not help his cause by being a reluctant and then cleverly diplomatic Crusader. In 1227, under threat of excommunication by Pope Gregory IX, he attempted a military expedition and was deterred by plague. His second attempt was resolved peacefully with the Sultan Al-Kamil, obtaining the kingship of Jerusalem but not the entire love of the papacy.

His home kingdom of Sicily became his focus; he was not overly impressed with his new Holy Roman Empire kingdom and its papal backing and seemed to think if God had known Sicily, he would not have chosen the holy lands. In 1230 Frederic reconquered Southern Italy in an alliance with the Pope that at least deferred the threat of excommunication; but the next year he promulgated the Constitutions of Melfi, rooted in natural and kingly rather than ecclesiastical law, and guaranteeing certain basic human rights, including the right to a speedy trial and divorce (which would not be legal in Italy in general until 1973).

Meanwhile, traveling his kingdom with his Magna Curia, he amazed the population not just with his retinue of poets, musicians, craftsmen, and even harem girls, but with a menagerie of exotic animals like elephants, lions, and camels, and, in an early example of mobile information, a mule train carrying his precious library of manuscripts.

Knowledge and particularly science was his passion, along with fencing, riding, hunting, and falconry, for which he actually wrote a *Dea Arte Venandi Cum Avibus* ("The Art of Hunting with Birds") as part of being, in effect, the western world's first ornithologist. Fascinated by mathematics, he befriended Fibonacci, who introduced Arabic numerals into Europe, and established the University of Naples in 1224. A poet himself, he created the first school of vernacular poetry in the Italian language, where Gicaomi da Lentini concocted the first sonetto (from *sonetta*, little poem). Moses Maimonides' *Guide for the Perplexed* and many other texts in ancient languages were translated at Frederick's brilliant court in Palermo.

Meanwhile he proposed a series of extremely rational questions about the afterlife—where's heaven and hell and how do you get there?—causing the Pope to finally excommunicate him. For all his accomplishments and despite his crusade, he literally never lived that down. Dante, although lauding in his *de vulgari eloquentia* Frederic II's "nobility and righteousness" and enlightened mind, still consigned him to hell in a fiery tomb with Epicureans, heretics, and afterlife deniers.

But perhaps Frederic's most enduring accomplishment, and most direct contribution to the Renaissance, derived from his guiding his builders to emulate the ruins of classical Rome rather than recycling them for building materials. His Castel del Monte, a unique octagonal limestone-walled fortress with eight corners crowned with octagonal towers, had an at-the-time groundbreaking gate with Greco-Roman temple motifs. It was declared a World Heritage site by UNESCO in 1996 and has magnificently endured the passage of empires and time, gaining a second life on the Italian Euro-cent.

Caught up in the Guelph-Ghibelline wars against the enemies in the papacy he could never escape, his fortunes seesawed until his army was destroyed and he died of dysentery. When the news reached Rome, Pope Innocent IV was delighted. "Let heaven exult and the earth rejoice," he proclaimed. But an anonymous Latin chronicle mourned that "the sun of the world has set, which illuminated all the people." The sight of Frederic's red porphyry sarcophagus standing on four carved lions in his grandfather's magnificent Cappella Palatina suggests that, while the fortunes of Italy's warring factions would rise and fall, the culture of Italy would forever be illuminated by that sunset glow.

◆YOU SAY XITOMATI
AND I SAY XITOMAHTO

◆   ◆   ◆

◆ZA'FARAN,
FROM PERSIA WITH LOVE

◆ZIN'S TWIN?

◆ZECCHINO

◆ZUCARRI MOSTRI MASHUP

◆THE ZANNI

◆ YOU SAY XITOMATI AND I SAY XITOMAHTO

Tomato is *the* ingredient most synonymous with Italy and Italian dining. It feels Old World, but really it is New World and has had a rather convoluted history, bouncing back and forth across the pond a couple of times. Formerly feared as poisonous, nowadays it's not only a cultural icon but a nutritional superstar with its powerful antioxidants.

Tomatoes originated in South America where the Incas were the first to cultivate this juicy fruit as early as 700 CE; it spread to Mexico where the Aztecs called it *xitomati,* meaning "plump thing with a navel." Golden tomatoes, thought to be ornamental plants, were taken back to Europe (along with squash and sunflowers) by the conquistadors; some crediting Cortez with this, his one benign act of cultural theft.

The first written account of the tomato in Italy dates to 1546, when Italian physician and botanist Pietro Andrea Mattioli classified it as a fruit and referred to it as *pomid'oro* or the "golden fruit." The French called it "the apple of love" and the Germans called it "the apple of paradise," in all likelihood due to its shape, color, and juiciness. It was further classified as a mandrake (aphrodisiac) and a nightshade, some of which are poisonous. An interesting choice—love or death!

According to Annabelle Smith writing for the Smithsonian, the "plump thing" struggled to catch on, not surprising due to these extreme misperceptions. Some believed the stalk was poisonous while the fruit was not, some reported that it attracted large worms that were toxic. Europeans feared the tomato was fatal in and of itself well into the late 1700's. There had been numerous incidents when aristocrats took ill and died after eating them; the actual cause was pewter plates which were high in lead content, and so when the tomatoes, high in acidity, were placed on this particular tableware, the fruit would leach lead from the plate, resulting in deaths from lead poisoning. No one made the connection with the plates so the plump juicy newcomer tomato was blamed as the culprit.

Time ultimately dispelled all the misinterpretations and tomatoes proliferated throughout Italy, especially in the South and in the San Marzano region located just outside of Naples. Their high acid content was ultimately a great advantage, good for preservation (see "Marinara"), and their popularity only increased with the development of pizza at the end of the 19th century (see "Queen of Pearls"). The San Marzano tomato was the original export tomato to America one hundred years ago and now enjoys protected agricultural status.

It was Thomas Jefferson who brought back tomato seeds from his days as ambassador to Paris (along with vines for wine), but both required time to gain a foothold and commercial trading status. The tomatoes needed the waves of southern Italian immigrants at the turn of the last century who were homesick for sunny *Italia* and the foods of their homeland. They first had to make do with what was here, canned tomatoes being the closest connection.

But today there are over 10,000 varieties of cultivated tomatoes throughout the world, and it is now the most widely grown of all produce, vegetable or fruit, in the United States. Perhaps it's history rewound, as Italy's tomato lovers, settling in the New World, brought the *xitomati* back home.

♦ ZA'FARAN, FROM PERSIA WITH LOVE

Italy cultivated it, then lost the knack, the Moors and Persians brought it back, and Italy then resumed marketing it to the rest of Europe. Very difficult to harvest, it has nonetheless never lost its appeal over the centuries.

We know it as saffron, a wonderfully aromatic spice and an essential ingredient of any Italian pantry, whether you're preparing *risotto Milanese*, Sicilian *arancini*, or fish soups typical of Marche and Liguria. It's the world's most expensive spice and not surprisingly its history is one of luxury.

Vibrant red-orange sweet-smelling saffron was highly prized by the ancients, who also used it as a perfume and in preparation for dyes for cloth and for paint for classical artists. The spice has been associated with curative powers, believed to help ease digestion, rheumatism aggravated by melancholy, and colds (and valued for its antioxidant properties today).

Saffron was considered a wonder drug long before you could actually tell if a drug worked wonders. Zeus was said to sleep on a bed of saffron. Both Greeks and Romans scattered saffron water in theatres and other public places—the Romans on the floors of banquet halls—and when Emperor Nero entered Rome he insisted on having saffron spread along the streets. Wealthy Romans used saffron in their baths and stirred it into wine. It was burned as a high offering to deities, and it  was even considered an aphrodisiac and sprinkled in the beds of newlyweds.

And its costliness was tolerated; saffron was, and still is, very expensive. Its red-orange threads are the stigmas from the center of the fall flowering purple crocus and each bloom provides only three stigmas each. An ounce of saffron requires approximately 14,000 of these tiny saffron threads and the threads must be hand-picked from the flowers and dried for only a limited number of days.

Saffron cultivation in Italy and Europe declined following the fall of the Roman Empire but it was revived when the Moors came from north Africa and settled in Sicily, southern Italy, southern Spain, and parts of France; the word "saffron" probably comes from the Persian *za'faran*. But there had been a Latin form, *safranum*, and Italy quickly got back into the swing of saffron, During the Renaissance, Venice was its most important commercial center for saffron and at that time saffron was actually worth its weight in gold.

Even today it remains the world's most expensive spice, as the threads are still picked by hand. But don't be put off by its super-luxe reputation. Most recipes call for a mere pinch of saffron, and as centuries of history and lore and Italian trade fortunes tell us, not to mention the taste of a good *risotto Milanese*, it's well worth the expense.

♦ ZIN'S TWIN?

DNA testing has made it into the world of viticulture, and predictably started a controversy. The question is whether an ancient southern Italian grape, the Primitivo, and a distinctively Californian newcomer, less than 200 years old, share virtually the identical genetic make-up such that they're basically time-traveling twins.

Both grapes are unquestionably descendants from the Crljenak Kastelanski grape, a rare Croatian varietal. The California Zinfandel appears to be an exact descendant while Italy's Primitivo qualifies more as a clone. Does that clear things up? Actually a clone in this viticultural context is not a scary dystopian notion but a reflection of natural adaptation to *terroir* (soil) and the normal genetic variations that result.

But all this really gets far more intriguing when you do a side-by-side of the vines, the grapes, and the wines they produce. Physically, they certainly don't look like twins or even second cousins. Primitivo and Zinfandel vines produce grapes that are different in most every way, especially size, shape, and cluster density. However, the wines they ultimately produce are virtually indistinguishable—high in alcohol content, lusciously juicy and full of ripe red fruit with a touch of black pepper. This has led the US Alcohol and Tobacco Tax and Trade Bureau to consider officially declaring that Primitivo and Zinfandel could be used interchangeably on labels. Predictably, since Italian Primitivos tend to be value-priced, the prospect of this has made many California vintners crazy.

But to begin at the very beginning, the Primitivo is a grape of gravitas with an illustrious history full of myth and lore. One of the legends suggests its name refers to it being the original grape, as in "In the beginning…" making it the proverbial "Adam" of grapes. In the same rather grandiose vein it has been suggested that Primitivo was the wine served at the Last Supper, also hard to believe and impossible to prove. We do know it dates back to seafaring Phoenicians who settled in Puglia. And a more logical albeit mundane explanation for its "primo" name is that it ripens and is harvested before other varietals. Nonetheless it's been around for a long time, is more ancient than Ancient Rome, and is venerable and much beloved.

By comparison Zinfandel is a whippersnapper and parvenu coming into prominence as the ubiquitous pink swill popular with the club hoppers of the 1980s—training wheels for novice wine lovers. It first arrived in the United States as clippings at the turn of the 19th century and made its way across the country. It was popular with gold miners and later Italian immigrants, reminding them of home. Its popularity is also due to it being a vigorous low-maintenance, high-yielding vine that propagates easily. The Zin's easy growing nature led to the huge surplus of the '80s which led to the production of white Zinfandel and the pink swill craze which nearly pushed the true full-body ruby red version into obscurity, but thankfully not. Nowadays you can experience some truly heady Zins that are world class.

But maybe not world-historical class. All things considered, DNA testing or not, the Italian Primitivo should be considered not a mere twin but a breed of its own. After all (as in one of the themes of this entire book), Rome wasn't built in a day, and neither was the august history of this classic wine.

♦ ZECCHINO

Sparkly sartorial splendor as a symbol of status and wealth dates back multiple millenia to as early as Tutankhamun in 1341–1323 BCE. Gold sequin-like disks were discovered sewn into his royal garments; it's assumed they'd ensure he would be financially and fashionably prepared for the hereafter.

The first "modern" sequins began as small obsolete coins of pure gold that were pierced and then sewn into dresses as decoration by creative and enterprising Venetian seamstresses to add dazzle and glitter to the fashions of the early 16th century. The small coin was a *zecchino* first issued in Venice in 1284 and, befitting the elegance the wardrobe mistresses strove for, the word 'sequin,' a "Frenchified" rendition of *zecchino*, came to be used to describe this fancy decoration. Needless to say, as sequins became hugely popular, all that glittered was no longer gold.

♦ ZUCCARI MOSTRI MASHUP

If you go to the Spanish Steps in Rome, then head down the Via Gregoriana toward the Church of the Trinità dei Monti, you'll soon come upon the Palazzo Zuccari and one of the strangest doorways you'll ever see.

Now a fine arts library, the Palazzo is the creation of Baroque Mannerist painter Federico Zuccari. He bought it in 1590 to build a studio and residence, and the question is: why did he make the doorway into a monstrous leonine mouth and use variations of that ominous design on the windows? To comment on his own bizarre urges? To discourage visitors?

No, it was actually in response to the Parco dei Mostri located in the hills of the Lazio region, just outside the little medieval town of Bomarzo. Zuccari found this "Park of the Monsters" absolutely inspiring in a way perhaps only artists, who are in some respect weavers of living dreams, can appreciate (for nightmares are dreams too, and sometimes even more illuminating.)

Vicino Orsini, the nobleman who created the park on his land, had a strong anarchic and artistic streak, and found a willing partner in architect/artist Pirro Ligorio. Beginning in 1550, they created from the landscape's peperino stone outcrops one of the all-time manifestations of the Mannerist and grotesque in Italian sculpture. These monsters, while based in classical art and mythology, were designed to arise out of the foliage by torchlight and disorient and shock their viewers, much like works of Dada and surrealist movies such as Luis Bunuel and Salvador Dali's *Un Chien Andalou* would do in the twentieth century.

The statues, especially the clash of the Titans, are often enormous. The images are archetypes manifesting power and sexuality as much as deep-rooted fears. At the giant mouth of one statue was originally carved "Lasciate ogni pensiero voi ch'entrate" ("Abandon all thought, ye who enter here"), similar to the famous words from the *Divina Commedia* written over the portal to hell: "Abandon all hope, ye who enter here."

In part because that inscription, like many in the park, has been eroded away, it's hard to know what the park was about. A vision of hell? Or, like Niki de Saint Phalle's Tarot Garden, which was inspired by the Park, a celebration of the liberating power of fantasy to embrace both the power and terror of the world? It contains on the one hand deliberately crooked houses and all those monsters, but also a mausoleum to Prince Orsini's beloved deceased wife. "Just set the heart free," says one of the epitaphs, and the mind as well: the place is anti-empire and all that means, as typified in a statue of Hannibal on an elephant whose trunk strangles a Roman soldier.

The park is also known as *Sacro Bosco*, Sacred Grove, as in "marvelous," and it suggests marvels of literature and scholarship, alluding not just to Dante but Ariosto, Petrarch, and Bernardo Tasso. Some have called it a "garden-book," poetic literature that challenges the old classical order with sculpture that can yield many readings and themes. Whatever you think about it, now that (since 1954) it's been restored to its former dark glory, it's certainly a place in which to think and dream and wonder.

♦ AND Z IS FOR THE ZANNI

He is the most primitive of clowns, earth spirit, creator, trickster, troublemaker. Not as light and clever and playful as *Arlecchino*, he can be a little darker, more primal, the embodiment of impulses of the "id" that come from below. But he is also all about levity, levity, levity, gravity defied, the momentary suspension of seriousness, the piercing of pretense (regardless of who's pierced, for none of us are immune to his silly slapstick gags, none of us can evade the laughter).

He is also very much part of a group, the *zanni,* the collective of servant characters, who displayed acrobatic and clown-like antics, of Commedia dell'Arte. *Arlecchino* can be graceful, but the *zanni* are just on the edge (or quite over the edge) of chaos, and that's why our word "zany" comes from them. The *zanni* invite us to joyfully engage in nonsense for no purpose other than the joy of being silly.

Arlecchino (who has *zanni* roots) is universally recognizable as an aspect of artful enjoyment, cast as a type in an artistic framework. The *zanni* are more universal. Their close cousins can be found everywhere: Benny Hill, the Marx Brothers, the Italian Tonto, Roberto Benigni, the Three Stooges. They're pure outlandish, incongruous, extravagantly comical fun.

The best Commedia performances meant the best *zanni*, and *zanni* were at their best when they were most in the moment. That was their job, to keep the stock stories interesting, fast-paced, and fresh with their gags and physical comedy. Their stock routines were the *lazzi*, which had no purpose other than laughter, gags that were their catechism of crazy, the "how to" for enacting nonsense. Acrobatic *lazzi*, like leaping back and forth from or running around the stage and the balconies (Harpo Marx); rough-and-tumble *lazzi* as when two clowns, kept from fighting each other, then pummel the intercessor (The Three Stooges); foreign language *lazzi*, as when a clown pretends to know a foreign nobleman's language and renders it to someone else as gibberish (Sid Caesar).

Federico Fellini's *The Clowns* begins with a sequence in which a little boy sees a circus tent rise from the night and, as the clowns spill out, he's terrified, showing how (especially to a child) there is something frightening about their *zanni* energy. But the movie ends with a clown funeral which, though it starts with the proper rituals, goes crazily wrong, from the assemblage of a coffin that just won't assemble, to a refractory "mule" that refuses to tow the hearse and turns its back to the clown master and expresses his defiance in no uncertain and very liquid terms. Ultimately the hearse does move on, but only to careen out of control in a wild musical celebration, until it breaks apart to reveal a champagne bottle and the ceremony becomes a confetti-laden uproarious dance and parade in the face of grief.

Fellini knows his *zanni*, and his sequence suggests that the clowns, the stooges, the *zanni* tell us life can purely (and maybe at its best) be silliness, as in the old Disney tune "Put 'em together and what have you got? Bibbity-bobbity-boo." It's not as if the Fairy Godmother isn't working hard to put it all together for Cinderella—to make a coach out of a pumpkin is no mean feat of fabrication. But ultimately, as the *zanni* tell us with their bodies and language, it may all just come down to something nonsensical, bibbity-bobbity-boo, that's fun to roll off the tongue and babble and be silly with, full of childlike nonjudgmental joy.

Roberto Benigni, after turning his Oscar acceptance into a *zanni* bit by walking on the seats of the audience on his way to the stage, quoted William Blake's "He who kisses the joy as it flies/Lives in eternity's sunrise." If, as that other (honorary) Italian, Shakespeare, said, "what fools these mortals be" and "We are such stuff as dreams are made of," the *zanni* put themselves right in the moment to invite us to kiss the joy, savor the foolishness, and embrace the dream.

And maybe, just maybe, their nonsense is one route toward the vision of Dante that Benigni also quoted: *L'amor che move il sole e l'altre stelle*, "the love that moves the sun and the other stars."

L'amor che move il sole e l'altre stelle.

Acknowledgments

Grazie mille to Michael Stein who shared my vision of the book, for his witty contributions, editing expertise, and the mind-meld we so naturally achieved, and to Lannie Hart, one of my dearest friends and long-time artistic collaborator, for her thoroughly enchanting illustrations that add such joy. Special thanks to Patrizia Calce, Perry Matsa, and Tom Dawson for being insightful "beta-readers"; to Deborah Schneider, Paul Vasi, Mark Nassuti, and Jim Tilley for their early encouragement when *La Dolce Vita "U"* was only a spark in my imagination; and to Scott Mason for his marvelous haiku and most especially for his unflagging support and belief in me and for keeping me laughing through my multitudinous life projects.

About the Author

Carla Gambescia's passion for Italy began early—with her mother's love of the Renaissance masters and her father's discourses on Italian geniuses of every calling. In the ensuing decades she has toured every region of Italy (often by bicycle) and immersed herself in its astonishing array of cultural treasures. In recent years Carla has combined her passion as an Italophile with her skills as a career marketer and branding expert, acting as a consultant to and a collaborator with boutique tour operators. She conceived and co-led the Giro del Gelato bicycle tour, winner of Outside Magazine's "Best Trip in Western Europe." In 2008 Carla founded Via Vanti! Restaurant & Gelateria, in Mount Kisco, New York, with the ambition of creating a unique environment and dining experience that would enable guests to feel as though they had stepped right into Italy. Via Vanti! quickly won plaudits not just for its innovative Italian cuisine, extraordinary gelato (named "Best Gelato Shop in New York") and dazzling jewel box interior but also, under Carla's direction, for its active program of culinary and cultural events. It is Carla's conviction that all of us, regardless of our inherited ethnicities, share an "inner Italian"—that part of our nature which is most expressive, festive, spontaneous, and fun—just waiting to be unlocked.

La Dolce Vita University: An Insider's Guide to Italian Culture from A to Z is the natural outgrowth of Carla's work and play in both the restaurant and boutique travel industries, as well as a lifelong love affair with the land of her ancestors.

References

♦ BOOKS

Abulafia, David. *Frederick II: A Medieval Emperor*. London: Pimlico, 2002.

Bull, George. *Michelangelo: A Biography*. New York: St. Martins Griffin, 1998.

Castiglione, Baldassarre. *The Book of the Courtier*. Translated and with an introduction by George Bull. Harmondsworth, UK: Penguin, 1967.

Clark, Kenncth. *Civilisation*. New York: Harper and Row, 1969.

Cole, Bruce. *The Scrovegni Chapel, Padua*. New York: George Braziller, 1993.

David, Elizabeth. *Italian Food*. London: Folio Society, 2006.

D'Epiro, Peter, and Mary Desmond Pinkowish. Sprezzatura: *50 Ways Italian Genius Shaped the World*. New York: Anchor, 2002.

Falcone, Linda. *Italian Voices: A Window on Language and Customs in Italy*. Jersey City, NJ: Florentine Press, 2006.

Graham-Dixon, Andrew. *Michelangelo and the Sistine Chapel*. New York: Skyhorse, 2016.

Halles, Diane. La Bella Lingua: *My Love Affair with Italian, The World's Most Enchanting Language*. New York: Broadway Books, 2009.

Hibbert, Christopher, Ursula Seiger, and Reg Piggott. *Florence: Biography of a City*. London: Penguin, 1994.

Hochkofler, Matilde. *Marcello Mastroianni: The Fun of Cinema*. Rome: Gremese, 2001.

Hooper, John. *The Italians*. London: Penguin, 2016.

Holmes, George. *The Florentine Enlightenment, 1400–50*. New York: Pegasus, 1969.

Hughes, Robert. *Rome: A Cultural, Visual, and Personal History*. New York: Vintage, 2011.

Jenkins, Jessica Kerwin. *Encyclopedia of the Exquisite: An Anecdotal History of Elegant Delights*. New York: Nan A.Talese / Doubleday, 2010.

Johnson, Hugh. *Vintage: The Story of Wine*. New York: Simon and Schuster, 1989.

Jones, Jonathan. *The Loves of the Artists: Art and Passion in the Renaissance*. London: Simon and Schuster UK, 2014.

Kent, Dale V. *Cosimo de Medici and the Florentine Renaissance: The Patron's Oeuvre*. New Haven, CT: Yale University Press, 2006.

King, Ross. *Brunelleschi's Dome: How a Renaissance Genius Reinvented Architecture*. New York: Penguin, 2000.

King, Ross. *Michelangelo and the Pope's Ceiling*. New York: Bloomsbury, 2014.

Manning, Henry Edward, trans. and ed. *The Little Flowers of Saint Francis of Assisi*. Old Saybrook, CT: Konecky & Konecky, 1915.

Meyer, G.J. *The Borgias: The Hidden History*. New York: Bantam, 2013.

Morris, Jan. *Ciao, Carpaccio! An Infatuation*. New York: Liveright, 2014.

Nagel, Alexander. *Cherubs: Angels of Love*. Boston: Bulfinch, 1994.

Norwich, John Julius. *A History of Venice*. London: Penguin, 2012.

Preston, Douglas, and Mario Spezi. *The Monster of Florence*. New York: Grand Central, 2008.

Schevill, Ferdinand. *The Medici*. Harper Torchbooks ed. New York: Harper & Row, 1960.

Sedgwick, Henry Dwight. *A Short History of Italy (476-1900)*. Boston: Houghton Mifflin, 1905.

Seymour, Charles, Jr., ed. *Michelangelo: The Sistine Chapel Ceiling*. Norton Critical Studies in Art History. New York: W.W. Norton, 1972.

Seymour, Charles, Jr. *Michelangelo's* David: *A Search for Identity.* The Norton Library. Pittsburgh, PA: University of Pittsburgh Press, 1974.

Steward, James Christen. *The Masks of Venice: Masking, Theater, and Identity in the Art of Tiepolo and His Time.* Berkeley: University of California, Berkeley Art Museum, in association with the University of Washington Press, 1996.

Strathern, Paul. *The Venetians, A New History: From Marco Polo to Casanova.* Pegasus, 2013.

Van Allen, Susan. *100 Places in Italy Every Woman Should Go*, 3rd Edition. Palo Alto, CA: Travelers' Tales, 2017.

Vasari, Giorgio. *The Lives of the Painters, Sculptors, and Architects.* Translated by A. B. Hinds. Edited with an Introduction by William Gaunt. 4 vols. London: Dent, 1963.

Vidal, Pierre, Myrtille Tibayrenc, and Jean-Paul Gonzalez. "Chapter 40: Infectious Disease and Arts". In *The Encyclopedia of Infectious Diseases: Modern Methodologies,* ed. Michel Tibayrenc, p. 680. New York: John Wiley & Sons, 2007.

Ward-Perkins, J. B. *Roman Imperial Architecture.* New Haven, CT: Yale University Press, 1994.

Watts, Alan. *Become What You Are.* Boston: Shambhala, 2003.

Willard, Pat. *Secrets of Saffron: The Vagabond Life of the World's Most Seductive Spice.* Boston: Beacon Press, 2001.

Wittkower, Rudolf. *Bernini: Sculptor of the Roman Baroque.* Photographs by Pino Guidolotti. New York: Phaidon, 1997.

♦ WEBSITES

"7 Facts about Marcus Vitruvius Pollio." *MyHarvardClassics.com.* N.a. 26 Feb. 2014. Accessed 04 June 2017.

"10 Facts about the Trevi Fountain in Rome." *Italian Notes.* N.a. 04 June 2017. Accessed 04 June 2017.

"A Cure for Road Rage and Other Modern Ailments." *Loving Italy's Gardens.* N.a. 01 Mar. 2015. Accessed 06 June 2017.

"Amalfi Coast Lemon." *ITG Vanvitelli*. ITG Vanvitelli, April 2009. Accessed 07 June 2017.

"Amarone Wine of the Italian Veneto & Valpolicella Wineries." *Wine Enthusiast Magazine*. N.a., 19 Jan. 2016. Accessed 09 Aug. 2017.

"Anita Ekberg Made Everyone Want to Live 'La Dolce Vita." *Hillplace. blogspot.com*. 22 June 2013. Accessed 04 June 2017.

Bagley, Mary. "Mount Vesuvius & Pompeii: Facts & History." *LiveScience*. 29 June 2016. Accessed 17 June 2017.

"Bomarzo, The Strange Garden of Monsters from the Renaissance." *Atlas of Wonders*. N.d. Accessed 06 June 2017.

Brown, Sunny. "Primitivo vs. Zinfandel." *Winegeeks*. N.d. Accessed 22 Nov. 2015.

Buttrose, Larry. "How Bad Were the Borgias Really?" *Writings*. 22 Nov. 2010. Accessed 04 June 2017.

Byers, Chuck. "Accidental Amarone Has Ancient Roots." *DurhamRegion. com*. 3 May 2013. Accessed 03 June 2015.

"Capo Testa Rock Formations." *Atlas Obscura*. N.d. Accessed 04 June 2017.

Cavendish, Richard. "Death of Emperor Frederick II." *History Today*. 12 Dec. 2000. Accessed 04 June 2017.

"Chess Game in Marostica Italy." *Bed-breakfast-Italy*. N.d. Accessed 04 June 2017.

"Christ Our Life." *The Patron Saints of the Culinary Arts*. N.d. Accessed 06 June 2017.

Clarke, Adam. "Some of the Best Things Are Discovered by Accident – Amarone Wine A Great Mistake!" *Majestic Wine*. 19 Sept. 2016. Accessed 16 July 2017.

Cohen, Jennie. "Is Rome's Pantheon a Giant Sundial?" *History.com*. A&E Television Networks, 04 Aug. 2011. Accessed 06 June 2017.

Crowther, Bosley. "The Screen: *Divorce Italian Style*: 'Dandy Satiric Farce' at Paris Theater, Marcello Mastroianni and Miss Rocca Star." *The New York Times*. 18 Sept. 1962. Accessed 04 June 2017.

"Dante Alighieri: *The Divine Comedy.*" *Maryourmother.net.* N.d. Accessed 03 June 2017.

D'Costa, Krystal. "From the Archives: Power, Confidence, and High Heels." *Scientific American Blog Network.* 13 Jan. 2012. Accessed 06 June 2017.

"Dolomites Via Ferrata." *Experience the Thrill of a Via Ferrata in the Dolomites with Expert Local Guides.* N.a. 26 June 2013. Accessed 09 Aug. 2017.

"Domus Aurea." *Atlas Obscura.* N.d. Accessed 06 June 2017.

Donadio, Rachel. "When Italians Chat, Hands and Fingers Do the Talking." *The New York Times.* The New York Times, 30 June 2013. Accessed 15 July 2017.

DreamDiscoverItalia.com. "Italian Art 101 – Lacoon and His Sons, Vatican Museum." *DreamDiscoverItalia.* Lizbert1. 25 May 2016. Accessed 16 July 2017.

"Easter in Florence: Explosion of the Cart." *Visit Florence—Fall in love with Florence, Italy!* N.d. Accessed 03 June 2017.

Ebert, Roger. "*Fellini's Roma* Movie Review and Film Summary (1972) | Roger Ebert." *RogerEbert.com.* 01 Jan. 1972. Accessed 04 June 2017.

The Editors of Encyclopædia Britannica. "Peggy Guggenheim." *Encyclopædia Britannica.* Encyclopædia Britannica, Inc. N.a., n.d. Accessed 17 June 2017.

"Eruption of Mount Vesuvius Begins." *History.com.* A&E Television Networks. N.a., n.d. Accessed 17 June 2017.

Eveleth, Rose. "The History of the Exclamation Point | Smart News . . . " *Smithsonianmag.com.* 9 Aug. 2012. Accessed 3 June 2017.

Falcone, Linda. "'*Arrangiarsi*." *The Florentine.* 07 Mar. 2007. 03 June 2017.

Gaiter, Dorothy J., and John Brecher. "Italy's Zinfandel Pretender." *The Wall Street Journal.* 03 Oct. 2008. Accessed 13 July 2017.

"Giorgio Vasari." *Encyclopædia Britannica.* Encyclopædia Britannica, Inc., N.a., n.d. Accessed 10 Aug. 2017.

"Giorgio Vasari." *PBS*. Public Broadcasting Service, N.a., n.d. Accessed 10 Aug. 2017.

Griffiths, Mark. "Having an Art Attack." *Psychology Today*. Sussex Publishers, 10 Mar. 2014. Accessed 09 Aug. 2017.

"Grotta Azzurra (Blue Grotto)." *Atlas Obscura*. N.d. Accessed 04 June 2017.

"Gubbio's Raucous and Saintly Festa dei Ceri ." *Postcards from Italy*. 14 May 2014. Accessed 04 June 2017.

Hainey, Michael. "Where the Wild Boars Are." *Departures*. 30 Mar. 2010. Accessed 03 Nov. 2015.

Hales, Linda. "Platforms: Height Of Impracticality." *The Washington Post*. WP Company, 18 Nov. 2006. Accessed 06 June 2017.

Hanlon, Mike. "The Scooter—The Short History of a Cultural Icon." *New Atlas—New Technology & Science News*. New Atlas, 18 Apr. 2005. Accessed 03 July 2015.

"Harry's Bar in Venice—Cipriani Bar & Restaurant Venezia." *Harry's Bar in Venice | Cipriani Bar & Restaurant Venezia*. N.d. Accessed 16 June 2017.

"History of Venetian Glass Making." *Big Bead Little Bead*. N.d. Accessed 06 June 2017.

Imboden, Durant. "Murano, the Glass Island." *A Travel Guide*. N.a., n.d. Accessed 09 Aug. 2017.

"Interesting Facts about the Trevi Fountain." *Around Rome Tours*. 24 Jan. 2014. Accessed 04 June 2017.

"Isabella d'Este." *Brooklyn Museum: Isabella d'Este*. N.d. Accessed 06 June 2017.

"Isabella D'Este, the Grand Lady of the Renaissance." *History and Women*. 29 May 2014. Accessed 15 July 2017.

Ivan. "The Hidden Messages of Michelangelo in the Sistine Chapel." *Ancient Code*. 11 Feb. 2015. Accessed 16 June 2017.

Korteman, Jessica. "Fit for a Peasant." *Notes of Nomads*. 03 Mar. 2014. Accessed 04 June 2017.

"Lacryma Christi del Vesuvio: Fabled Campagna Wine is Great Paired with Pizza." *Into Wine*. N.d. Accessed 03 June 2017.

LaFrance, Adrienne. "Pompeii's Graffiti and the Ancient Origins of Social Media." *The Atlantic*. Atlantic Media Company, 29 Mar. 2016. Accessed 04 June 2017.

"Laocoon and His Sons (*c*. 42–20 BCE)." *Laocoon and His Sons, Greek Statue: History, Interpretation: Encyclopedia of Sculpture. visual-arts-cork. com*. N.d. Accessed 03 June 2017.

Lee, Alexander. "Were the Borgias Really So Bad?" *History Today*. 1 Oct. 2013. Accessed 19 Dec. 2015.

Lewis, Jone Johnson. "Isabella dEste—Renaissance Arts Patron." *Thought-Co*. 11 Mar. 2017. Accessed 06 June 2017.

Lillie, Barry. "History of an Icon: *La Vespa*." *ITALY Magazine*. 04 Aug. 2014. Accessed 06 June 2017.

Mackrell, Judith. "Sex and Art by the Grand Canal: How Peggy Guggenheim took Venice." *The Guardian*. Guardian News and Media, 10 May 2017. Accessed 17 June 2017.

"Marcello Mastroianni, Known as 'Latin Lover' Dies." *CNN*. Cable News Network, 19 Dec. 1996. Accessed 04 June 2017.

Mariani, John. "Harry's Bar ... The One and Only." *Virtual Gourmet*. 06 Nov. 2011. Accessed 03 Jan. 2014.

Matthiesen, Dawn, and Linda Moore. "Trulli Extreme Tax Dodging." *Love art travel*. 20 June 2015. Accessed 04 June 2017.

McGrath, Peter. "Salt: Sicily's White Gold." *ITALY Magazine*. 11 Dec. 2015. Accessed 06 June 2017.

McMahon, Mary, and Bronwyn Harris. "What is Ciabatta Bread?" *Wise-GEEK*. Conjecture Corporation, 26 May 2017. Accessed 08 June 2017.

McNamara, Jeremy. "'Ovidius Naso Was the Man': Shakespeare's Debt to Ovid." *The 1992–93 Fox Classics Lecture, 1992*. Accessed 06 June 2017.

McNearney, Allison. "How Peggy Guggenheim Became The Queen of Modern Art." *The Daily Beast*. The Daily Beast Company, 02 May 2015. Web. 15 July 2017.

McNeill, Maggie. "Veronica Franco." *The Honest Courtesan*. N.d. Accessed 06 June 2017.

Mendola, Luigi. "King Roger II Hauteville, King of Sicily—Best of Sicily Magazine." *Visit Best of Sicily*. N.d. Accessed 06 June 2017.

Mitzman, Dany. "Nutella: How the World Went Nuts for a Hazelnut Spread." *BBC News*. BBC, 18 May 2014. 16 July 2017.

Morris, Roderick Conway. "Under Frederick II, the First Rebirth of Roman Culture."" *The New York Times*. 5 July 2008. Accessed 04 June 2017.

Moses, Sarah. "Ancient Digger Archaeology." *Veronica Franco and Venetian Courtesans*. 13 Apr. 2011. Accessed 06 June 2017.

Muñoz-Alonso, Lorena. "$170 Million Da Vinci Seized from Swiss Vault." *Artnet News*. 11 Feb. 2015. Accessed 06 June 2017.

"Palazzo Zuccari—Portal to Hell or Mannerist Facade?" *GlobalizeYourself*. N.a. 30 Aug. 2015. Accessed 06 June 2017.

"Paolo Uccello." *Italian Renaissance Art.com*. N.p., n.d. Accessed 09 Aug. 2017.

"Paradise Regained: The Painted Garden of Livia at Palazzo Massimo." *Understanding Rome*. N.a. 08 Jan. 2014. Accessed 17 June 2017.

Parker, Freda. "The Pantheon—Rome—126 AD." *Monolithic Dome Institute*. 12 May 2009. Accessed 06 June 2017.

Pensabene, Patrizio, and Enrico Gallocchio. "The Villa del Casale of Piazza Armerina." *Penn.Museum*. University of Pennsylvania. N.d. Accessed 04 June 2017.

Perrottet, Tony. "Who Was Casanova?" *Smithsonian.com*. Smithsonian Institution, 01 Apr. 2012. Accessed 06 June 2017.

"Pliny the Elder, Natural History." *Pliny the Elder, Natural History—Livius. org*. N.a,, n.d. Accessed 08 June 2017.

"Pliny the Elder." *Strangescience.net/*. N.a., n.d. Accessed 08 June 2017.

"Pliny's World: All the Facts and Then Some." *Smithsonian.com*. Smithsonian Institution, 01 Nov. 1995. Accessed 15 July 2017.

Poggioli, Sylvia. "Tortellini, The Dumpling Inspired By Venus' Navel." *NPR*. NPR, 27 Aug. 2013. Accessed 17 June 2017.

Pollack, Rufus. "'Everything is so difficult Marcello': Fellini's *La Dolce Vita*." *Rufus Pollock Online*. 1977. Accessed 04 June 2017.

"Pompeii." *Ancient History Encyclopedia*. N.p., n.d. Accessed 09 Aug. 2017.

"Pope Julius II (1453–1513: reigned 1503–1513) Renaissance Patron of the Arts in Rome." *visual-arts-cork.com* N.a., n.d. Accesed 06 June 2017.

"Purpose of the Roman Pantheon." *Mariamilani*. N.d. Accessed 06 June 2017.

Revolvy, LLC. "'Volare (song)' on Revolvy.com." *Revolvy*. N.a,, n.d. Accessed 07 June 2017.

Roberts, Hannah. "Found in a Swiss bank vault, the £90 million long-lost Leonardo da Vinci masterpiece that vanished TWICE." *Daily Mail Online*. 10 Feb. 2015. Accessed 06 June 2017.

"Rome in the Footsteps of an XVIIIth Century Traveller." *Tivoli—The Palace of Villa dEste*. N.a., n.d. Acceessed 06 June 2017.

Russo, Simona. "The Jewels of Queen Margherita of Savoy" royalista.com. N.d. Accessed 01 July 2014.

Sanderson, Rachel. "Michele Ferrero, Confectioner and Nutella Creator, 1925–2015." *Financial Times*. 15 Feb. 2015. Accessed 17 June 2015.

"Savonarola and the Lasting Effects of the Bonfire of the Vanities on Painters of the Italian Renaissance." *Historyofpainters.com*. N.a., n.d. Accessed 04 June 2017.

"Simonetta Vespucci—The Top Model of the Renaissance." *DailyArtDaily. com*. N.a, 15 Jan. 2017. Accessed 03 June 2017.

Smith, K. Annabelle. "Why the Tomato Was Feared in Europe for More Than 200 Years." *Smithsonian.com*. Smithsonian Institution, 18 June 2013. Accessed 09 Aug. 2017.

"Socrates." "The Dirty World of Ancient Graffiti." *Classical Wisdom Weekly*. 15 Jan. 2014. Accessed 04 June 2017.

Squires, Nick. "Italian Regions Battle over Who Invented Tiramisu." *The Telegraph*. Telegraph Media Group, 17 May 2016. Accessed 08 June 2017.

Stradley, Linda. "Tiramisu Recipe and History, What's Cooking America." *What's Cooking America*. 26 Apr. 2017. Accessed 08 June 2017.

"St. Roch." *Catholic Encyclopedia: NewAdvent.* N.a., n.d.. Accessed 06 June 2017.

Stout, Hilary. "Michele Ferrero, Tycoon Who Gave the World Nutella, Dies at 89." *The New York Times.* The New York Times, 15 Feb. 2015. Accessed 17 June 2015.

"Terrazzo dell'Infinito—The Belvedere." *The Pinnacle List.* N.a., n.d. Accessed 04 June 2017.

Thayer, Laura. "Church of San Michele on the Island of Capri." *Charming Italy.* 9 Nov. 2010. Accessed 04 June 2017.

Thayer, Laura. "Lemons of Sorrento and the Amalfi Coast." *Charming Italy.* 14 Oct. 2015. Accessed 06 June 2017.

Thayer, Laura. "Overlooking the Amalfi Coast—Ravello's Villa Cimbrone Gardens." *Charming Italy.* 12 Jan. 2011. Accessed 04 June 2017.

"The Art of Marbling—Marbled Paper & Marbling Supplies." *The Art of Marbling—Marbled Paper & Marbling Supplies.* N.a., n.d. Accessed 09 Aug. 2017.

"The Brain on the Sistine Chapel Ceiling." *Thecaveonline.com.* N.a., n.d. Accessed 16 June 2017.

"The Mysterious Park of the Monsters of Bomarzo." *Slow Italy.* N.a. 20 Feb. 2013. Accessed 06 June 2017.

"The Palatine Chapel in Palermo (Cappella Palatina)." *The Wonders of Sicily.* N.d. Accessed 04 June 2017.

Poggioli, Sylvia. "Tortellini, The Dumpling Inspired By Venus' Navel." *NPR.* NPR, 27 Aug. 2013. Accessed 10 Aug. 2017.

"The Priceless Peggy Guggenheim." *The Independent.* Independent Digital News and Media, 20 Oct. 2009. Accessed 15 July 2017.

"The Secret Life of Ciabatta." *The Guardian.* Guardian News and Media. N.a. 29 Apr. 1999. Accessed 08 June 2017.

"Top 25 Quotes by Pliny The Elder (Of 131)." *A-Z Quotes.* N.a,, n.d. Accessed 03 June 2017.

"Trulli—How Did They Come About?" *Trullipuglia.* N.a,, n.d. Accessed 04 June 2017.

"Two Famous Italian Temptresses." *Two Famous Italian Temptresses | Italy.* N.a, n.d. Accessed 6 June 2017.

"Uccello, The Battle of San Romano." *Khan Academy.* N.a,, n.d. Accessed 03 June 2017.

"The Vasari Corridor." *Visit Florence—Fall in Love with Florence, Italy!* N.a, n.d. Accessed 08 June 2017.

VH. "How Do You Get Edible Salt out of the Sea?" *The Dangerously Truthful Diary of a Sicilian Housewife.* 20 Jan. 2014. Accessed 06 June 2017.

"Villa San Michele." *Capri.com.* N.a., n.d. Accessed 04 June 2017.

"Were the Borgias as Bad as We Have Always Thought?" N.a. 30 Oct. 2013. Accessed 4 June 2017.

"What does 'Vitruvian' Mean Anyway?" *Vitruvian Studio.* N.a., n.d. Accessed 04 June 2017.

"What's the Difference Between Bacon, Pancetta, and Prosciutto?" *Kitchn.* N.a., n.d. Accessed 12 July 2017.

"Why Ancient Roman Graffiti Is So Important to Archaeologists." *Redorbit.* N.a. 05 Jan. 2016. Accessed 04 June 2017.

Wiener, Scott. "Happy Birthday, Pizza Margherita!" *Scott's Pizza Journal.* 10 June 2011. Accessed 17 June 2017.

Winton, Patricia. "August Snow in Rome." *ItalianIntrigues.blogspot.com.* 08 Aug. 2013. Accessed 03 June 2017.

Zwingle, Erla. "The High Art of the Mask." *Craftsmanship Quarterly.* 26 May 2017. Accessed 06 June 2017.

◆ MOVIES

Divorce Italian Style. Dir. Pietro Germi. 1961. DVD. Los Angeles: Twentieth-Century Fox, Embassy Pictures. Criterion Collection. 2005. Perf. Marcello Mastroianni, Daniela Rocca, Stefania Sandrelli, and Leopoldo Trieste.

La Dolce Vita. Dir. Federico Fellini. 1960. DVD. New York: Astor Pictures Corporation. Koch Lorber. 2004. Perf. Marcello Mastroianni, Anita Ekberg, Anouk Aimée, and Yvonne Furneaux.

Fellini's Roma. Dir. Federico Fellini. 1972. DVD. Los Angeles: United Artists. Criterion Collection. 2016.

Traveler's Topic Index

◆ ◆ ◆

CITIES ◆ REGIONS

ANTIQUITY ◆ HISTORY

ARCHITECTURE ◆ ART HISTORY

CUISINE & AGRICULTURE ◆ WINE & SPIRITS

LANGUAGE & LITERATURE

ITALIAN CHARACTER

TRADITIONS & FESTIVALS

UNIQUE PLACES, VIEWS, GARDENS

THEATRE, MUSIC, CINEMA

STYLE & APPLIED ARTS

PEOPLE

CANINES

CITIES/REGIONS

HISTORY

ARCHITECTURE

ART HISTORY

CUISINE & AGRICULTURE

WINE & SPIRITS

LANGUAGE & LITERATURE

ITALIAN CHARACTER

TRADITIONS & FESTIVALS

PEOPLE

CANINES